Crusaders and Kings of Jerusalem

Crusaders and Kings of Jerusalem

The Beaumonts

Kathryn Warner

PEN & SWORD
HISTORY

First published in Great Britain in 2024 by
Pen & Sword History
An imprint of Pen & Sword Books Limited
Yorkshire – Philadelphia

ISBN 978 1 52677 633 4

A CIP catalogue record for this book is available from the British Library

Typeset by Mac Style
Printed in the UK by CPI Group (UK) Ltd, Croydon, CR0 4YY.

MIX
Paper | Supporting responsible forestry
FSC® C013604

Pen & Sword Books Limited incorporates the imprints of After the Battle, Atlas, Archaeology, Aviation, Discovery, Family History, Fiction, History, Maritime, Military, Military Classics, Politics, Select, Transport, True Crime, Air World, Frontline Publishing, Leo Cooper, Remember When, Seaforth Publishing, The Praetorian Press, Wharncliffe Local History, Wharncliffe Transport, Wharncliffe True Crime and White Owl.

For a complete list of Pen & Sword titles please contact

PEN & SWORD BOOKS LIMITED
47 Church Street, Barnsley, South Yorkshire, S70 2AS, England
E-mail: enquiries@pen-and-sword.co.uk
Website: www.pen-and-sword.co.uk
or
PEN AND SWORD BOOKS
1950 Lawrence Road, Havertown, PA 19083, USA
E-mail: uspen-and-sword@casematepublishers.com
Website: www.penandswordbooks.com

Contents

Royal House of Jerusalem

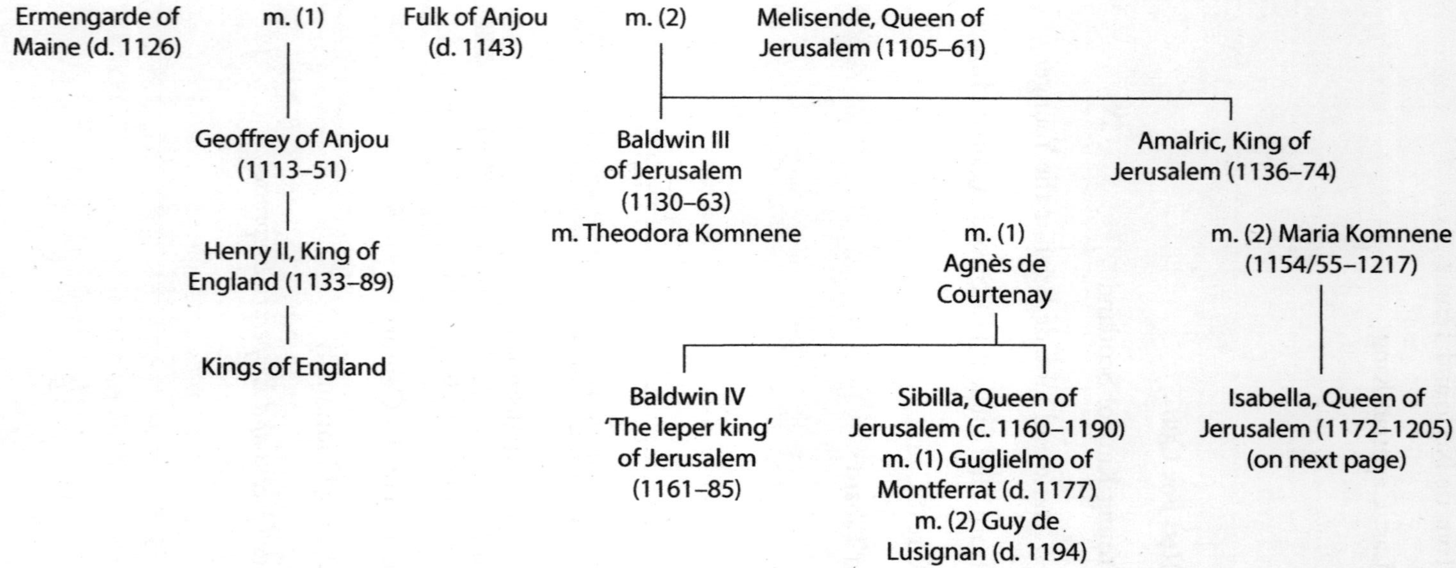

Royal House of Jerusalem

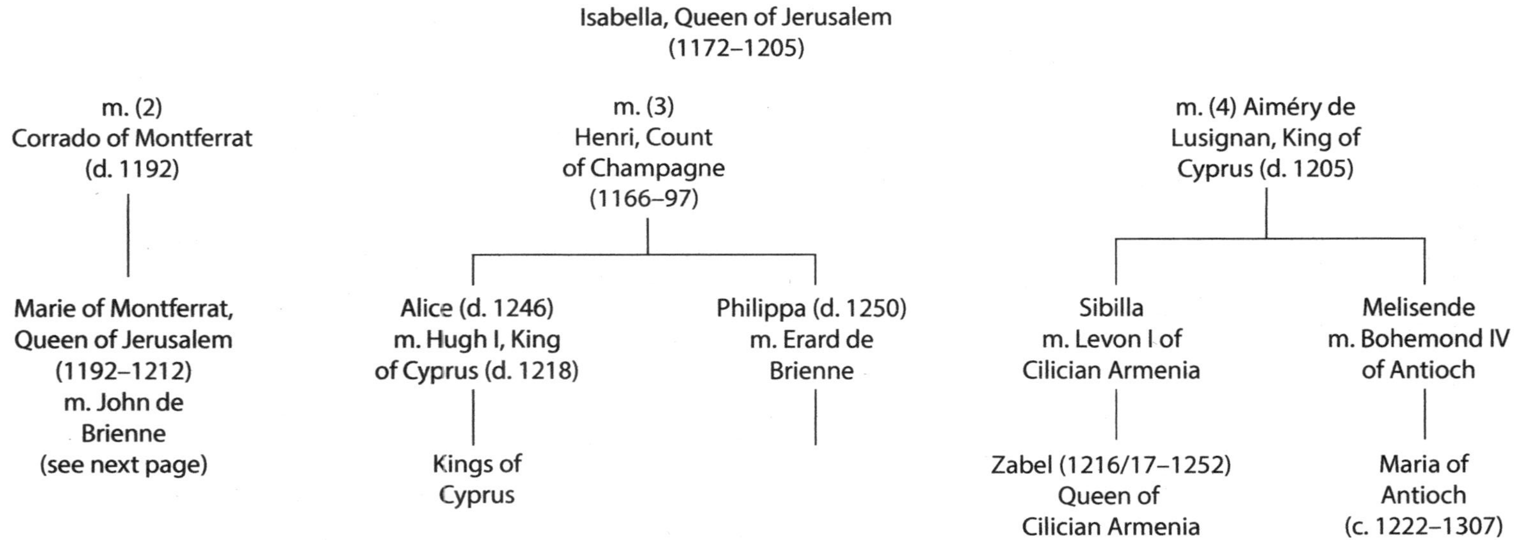

Royal House of Jerusalem

John de Brienne, Emperor of Constantinople (c. 1175/78–1237)

m. (1) Marie of Montferrat, Queen of Jerusalem (1192–1212)

Yolande de Brienne, Queen of Jerusalem (1212–28)
m. Friedrich II. Holy Roman Emperor (1194–1250)

Konrad von Hohenstaufen, King of Jerusalem, Germany, Italy and Sicily (1228–54)

Konradin von Hohenstaufen (1252–68)

m. (2) Stephanie of Armenia (d. 1220)

John (c. 1216–20)

m. (3) Berenguela of León (c. 1204/05–1237) (on next page)

Royal House of Jerusalem

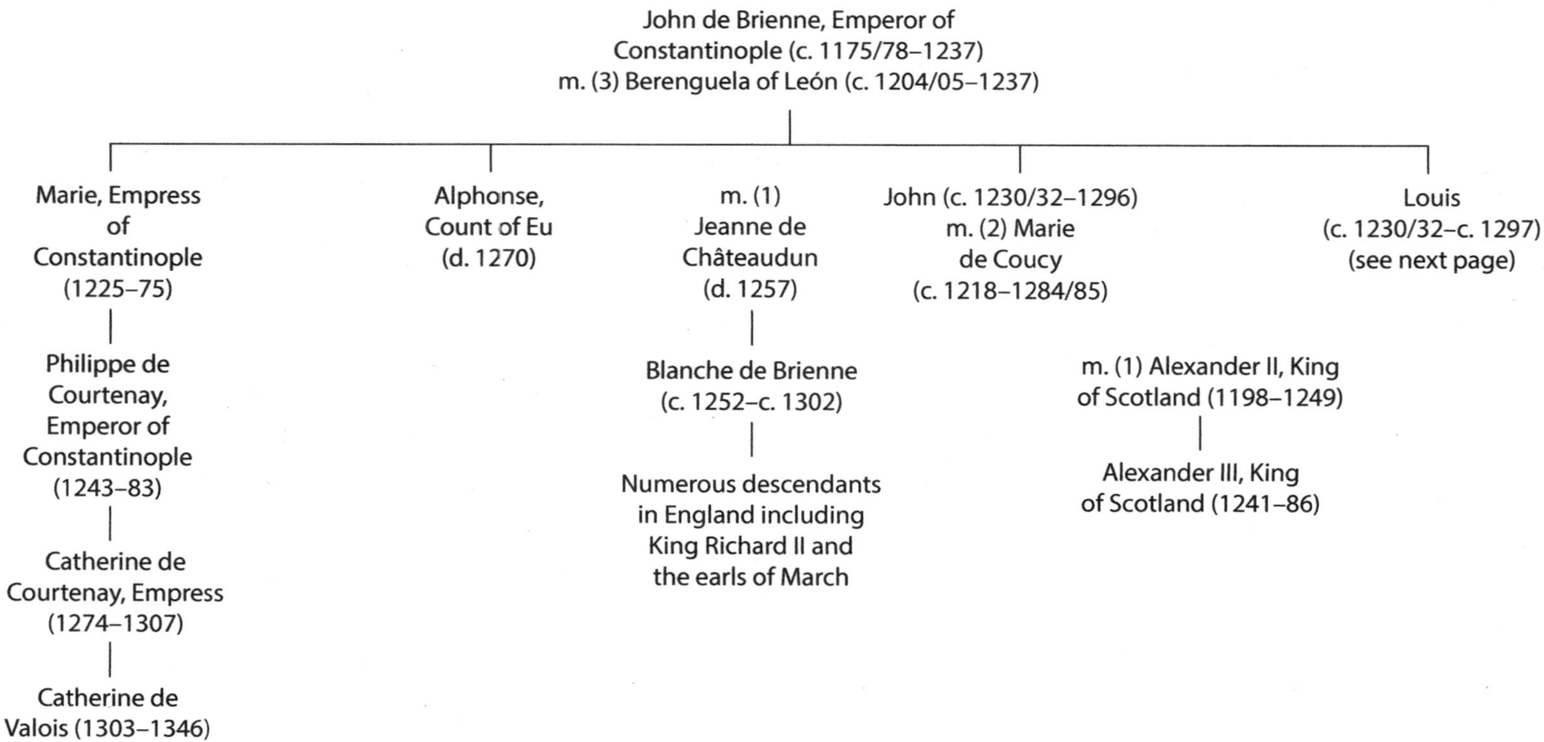

Royal House of Jerusalem

- John de Brienne, Emperor m. (3) Berenguela of León
  - Louis de Brienne (c. 1230/32–c. 1297) m. Agnes de Beaumont (d. 1304)
    - Isabelle (d. 1334)
Louis (d. 1333)
Marguerite (d. 1328)
Others
    - Henry (d. 1340) de Beaumont m. Alice Comyn (d. 1349)
      - Isabella (d. c. 1359/60) m. Henry, first duke of Lancaster (d. 1361)
        - Blanche (1342–68) m. John of Gaunt (1340–99)
          - Philippa (1360–1415) Queen of Portugal
          - Henry IV, King of England (1367–1413)
      - Others including Elizabeth (d. 1400)
      - John (d. 1342) de Beaumont m. Eleanor of Lancaster (d. 1372)
        - Henry de Beaumont (1339–69) m. Margaret de Vere
          - Beaumont family

Byzantium

- Alexios I Komnenos, Byzantine Emperor (1057–1118) m. Eirene Doukaina
  - Anna (1083–1153)
  - Ioannes II. Byzantine Emperor (1087–1143)
    - Isaakios (d. after 1146)
      - daughter
        - Isaakios Doukas Komnenos, Emperor of Cyprus (d. 1195)
          - The Damsel of Cyprus
    - Manuel I, Byzantine Emperor (1118–1180)
      - Maria Komnene (c. 1152–c. 1183) and Alexios II Komnenos, Byzantine Emperor (1169–1183) m. Agnes of France (1170/71–c. 1220)
    - Andronikos (d. 1142)
      - Ioannes Doukas Komnenos (d. 1176)
        - Maria Komnene (1154/55–1217)
          - Isabella, Queen of Jerusalem (1172–1205)
  - Isaakios (1093–after 1136)
    - Andronikos I Komnenos, Byzantine Emperor (c. 1118–1185) m. Agnes of France (1170/71–c. 1220)
  - Theodora (1096–after 1136)
    - Andronikos Angelos (d. before 1185)
      - Isaakios II Angelos (d. 1204), + Alexios III Angelos (d. 1211) + Theodora Angelina m. Corrado of Montferrat (d. 1192)

Castile-León

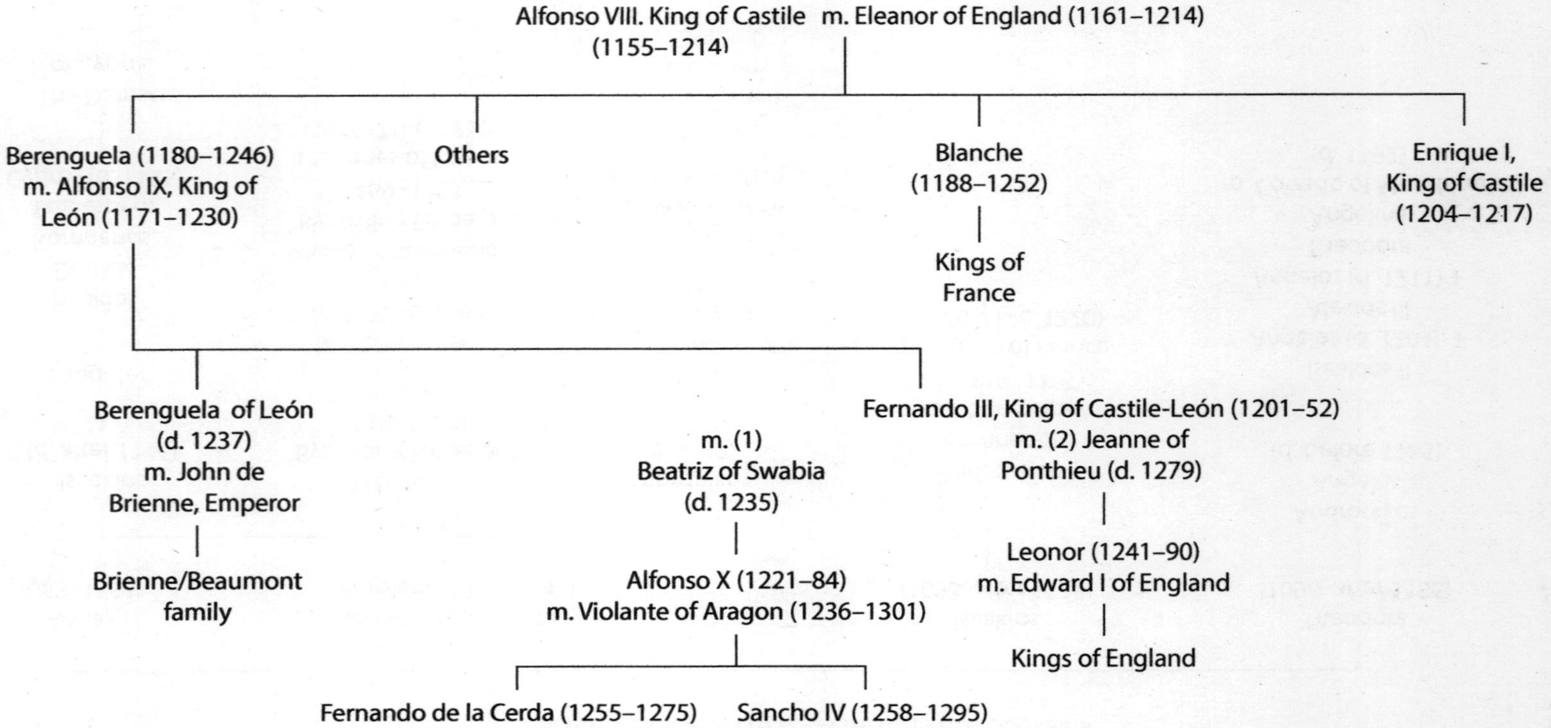

Castile-León 2

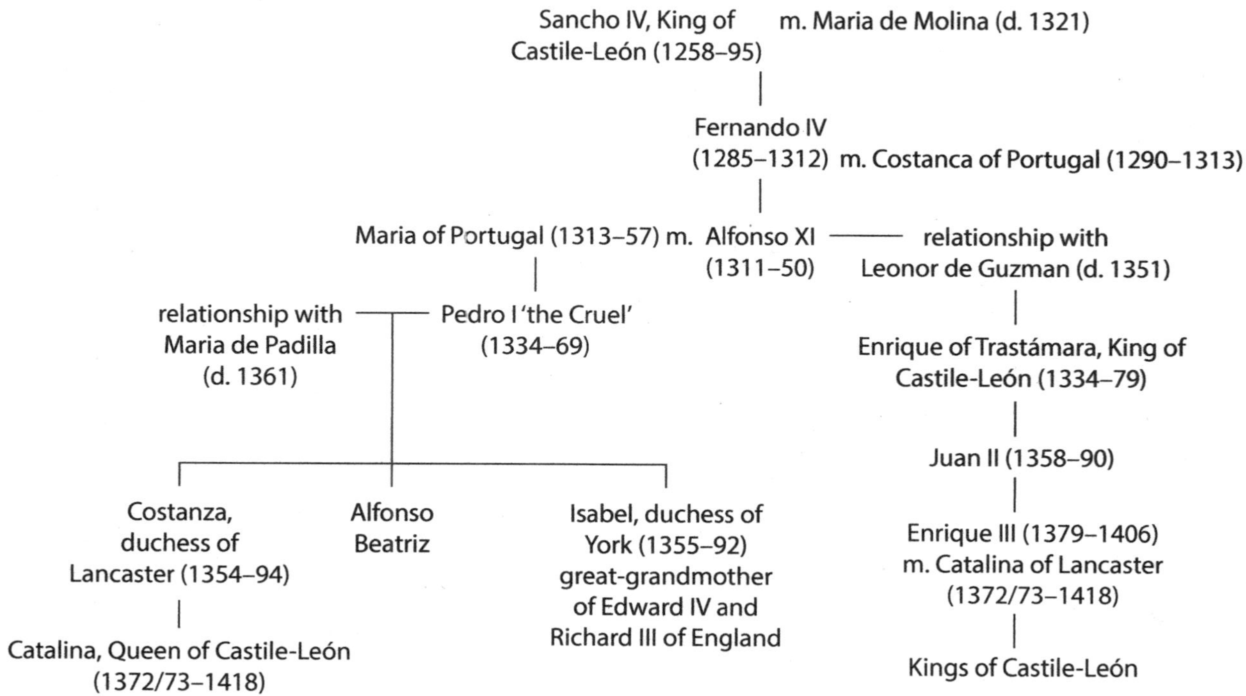

Aragon-Sicily

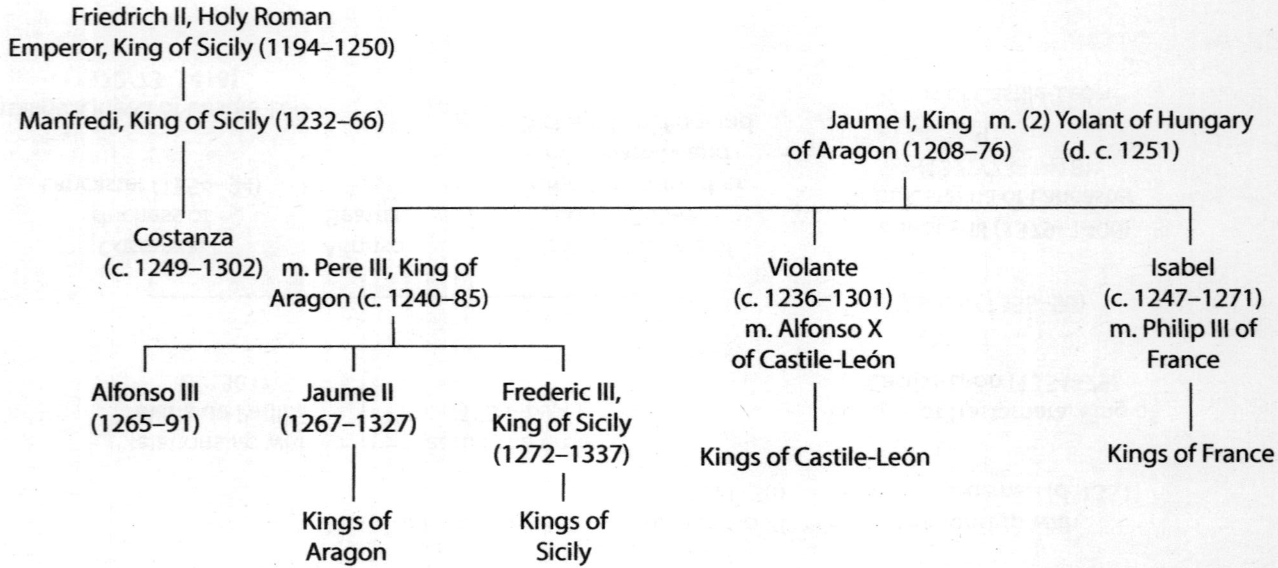

France

Philip II Augustus, King of France
(1165–1223) m. (1) Isabelle of Hainault (1170–1190)

Louis VIII, King of France
(1187–1226) m. Blanche of Castile (1188–1252)

Louis IX (1214–70)
m. Marguerite of Provence
(1221–1295)

Philip III (1245–85)
m. (1) Isabel of Aragon (d. 1271)

Philip IV (1268–1314)
m. Juana I of Navarre
(1273–1305)

Louis X (d. 1316)
Philip V (d. 1322)
Charles IV (d. 1328)
Isabella, Queen of England

Charles de Valois (1270–1325)

Philip VI, King of France
(1293–1350)
and
Catherine de Valois,
Empress of Constantinople
(1303–1346)
and others

Others including
Robert de Artois
and Alphonse of
Poitiers

Charles of Anjou,
King of Sicily (1227–85)
m. Beatrice of
Provence (d. 1267)

Charles of Salerno, King
of Naples (1254–1309)
m. Marie of Hungary (d. 1323)

Charles Martel of Hungary (1271–95)
and
Marguerite of Anjou – Naples (1272–99)
and
Robert, King of Naples (1276–1343)
and
Philip of Taranto (1278–1331)
and
Others

Scotland

- David I, King of Scotland (d. 1153) m. Maud of Huntingdon (d. 1130/31)
  - Henry, Earl of Northumbria and Huntingdon (d. 1152) m. Ada de Warenne (d. 1175)
    - Malcolm IV, King of Scotland (d. 1165)
    - William the Lion, King of Scotland (d. 1214)
      - Alexander II (1198–1249)
        - Alexander III (1241–86) m. (1) Margaret of England (1240–75)
          - Maighread, Queen of Norway (1261–83)
            - Margrete, the Maid of Norway (1283–90)
    - David, Earl of Huntingdon (d. 1219)
      - Margaret (d. c. 1228)
        - Devorguilla of Galway (d. 1290)
          - John Balliol, King of Scotland (d. 1314)
            - Edward Balliol (c. 1283–1364)
      - Isobel (d. 1251)
        - Robert Bruce (d. 1295)
          - Robert Bruce (d. 1304)
            - Robert Bruce, King of Scotland (1274–1329)

England

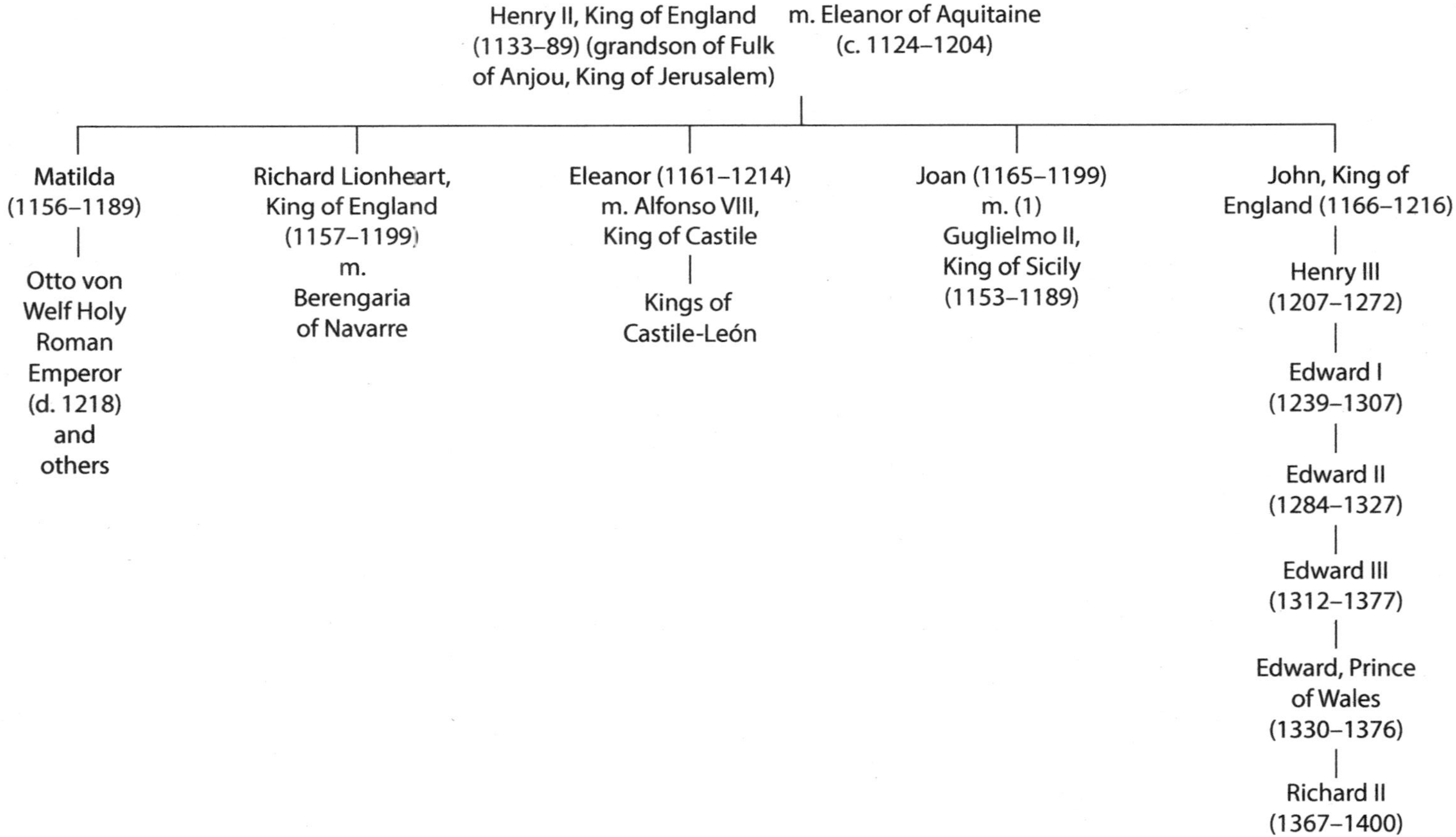

Henry II, King of England (1133–89) (grandson of Fulk of Anjou, King of Jerusalem)
m. Eleanor of Aquitaine (c. 1124–1204)
Matilda (1156–1189)
Otto von Welf Holy Roman Emperor (d. 1218) and others
Richard Lionheart, King of England (1157–1199) m. Berengaria of Navarre
Eleanor (1161–1214) m. Alfonso VIII, King of Castile
Kings of Castile-León
Joan (1165–1199) m. (1) Guglielmo II, King of Sicily (1153–1189)
John, King of England (1166–1216)
Henry III (1207–1272)
Edward I (1239–1307)
Edward II (1284–1327)
Edward III (1312–1377)
Edward, Prince of Wales (1330–1376)
Richard II (1367–1400)

Introduction

The Brienne/Beaumonts, a noble family originally from the Champagne region of France, spread across Europe and the Eastern Mediterranean in the Middle Ages. Their story begins with John de Brienne (*c*.1175–1237), who grew up in his father's county of Brienne 115 miles from Paris. He was the elected emperor of Constantinople, became king of Jerusalem by marriage, claimed the throne of a kingdom in modern-day Turkey called Armenian Cilicia, and was the brother-in-law of a Spanish king later canonised as a saint of the Catholic Church. Born as the youngest son of a comparatively minor French noble family, John made no fewer than three royal marriages, and by the mid-1220s was the father of the queen regnant of Jerusalem, father-in-law of the Holy Roman Emperor, son-in-law of the king of León, brother-in-law of the king of Castile and the queen regnant of Armenian Cilicia, and nephew-in-law of the king and queen of France. His and his children's lives were remarkably international. At the age of about fifty, John became an emperor, and his capital was the city of Constantinople, now called Istanbul; his two daughters, born in what is now Lebanon in 1212 and in Italy in 1225, were both empresses; one of his sons, who grew up in Constantinople, France and Spain, was the stepfather of the king of Scotland; one of his grandchildren was the king of Germany, Italy and Sicily; and several other grandchildren settled in England, where one became a great nobleman of the realm, married a Scottish heiress, and was the great-grandfather of a king of England and an English-born queen consort of Portugal.

John's son, the *Porphyrogennetos* Louis de Brienne, born to John's third wife Berenguela of León in the early 1230s, married the French heiress Agnès de Beaumont, viscountess of Beaumont-sur-Sarthe in her own right, in 1253. Three of Louis and Agnès's children moved to England in the last two decades of the thirteenth century and adopted their mother's last name. In England, the family were and are known as the Beaumonts, though most of Louis de Brienne's children who remained in France kept their father's and grandfather's family name. The Brienne/Beaumont family were influential across Western Europe and the Eastern Mediterranean, and *Crusaders and Kings of Jerusalem* tells the story of the places where they settled and held influence between the twelfth and fourteenth centuries. It begins in Outremer, the Crusader states that existed between the late eleventh and late thirteenth century, including the kingdoms of Jerusalem and Armenian Cilicia, and moves to the Latin Empire of Constantinople and the Holy Roman Empire. Emperor John de Brienne and his children and grandchildren also lived and were active in Spain, France, Scotland, and England.

Glossary

Armenian Cilicia: A Christian, Armenian state in southern Anatolia in what is now Turkey, created in the 1000s by refugees fleeing the Seljuks' invasion of Armenia. It is also sometimes known as Little Armenia or Lesser Armenia. Originally a principality, it became a kingdom in 1199 with the coronation of Levon I, first king of Armenian Cilicia. Its last king was Levon V de Lusignan, who died in exile in Paris in 1393.

Atabeg: Turkic word meaning ruler or governor.

Basileus: Greek word for emperor.

Byzantine Empire/Byzantium: A later name for the Eastern Roman Empire, which remained intact for a millennium after the collapse of Roman authority in Western Europe in the fifth century. The Byzantine Empire covered much of modern-day Turkey and Greece, much of southern Italy and the Balkans, and part of North Africa and the Middle East, and its capital was Constantinople, now Istanbul. Its ruling dynasties were the Komnenoi (1081–1185), the Angeloi (1185–1204) and the Palaiologoi (1259–1453). The Empire's thousand-plus years of existence ended when Constantinople fell to the Ottomans in 1453. See also 'Latin Empire of Constantinople' below.

Capetian: The name of the royal dynasty which ruled France from 987 to 1328, named after its founder Hugues Capet (d.996). They were succeeded by the Valois dynasty, named after Charles de Valois (1270–1325), son of Philip III, brother of Philip IV and father of Philip VI; the latter became the first Valois king in 1328. Until the late twelfth century, French monarchs were known as 'king of the Franks', then styled themselves 'king of France'.

Despot: The Greek word for 'lord', akin to the Latin *Dominus*. It was a title bestowed on the sons and sons-in-law of the Byzantine Emperors, usually on those men considered the emperor's heir apparent, with none of the modern connotations of the word.

Despotate: Territory ruled by a Despot.

Doge: The elected leader of the city-state of Venice.

Frankish: The adjective used for western European, predominantly French-speaking, settlers in Outremer and the Byzantine Empire, who were professed to the western Roman Church rather than subscribing to eastern Orthodox beliefs.

Frankokratia/Latinokratia: Meaning 'rule of the Franks' and 'rule of the Latins', a name for the period when western Europeans, mostly French and Italian men, created and governed several successor states of the Byzantine Empire. See also 'Latin Empire of Constantinople' below.

Holy Roman Empire (*Sacrum Romanum Imperium*): The Empire's history dates from the coronation of Charlemagne (*Charles le Magne*, meaning 'Charles the Great' in Old French) as Holy Roman Emperor in 800, the first emperor in western Europe since the collapse of Rome's western empire a few centuries earlier. It endured until the early 1800s, and consisted of modern-day Germany plus parts of ten other modern countries: Austria, Belgium, the Czech Republic, Denmark, France, Italy, Luxembourg, the Netherlands, Poland, and Switzerland.[1]

Kaisar (m)/**Kaisarissa** (f): Greek for 'Caesar', a senior Byzantine court title.

King of the Romans: A title that essentially meant the Holy Roman Emperor-elect, and the King of the Romans was usually, though not invariably, promoted to emperor by being crowned as such by the Pope. It was an elected position, and each king was chosen by a group of *Kurfürsten* or Prince-Electors: the archbishops of Cologne, Mainz and Trier, the king of Bohemia, the duke of Saxony, the count palatine of the Rhine, and the margrave of Brandenburg.

Latin: As an adjective, used to describe people of western European origin who were followers of the Roman Church; see also 'Frankish' above.

Latin Kingdom of Jerusalem: A Christian state established in 1099 after the First Crusade. The Kingdom was vastly diminished in 1187 after Salah al-Din overran almost all of it, including the city of Jerusalem itself, and ceased to exist in 1291, when its last remaining cities fell to the Mamluks.

Latin Empire of Constantinople: One of the successor states of the Byzantine Empire created after Crusaders sacked the city of Constantinople in 1204. Constantinople was recaptured and the Byzantine Empire re-established in 1261, after the victory of Mikhael Palaiologos at the battle of Pelagonia in 1259. Other rump states of the Byzantine Empire established in the early thirteenth century included the empires of Nicaea and Trebizond, the despotate of Epirus, the kingdom of Thessaloniki, and the principality of Achaea. The period of these territories' existence is known as the *Frankokratia* or *Latinokratia*, and the Latin Empire was known to contemporaries as *Romania* (printed here in italics to distinguish it from the country of Romania).

Mamluks: A sultanate and Muslim warrior class of former slaves which ruled much of the Levant (the Eastern Mediterranean), the Hejaz (the westernmost area of modern-day Saudi Arabia) and Mesopotamia (modern Iraq) from the mid-thirteenth century until overthrown by the Ottomans in the early 1500s.

Ottomans/Ottoman Empire: A dynasty founded in Turkey in the late thirteenth century, the Ottomans ruled much of the Balkans, the Caucasus, North Africa and the Middle East until the early twentieth century. Their capture of Constantinople in 1453 brought down the Byzantine Empire.

Outremer: Meaning 'overseas' or 'beyond (the) sea' in French, the name refers to the various territories created and settled by European Christians in the Eastern Mediterranean between the late eleventh and late thirteenth century: the Latin Kingdom of Jerusalem, the counties of Tripoli and Edessa, and the principality of Antioch. Outremer is also often known to posterity as the Latin East or the Crusader States.

Porphyrogeniture: A system of inheritance in which children born during their father's reign as king or emperor are preferred as heirs over their older siblings born before their father's accession to the throne. In 1100, Henry

I used porphyrogeniture to claim the English throne, on the grounds that he, unlike his eldest brother Robert Curthose, duke of Normandy, was born after their father William the Conqueror became king of England in 1066.

Porphyrogennete (f)/**Porphyrogennetos** (m): Greek, meaning 'born in the purple'; the title given to a child born during their father's reign as Byzantine Emperor. Originally it meant that the person was born in the Porphyry Chamber in the imperial palace of Constantinople, which was lined with a hard purplish rock called imperial porphyry.

Primogeniture: From the Latin meaning 'firstborn', a system of inheritance in which the eldest son inherits everything. In medieval England, female heirs inherited equal portions of an estate in the absence of a male heir, whereas in medieval France, the eldest daughter inherited everything if she had no brothers.

Protosebastos: literally 'first *Sebastos*' or 'venerable one', the Greek equivalent of the Latin word *Augustus*; a title given to high-ranking relatives of the Byzantine emperors and empresses.

Romania: See 'Latin Empire of Constantinople' above.

Sebastokrator: Greek for 'venerable ruler', used in the Byzantine Empire and its successor states; the highest title after emperor. The wife of a *Sebastokrator* was a *Sebastokratorissa*.

Seljuks/Seljuk Empire: A dynasty of Turkish/Persian, Sunni Muslim rulers in the eleventh and twelfth centuries, founded by Seljuk Beg (d. early 1000s). At its height, the Seljuk Empire stretched from Turkey to the Hindu Kush, and they captured Baghdad in the 1050s.

Seljuk Sultanate of Rûm: A Sunni Muslim state in Anatolia, established on land captured from the Byzantine Empire, which lasted from the 1070s until the early 1300s. Rûm means Rome. It is sometimes also called the Sultanate of Iconium, which was its capital and is now a Turkish city called Konya.

Sicily: From 1130 until 1282, the kingdom of Sicily consisted of not only the island of Sicily, but also the Italian mainland below Rome. After the War of the Sicilian Vespers in 1282, the island of Sicily remained the kingdom of Sicily and the area of the Italian mainland formerly joined to it in one realm became the kingdom of Naples.

Ultimogeniture: A rare system of inheritance in which the youngest sibling inherits everything.

Part I

Outremer

Dramatis Personae

John de Brienne, born *c.*1175/78, nobleman of Champagne in France; king of Jerusalem by his first marriage, and claimant to the throne of Armenian Cilicia by his second; marries 1) Marie of Montferrat, queen regnant of Jerusalem, in 1210, and 2) Stephanie of Armenia in 1214; founder of the Brienne/Beaumont family

Baldwin III, b.1130, king of Jerusalem jointly with his mother Queen Melisende from 1143 to 1161, and alone from 1161 to 1163; marries Theodora Komnene of Byzantium, niece of the Byzantine Emperor Manuel I Komnenos (r.1143–80)

Amalric (or Amaury), b.1136, king of Jerusalem 1163 to 1174; brother and successor of Baldwin III; marries firstly Agnès de Courtenay, daughter of Joscelin II, count of Edessa, and secondly Maria Komnene of Byzantium

Baldwin IV, b.1161, king of Jerusalem 1174 to 1185; son of Amalric and Agnès de Courtenay; known as the Leper King and never marries

Sibilla, b. *c.*1159/60, countess of Jaffa and Ascalon, queen regnant of Jerusalem 1186 to 1190; daughter of Amalric and Agnès; sister of Baldwin IV

Baldwin V, b.1177, Sibilla's son from her first marriage to Guglielmo (William) of Montferrat (d.1177); king of Jerusalem 1185 to 1186

Guy de Lusignan, b. *c.*1150, a younger son of Hugues de Lusignan, baron of Poitou in western France; Sibilla's second husband and co-ruler of Jerusalem; later lord of Cyprus

Maria Komnene, b. *c.*1154/55, queen consort of Jerusalem; daughter of the *Protosebastos* Ioannes Doukas Komnenos (d.1176), and great-niece of Emperor Manuel I Komnenos; marries King Amalric as his second wife in 1167, and secondly the Frankish nobleman Balian d'Ibelin in 1177

Isabella, b.1172, queen regnant of Jerusalem 1190 to 1205; only child of Amalric and Maria Komnene; half-sister of Baldwin IV and Sibilla; Sibilla's successor

John d'Ibelin, b. *c.*1178, elder son of Queen Maria Komnene and Balian d'Ibelin; half-brother of Queen Isabella; lord of Beirut, and regent of Jerusalem 1205 to 1210; his brother is Philip d'Ibelin, b. *c.*1180

Humphrey of Toron, b. *c.*1166, heir to the lordships of Toron and Oultrejourdain; first husband of Queen Isabella of Jerusalem; their marriage is annulled in 1190

Corrado (Conrad) **of Montferrat**, b.1140s, marquis of Montferrat in northern Italy, king of Jerusalem by marriage; brother of Queen Sibilla's first husband Guglielmo; marries Theodora Angelina of Byzantium in 1187, then Queen Isabella as her second husband in 1190

Marie of Montferrat and Jerusalem, b.1192, queen regnant of Jerusalem 1205 to 1212; only child of Corrado; eldest of Queen Isabella's five daughters, and her successor; marries John de Brienne in 1210

Henri, count of Champagne, b.1166; nephew of both King Richard I Lionheart of England and King Philip II Augustus of France; marries Queen Isabella as her third husband in 1192

Alice of Champagne and Jerusalem (b. *c.*1193/95), queen consort of Cyprus, and **Philippa of Champagne and Jerusalem** (b. *c.*1195/97), lady of Ramerupt; daughters of Queen Isabella and Henri of Champagne; half-sisters of Marie of Montferrat

Aiméry de Lusignan, b. *c.*mid-1140s, first king of Cyprus; older brother of Guy de Lusignan; marries Queen Isabella as her fourth and last husband in 1198

Hugh I de Lusignan, b. *c.*1195, king of Cyprus 1205 to 1218; Aiméry's son from his first marriage to Eschiva d'Ibelin; marries his stepsister Alice of Champagne and Jerusalem

Sibilla of Cyprus and Jerusalem (b. *c.*1198/99), queen consort of Armenian Cilicia, and **Melisende of Cyprus and Jerusalem** (b. *c.*1200), princess of Antioch and countess of Tripoli; daughters of Queen Isabella of Jerusalem and King Aiméry of Cyprus; half-sisters of both Marie of Montferrat, queen of Jerusalem, and Hugh I de Lusignan, king of Cyprus

Amaurion of Cyprus and Jerusalem, dies in childhood; son of Isabella and Aiméry

Yolande de Brienne, b.1212, queen regnant of Jerusalem 1212 to 1228; Holy Roman Empress and queen of Sicily by marriage; only child of Marie of Montferrat and John de Brienne; granddaughter of Queen Isabella and Corrado of Montferrat

Konrad von Hohenstaufen, b.1228, son and heir of Yolande de Brienne and grandson of John de Brienne, and his son and heir **Konradin,** b.1252, titular kings of Jerusalem

Isaakios Doukas Komnenos, b. mid or late 1150s, self-proclaimed *Basileus* of Cyprus 1185 to 1191; great-nephew of the Byzantine Emperor Manuel I Komnenos; his daughter and heir, given name unknown, is called the Damsel of Cyprus

Levon I, b. *c.*1150, prince of Armenian Cilicia from 1187, and its first king from 1199 to 1219; marries firstly Isabelle of Antioch and secondly Sibilla of Cyprus and Jerusalem (b. *c.*1198/99)

Stephanie of Armenia, b. after 1195, daughter of Levon I and Isabelle of Antioch; marries John de Brienne as his second wife in 1214, and mother of his son, probably also called John de Brienne (b. *c.*1216), half-brother of Queen Yolande of Jerusalem

Zabel of Armenia, b.1216/17, queen regnant of Armenian Cilicia 1219 to 1252; half-sister of Stephanie; daughter of Levon I and Sibilla of Cyprus and Jerusalem; granddaughter of Queen Isabella of Jerusalem and King Aiméry of Cyprus; marries firstly Philip of Antioch and secondly Hethum of Baberon

Bohemond III, b.1140s, prince of Antioch; brother-in-law of Emperor Manuel I Komnenos; father of Raymond IV, count of Tripoli, and Bohemond IV, prince of Antioch and count of Tripoli

Bohemond IV 'the One-Eyed', b. *c.*1175, prince of Antioch and count of Tripoli; marries firstly Plaisance of Jebail and secondly Melisende of Cyprus and Jerusalem (b. *c.*1200)

Bohemond V, b. late 1190s, prince of Antioch and count of Tripoli; son of Bohemond IV and Plaisance of Jebail; father of **Plaisance of Antioch**, queen consort of Cyprus

Raymond-Roupen of Antioch, b.1197/98, posthumous son of Raymond IV, count of Tripoli, and Alice of Armenia; nephew of Bohemond IV; claimant to the throne of Armenian Cilicia as the great-nephew of Levon I

Philip of Antioch, b. early 1200s, son of Bohemond IV and Plaisance of Jebail; younger brother of Bohemond V, and cousin of Raymond-Roupen; marries Zabel, queen regnant of Armenian Cilicia, in the early 1220s

Henry I de Lusignan, b.1217, king of Cyprus 1218 to 1253; son of Hugh I de Lusignan and Alice of Champagne and Jerusalem; grandson of Queen Isabella of Jerusalem and Henri of Champagne; his third wife is Plaisance of Antioch

Hugh II de Lusignan, b.1252, king of Cyprus 1253 to 1267, son of Henry I and Plaisance of Antioch; dies in his teens and has no children

Hugh III of Antioch-Lusignan, b. *c.*1235, king of Cyprus 1267 to 1284 and king of Jerusalem 1268 to 1284; cousin and successor of Hugh II; father of **John I** and **Henry II**, kings of Cyprus, and **Amalric**, lord of Tyre

Maria of Antioch, b. *c.*1222, daughter of Bohemond IV and Melisende of Cyprus and Jerusalem; half-sister of Bohemond V: granddaughter of Queen Isabella of Jerusalem and King Aiméry of Cyprus; claimant to the throne of Jerusalem

Salah al-Din, known as Saladin, birth name Al-Malik al-Nasir Salah al-Din Abu'l Muzaffar Yusuf ibn Ayyub, b.1137/38, first sultan of Egypt and Syria, and founder of the Ayyubid dynasty; warrior against the Crusaders, and captures most of the Latin Kingdom of Jerusalem in 1187

Henry II, b.1133, king of England 1154 to 1189; marries Eleanor of Aquitaine in 1152; cousin of Baldwin IV, Queen Sibilla and Queen Isabella of Jerusalem

Richard I Lionheart, b.1157, king of England 1189 to 1199; son of Henry II and Eleanor of Aquitaine; marries **Berengaria of Navarre** (b. *c.*1165/70), eldest daughter of King Sancho VI of Navarre, in Cyprus in 1191

Joan of England, b.1165, youngest daughter of Henry II and Eleanor of Aquitaine; sister of Richard Lionheart; marries Guglielmo II de Hauteville, king of Sicily

Philip II Augustus, b.1165, king of France 1180 to 1223; son of Louis VII and his third wife Adèle of Champagne

Friedrich Barbarossa ('Redbeard'), b.1122, Holy Roman Emperor 1155 to 1190, king of Germany, Italy and Burgundy

Chapter 1

Vivacity of Disposition

The ancient port of Tyre, which stands on the coast of the Mediterranean in southern Lebanon, is one of the oldest continually inhabited settlements in the world, probably founded around 2750 BCE. During its millennia of existence, Tyre has been ruled by, among others, the pharaohs of Ancient Egypt, the Phoenicians, the Neo-Assyrians, the Persian kings Cyrus the Great and Darius the Great, the Macedonian king Alexander the Great, the Ancient Greeks, the Romans, the emperors of Byzantium, the Rashidun, Umayyad and Abbasid caliphates, the Latin kings of Jerusalem, the Mamluks, and the Ottomans. The twelfth-century historian William of Tyre described the residents of his birthplace as being 'noted for their keenness of mind and vivacity of disposition' and pointed out how Tyre 'dates from very remote times'.[1] Among the many delights which entice visitors to this UNESCO World Heritage Centre today are a causeway built by Alexander the Great in 332 BCE, a Roman hippodrome and aqueduct, a triumphal arch which is more than 2,000 years old, and, at Al Mina, the red granite columns that are now all that remain of the huge Crusader Cathedral of Tyre. It was built in the 1120s when the city fell under the control of the Crusaders and became part of the Latin Kingdom of Jerusalem, and was destroyed by the Mamluks in the late 1200s when they captured Tyre.

In the twelfth and thirteenth centuries, numerous men from western Europe sought and found their fortune in Outremer. One of them was John de Brienne, a French nobleman who began what was to be an astonishingly successful career in Outremer in the early 1200s. He was born in the mid or late 1170s as the youngest son of Érard II, count of Brienne, which in the Middle Ages was a small county in the Champagne region, 115 miles east of Paris and 25 miles from Troyes. John de Brienne, with few prospects of advancement in his homeland and a man of 'genteel poverty', managed to make a brilliant marriage to Marie of Montferrat, the eighteen-year-old queen regnant of Jerusalem, the first important step in his remarkable career. John and Marie married in the port of Acre, then in the Latin Kingdom of

Jerusalem and now in northern Israel, and now called Akko, on 14 September 1210. Six years later, in 1216, the French churchman Jacques de Vitry visited Acre and hated it: he called it 'this horrible city… full of countless disgraceful acts and evil deeds', and full also of 'foreigners who had fled from their own lands as outlaws because of various appalling crimes'. One wonders if John de Brienne was rather more impressed. He and Marie were jointly crowned king and queen of Jerusalem at the beginning of October 1210 by Albert, Patriarch of Jerusalem, in Tyre Cathedral. Present during the coronation were the archbishops of Tyre and Nazareth, the bishops of Sidon and Acre, and Queen Marie's uncle and her former regent during her minority, John d'Ibelin, lord of Beirut.[2]

The states created by western Europeans in what is now Lebanon, Israel, Palestine, Syria and Turkey began their existence with the First Crusade in the late 1090s. The French nobleman Godfrey de Bouillon, duke of Lower Lotharingia (or Lorraine) and a son of the count of Boulogne, was one of the many European noblemen and knights who heeded Pope Urban II's call to a holy war in 1095, and their aim was to capture the city of Jerusalem and the Holy Land from its Muslim rulers. Jerusalem duly fell to them in July 1099 after a six-week siege, and horrifying carnage ensued: the bodies of human beings were piled 'on mounds as big as houses', wrote one author, and another declared that 'if you had been there, your feet would have been stained to the ankles with the blood of the slain'. Men, women and children were slaughtered without mercy; some were forced to jump to their deaths from towers.[3]

Godfrey de Bouillon was the first ruler of the Latin Kingdom of Jerusalem created by the Crusaders at the end of the 1090s, though he eschewed the title of king and had ruled for barely a year when he died in 1100. His brief reign, and his and the other Crusaders' bloody exploits in Outremer, were detailed for posterity by William of Tyre (d.1186), one of the greatest of all medieval historians, in his *Historia Rerum in Partibus Transmarinis Gestarum* or 'History of Deeds Done Beyond the Sea'. Godfrey, a childless bachelor, was succeeded as ruler of the nascent Kingdom of Jerusalem by his younger brother Baldwin of Boulogne, who did use the title of king, then by their kinsman Baldwin of Le Bourcq, son of the count of Rethel in northern France and himself count of Edessa, who succeeded as King Baldwin II of Jerusalem in 1118. In 1124, during Baldwin II's thirteen-year reign, European settlers captured the port of Tyre from Tughtekin, *Atabeg* of Damascus, after a siege of five months. Over the years and decades following the capture of Jerusalem in 1099, they created territories in the Holy Land which they named the counties of Edessa and Tripoli and the principality of Antioch. The settlers did not, however, have everything their own way; in 1119 a Crusader army from Antioch was heavily defeated by the Muslim ruler of Aleppo in a battle known as the Field of Blood, during which the regent of Antioch was one of the many Frankish men killed, and in the 1140s the Second Crusade was triggered when Zengi, *Atabeg* of Mosul, captured Edessa.

Baldwin II of Jerusalem and his wife Morfia of Melitene – a city located in Cappadocia in the eastern Anatolian region of what is now Turkey, though Morfia herself was the daughter of an Armenian nobleman named Gabriel – had four daughters, of whom the eldest was Melisende. She was born in Edessa, a city also in modern-day Turkey now called Şanlıurfa, probably in 1105, and was thirteen when she witnessed her parents' coronation as king and queen of Jerusalem on Christmas Day 1118 in the Church of the Holy Nativity of Bethlehem.[4] King Baldwin searched among the nobility of his native France for a suitable husband for his and Morfia's eldest daughter and heir, and settled on Fulk or Foulques, count of Anjou, who declared himself amenable to the idea of moving from France to the Holy Land and becoming king of Jerusalem. He and Melisende wed in 1129. This marriage gave the royal family of Jerusalem a close connection to the royal family of England, as in 1128, Fulk's son and heir from his first marriage to Ermengarde of Maine, Melisende's stepson Geoffrey of Anjou (b.1113), made a brilliant marriage to Matilda, the dowager empress of Germany and the only surviving legitimate child of Henry I, king of England (r.1100–35). William of Tyre described Fulk of Anjou as 'a ruddy man… faithful and gentle, affable, kind and compassionate, unusual traits in people of that complexion… an experienced warrior full of patience and wisdom in military affairs'.[5]

Melisende and Fulk became king and queen of Jerusalem on Baldwin II's death in August 1131. After Fulk's death in a hunting accident twelve years into their joint reign – his horse stumbled and sent him to the ground, and he was killed by his heavy saddle falling on his head – Melisende and the barely thirteen-year-old Baldwin III, the elder of her and Fulk's two sons, became joint rulers of Jerusalem. Mother and son were crowned together on Christmas Day 1143, and during Baldwin's minority there is little doubt that Melisende ruled the Latin Kingdom of Jerusalem as queen regnant. She gradually gave more of a role to her son as he grew older, though a civil war broke out in the early 1150s as Baldwin reached his majority and demanded that he rule alone. Melisende refused, though eventually she was compelled to back down.[6] According to William of Tyre, Melisende was 'a woman of great wisdom' who had 'risen so far above the normal status of women that she dared to undertake important measures'. Despite this rather patronising assertion, William was highly impressed with Queen Melisende: 'she ruled the kingdom and administered the government with such skilful care that she may be said truly to have equalled her ancestors in that respect'.[7] Melisende's two granddaughters, a great-granddaughter and a great-great-granddaughter reigned as queens regnant of Jerusalem and another great-granddaughter was regent of Cyprus, while Melisende's younger sisters Hodierna and Alice, Alice's daughter Constance, princess of Antioch in her own right, and Constance's daughter Maria, Byzantine Empress, were also powerful and influential women. Back in France, meanwhile, Fulk's heir to his county of Anjou was his son Geoffrey, Baldwin III's much older half-brother. Geoffrey died in 1151, and his and Empress Matilda's eldest son Henry of Anjou, Baldwin's nephew though close to his own age, succeeded him in Anjou and in 1154 also became King Henry II of England.

Baldwin III married Theodora Komnene of Byzantium in 1158 in the hope that her wealthy and powerful uncle, the Byzantine Emperor Manuel I Komnenos, would provide a fabulous dowry.[8] When Baldwin died in 1163, two years after his mother Queen Melisende, he and the still very young Theodora had produced no children, and he was succeeded by his brother Amalric, the second son of Queen Melisende and Fulk of Anjou. As a widow, the dowager queen Theodora Komnene had a long and infamous relationship with her kinsman Andronikos Komnenos, which resulted in two out-of-wedlock children; see Part 3 below. Within months of his accession, King Amalric launched an invasion of Egypt in an attempt to strengthen his kingdom at the expense of the weak state of Egypt under the Fatimid caliphate, though the accession of Salah al-Din as the first sultan of Egypt and Syria a few years later tipped the balance of power in Egypt's favour.

In 1157, King Amalric had married the Frankish noblewoman Agnès de Courtenay, daughter of the count of Edessa, and they had two children: a daughter named Sibilla, born in 1159 or 1160, and a son, Baldwin, born in 1161 a few weeks before the death of his grandmother Queen Melisende. Before the Frankish nobility of the Kingdom of Jerusalem permitted Amalric to accede to his late brother's throne in 1163, however, they forced him to annul his marriage to Agnès, for reasons which remain unclear but probably had something to do with consanguinity. Agnès's daughter Sibilla subsequently grew up in the convent of Bethany near Jerusalem where her great-aunt Iveta, the fourth and youngest daughter of Baldwin II and his Armenian wife Morfia of Melitene, and the sister of Queen Melisende, was abbess.[9] As for young Baldwin, his tutor William of Tyre, the great historian who was then archdeacon of Tyre and served as the city's archbishop from 1175 to 1186, realised that the boy had leprosy when he was nine years old and felt no sensation in his right arm.[10]

Keen to maintain cordial relations with the Byzantine Empire, a useful ally in the ever-shifting political scene in the region, Amalric sent envoys there to negotiate a second marriage for him. His new bride was Maria Komnene, whose father Ioannes Doukas Komnenos was a *Protosebastos* and governor of Cyprus, a grandson of the Byzantine emperor Ioannes II Komnenos (d.1143), and nephew of the reigning emperor, Manuel I. After two apparently tortuous years of negotiations, Maria, who was still only twelve or thirteen, married Amalric in Tyre Cathedral in August 1167. Their only surviving child, Isabella, was born in 1172, and like her half-sister Sibilla grew up in the convent of Bethany with her great-aunt Iveta.[11] As a member of the Byzantine royal family, Queen Maria Komnene had grown up in fabulous luxury, possibly in the great imperial palace of Constantinople, and received an excellent education, as was usually the case among the Byzantine imperial family, including the women. Maria's great-great-aunt, the *Porphyrogennete* Anna Komnene (1083–1153), wrote, in Greek, a text known as the *Alexiad* about the life and reign of her father, Emperor Alexios I Komnenos (r.1081–1118). A Byzantine chronicler declared that Anna, whom he called *Kaisarissa Anna*, was 'ardently devoted to philosophy, the queen of all the sciences, and was educated in every field of learning'.[12] Some of the women who married into the imperial family of Constantinople were also highly educated: Emperor Manuel I Komnenos's sister-in-law Dobrodjeja Mstislavna of Kievan Rus studied Galen and translated some of his works into her native Old Russian, and wrote a long treatise called 'Ointments'.[13]

The wealth of Queen Maria Komnene's native Constantinople astonished all who saw it. When William of Tyre visited the city some years later in 1179/80 (see Part 3 below), he was so overawed by what he saw that he wrote 'any attempt to describe in detail all the wonders of those days would be utterly futile'. He did talk about the 'royal robes adorned with a profusion of precious stones' and the 'vast amount of massive gold and silver furniture' in the imperial palace. A French nobleman who visited the Boukoleon Palace in Constantinople at the beginning of the 1200s also wrote '[w]ords fail me when it comes to describing the treasures found in that palace, for there was such a store of precious things that one could not possibly count them', and another added '[n]or do I think, myself, that in the forty richest cities of the world there had been so much wealth as was found in Constantinople'. He stated, with some exaggeration, that in the Boukoleon Palace 'there were fully five hundred halls, all connected with one another and all made with gold mosaic', as well as thirty chapels whose door hinges were all made of silver. Despite her highly impressive and wealthy background, however, Queen Maria did not impress everyone after her arrival in Jerusalem: one chronicler, who loathed her, stated that she was 'steeped in Greek filth from the cradle'.[14]

Chapter 2

The Leper King

On King Amalric's death from dysentery in 1174, only in his late thirties, he left his leprous son Baldwin and his two daughters, Sibilla and Isabella. Despite the thirteen-year-old boy's severe health issues, the Frankish nobility elected him as their king, and he was crowned as Baldwin IV in the Church of the Holy Sepulchre in Jerusalem.[1] The Latin Kingdom of Jerusalem certainly permitted female succession, and Baldwin's sister Sibilla and their half-sister Isabella were also possible candidates for the throne; Sibilla as she was older than Baldwin, and Isabella by porphyrogeniture, as she, unlike her older half-siblings, was born after Amalric became king. As she was only two years old when her father died, however, she was not deemed a suitable candidate. Baldwin and Sibilla's claim to the throne was perhaps somewhat dubious as their parents' marriage had been annulled, and although they had a better claim than their infant half-sister by primogeniture, this system of inheritance did not always hold sway in Outremer. If Maria Komnene had borne Amalric a son, it seems highly likely that he would have been elected as king in preference to Baldwin, however young the putative boy might have been in 1174. That Baldwin's subjects were prepared to give their loyalty to a young man with leprosy seems astonishing, though as Helena Schrader points out, Outremer culture was heavily influenced by Byzantine and Orthodox traditions, and in Orthodox belief, leprosy was a sign of God's grace rather than a manifestation of sin and divine punishment. It is also likely that Baldwin's condition was suspected though still unconfirmed at the time of his election and coronation, and William of Tyre's opinion was that his affliction was worthy of compassion and did not indicate God's displeasure.[2]

Baldwin IV is known to posterity as the Leper King of Jerusalem, and was played by Edward Norton in the Hollywood film *Kingdom of Heaven*. In the film, his sister Sibilla has a relationship with the character played by Orlando Bloom, Balian d'Ibelin, who did exist but married Baldwin and Sibilla's widowed stepmother Queen Maria Komnene, not Sibilla (and never worked as a blacksmith in France, as his character in the film does; Balian was a Frankish nobleman born in the Kingdom of Jerusalem). King Baldwin and his stepmother seem to have a rather formal and not very close relationship, and Maria withdrew from court after her husband Amalric's death and retired to her own city of Nablus. She raised a family there with Balian d'Ibelin, whom she married in 1177.[3] Among their children, the younger half-siblings of Maria and Amalric's daughter Isabella, was John d'Ibelin, later known as the Old Lord of Beirut and regent of the kingdom for Maria's underage granddaughter in the early 1200s.

During Baldwin IV's minority, the Kingdom of Jerusalem was ruled by a regent, his father's cousin the count of Tripoli, though Baldwin came of age on his fifteenth birthday in 1176. Despite his deteriorating physical condition as the leprosy spread through his body, to the point where he became blind and unable to use either his feet or his hands in the early 1180s, Baldwin was a strong and courageous leader who personally led an army against the forces of Salah al-Din, sultan of Egypt and Syria, at the battle of Mont Gisard in November 1177 when still only sixteen years old, and routed his forces. Baldwin defeated Salah al-Din again in 1182, despite the devastating progression of his condition. The history written by his tutor William of Tyre paints a vivid picture of him in childhood as a bright, able and attractive boy with a stammer inherited from his father, who despite the lack of feeling in his arms became a skilled rider and was, like his father, passionately interested in history and reading.[4]

Baldwin succumbed to his illness in 1185 at not quite twenty-four. For obvious reasons he had been unable to marry and father children, and was succeeded as king by his young nephew Baldwin V, the son of Sibilla and her late Italian husband Guglielmo (or William) of Montferrat, who had died in 1177 while Sibilla, seventeen or eighteen years old, was pregnant.[5] She subsequently married Guy de Lusignan, a nobleman from Poitou, in what was a somewhat bizarre mismatch given that she was the daughter, sister and mother of kings while he was merely the younger son of a baron. A more suitable marriage to Étienne, count of Sancerre, son of the count of Blois and brother-in-law of Louis VII (d.1180), king of France, had previously been suggested for her.[6] Guy de Lusignan was grossly unpopular in Outremer, and William of Tyre talks of the hatred between him and his brother-in-law the Leper King.[7] There was a storm of discontent when Sibilla's nine-year-old son the king passed away in 1186 and Sibilla herself succeeded as queen regnant, and elected Guy as her co-ruler. Sibilla's reign was another short one, however, and she and her two young daughters by Guy de Lusignan died of fever outside the walls of Acre in 1190, during a siege of the port.

As was often the way with things in the Latin East at the time, Guy de Lusignan was compensated for losing Jerusalem on the death of his wife and daughters by being given the lordship of Cyprus instead. He ruled the island until he died in 1194, and was succeeded by his elder brother, Aiméry de Lusignan, who was crowned the first king of Cyprus in early 1198. The Lusignans were vassals of Richard Lionheart, king of England, in his capacity as duke of Aquitaine in south-west France, and Richard secured Cyprus for Guy after defeating the self-proclaimed emperor of the island in 1191; see Chapter 4 below. Guy was rewarded with Cyprus despite his personal responsibility for the loss of most of the territory of the Latin Kingdom of Jerusalem in 1187, and despite the undeniable fact that he was, as described by a modern historian, 'a catastrophically inept leader'.[8] He dragged an army through the desert without adequate water in the heat of July, and unsurprisingly, lost the battle of Hattin to Salah al-Din. Al-Din and his forces subsequently overran most of the Kingdom until all that remained of it was a narrow strip of coastal territory, including the port of Tyre. Salah al-Din took Guy captive after Hattin though spared his life and did not execute him, stating 'a king does not kill a king'.[9]

The loss of the city of Jerusalem, despite the stout defence of it led by Queen Sibilla, her stepmother Maria Komnene and Maria's husband Balian d'Ibelin, triggered the Third Crusade, which took place from 1189 to 1192. The Crusade was led by the king of England, Richard I Lionheart – son of Henry II of Anjou (d.1189) and thus a kinsman of the royal family of Jerusalem – and Louis VII of France's son and successor Philip II Augustus. Friedrich Barbarossa, Holy Roman Emperor and king of Germany, Italy and Burgundy, was also on his way to the Holy Land in June 1190 to take part in the Crusade when he drowned in a river near Silifke (or Seleucia) Castle in Armenian Cilicia. 'He who had so often escaped great dangers died miserably', lamented one chronicler, and indeed dying by falling into a river seems a curiously anticlimactic passing for such a towering personality as Barbarossa.[10] The Third Crusade failed in its main objective of recapturing Jerusalem from Muslim hands, though did eventually succeed in retaking the important port of Acre and the city of Jaffa. Queen Sibilla and her young daughters died during the Crusaders' exhaustingly long siege of Acre, as did Friedrich, duke of Swabia, who had taken over command of the German forces after his father Barbarossa's death, and Étienne, count of Sancerre and Philip II's uncle, once suggested as Sibilla's second husband. King Philip himself fell seriously ill, though recovered.

Chapter 3

Queen Isabella and Queen Marie

Isabella, the now eighteen-year-old daughter of King Amalric and Queen Maria Komnene, succeeded her half-sister Sibilla in 1190 and became queen regnant of the vastly diminished Latin Kingdom. Although Isabella was always called the queen of Jerusalem, it was an empty title as she never set foot in the city again, though her grandson-in-law recaptured it in the late 1220s and it fell once again into Christian hands for a few years. As a child of eleven in the autumn of 1183, Isabella had been married by her half-brother Baldwin IV to Humphrey of Toron, who inherited the lordship of Toron from his grandfather and was also heir to his mother Stephanie de Milly's lordship of Oultrejourdain (or Transjordan). Isabella moved from the convent of Bethany to her mother-in-law's massive fortress of Kerak east of the Dead Sea, where her wedding took place. In a case of desperately unfortunate timing, Salah al-Din and his army arrived outside the castle and began besieging it during the celebrations, though on learning of the nuptials, al-Din ordered his catapults not to fire during the wedding banquet and spared the tower where the young couple were lodged.[1] Isabella's new mother-in-law Stephanie de Milly and Stephanie's powerful third husband Raynald de Châtillon prevented her from visiting her mother Maria Komnene and stepfather Balian d'Ibelin, apparently to thwart any attempts by the ambitious dowager queen and her allies to make Isabella the queen regnant of Jerusalem when it became obvious that Baldwin IV's leprosy would kill him sooner rather than later.[2]

After Isabella succeeded to the throne anyway after the deaths of her half-siblings, her nephew Baldwin V and her little de Lusignan nieces, her strong-willed mother decided that Humphrey of Toron was too weak to be entrusted with the rule of the Latin Kingdom. She therefore declared that Isabella had been too young to consent to her marriage, and that it was invalid. Isabella and Humphrey's marriage was annulled against their own wishes. This fact was to cause much unease at the papal court in later years, and the legality of Isabella's subsequent marriages and the legitimacy of her children were questioned. After the annulment, Isabella was married instead, in late 1190, to Corrado or Conrad, who succeeded his father as marquis of Montferrat in northern Italy in 1191 and was the younger brother of Queen Sibilla's first husband Guglielmo of Montferrat.[3] Corrado had played an active role in almost single-handedly saving Tyre from Salah al-Din in 1187 shortly after he arrived in Outremer, and was extremely well-connected, being a first cousin of the late king of France, Louis VII, the recently-drowned Holy Roman Emperor, Barbarossa, and Leopold von Babenberg, the duke of Austria.

Although much English-language fiction in the nineteenth and twentieth centuries maligned Corrado as a villainous, treacherous and even violently sadistic character, in reality he was a rather dashing figure whom contemporaries praised as 'valiant and worthy' and 'brave and prudent beyond measure, flourishing in vigour and bodily strength… He so excelled in bravery and sagacity that he was far-famed'. Chroniclers' judgement of him would appear, from his staunch defence of Tyre and its inhabitants, to be accurate.[4] William of Tyre described Corrado's eldest brother Guglielmo as 'a rather tall, good-looking man with blond hair', while their youngest brother Ranieri's 'hair shone like the sun' and he was 'pleasant to look at'. This gives some idea of what Corrado, of northern Italian, Austrian and German origin, must have looked like, though the great twentieth-century historian of the Crusades, Steven Runciman, once talked rather unfairly of 'the grimness of the ageing Piedmontese'.[5] Fair hair also ran in Queen Isabella's family: her uncle Baldwin III had 'straight yellowish hair' and her father King Amalric was blond and bearded. Amalric was 'altogether too fat' with 'breasts like those of a woman hanging down to his waist' in the harsh evaluation of William of Tyre, though William also conceded that he had 'a rather unusual beauty'.[6]

It seems highly likely that Corrado of Montferrat's previous wife Theodora Angelina, sister of the reigning Byzantine Emperor Isaakios II Angelos (r.1185–95), was still alive when he married Isabella, and according to a Byzantine chronicler, Corrado's first wife, whose identity is not known, had died not long before he married Theodora in early 1187.[7] In addition to the difficulties caused by a living wife, and the fact that Isabella was still married to Humphrey of Toron when her marriage to Corrado was planned, Corrado's brother had once been wed to Isabella's half-sister. By the standards of the time, this meant that the couple were, without a papal dispensation, committing incest. As historian Jonathan Phillips says, their marriage was 'a move of breathtaking opportunism' on Corrado's part, as well as being 'both incestuous and doubly bigamous'.[8]

Isabella and Corrado's only child, Marie of Montferrat and Jerusalem, was born several months after Corrado was murdered in Tyre on 28 April 1192, shortly before his planned coronation as king of Jerusalem. This act was possibly carried out by the Assassins, a sect active in Syria and Persia between the eleventh and thirteenth century. The motive for the murder cannot be determined with any certainty, though one contemporary German chronicler suggested, rather improbably, that Corrado was murdered with the connivance of King Richard Lionheart of England, who despised him.[9] The young queen regnant was not widowed for long: whether willingly or not, Isabella was married to her third husband, Henri, count of Champagne, on 5 May 1192, a mere week after Corrado's assassination and while she was pregnant. One chronicler wrote sardonically, though with only slight exaggeration, that Corrado was killed on Tuesday and Isabella married Henri on Thursday. For reasons which are unclear, Henri was never crowned as king of Jerusalem, though over the next five years he proved a competent and effective leader of the Latin Kingdom.[10]

Henri of Champagne's mother Marie was one of the two daughters of Louis VII of France from his first marriage to Eleanor of Aquitaine, who subsequently married King Amalric's kinsman Henry II of England. This made Henri a nephew of both Philip Augustus of France and Richard Lionheart of England, the leaders of the Third Crusade, and he was therefore acceptable to both men as the queen of Jerusalem's husband. Perhaps understandably, Henri was dubious about marrying a pregnant woman who might give birth to a son; he had no wish to leave his own lands in Champagne to look after a kingdom when he might be ousted by his stepson a few years later, and a son of Corrado would take precedence over his own children.[11] He was, therefore, surely relieved when his wife gave birth to Corrado's posthumous daughter, another Marie, some months after their wedding. Isabella perhaps named her daughter in honour of her own mother Maria Komnene and her husband's royal French mother as well.

Isabella and Henri had had two daughters, Alice and Philippa – as well as another daughter who died in infancy, though no sons – when Henri was killed in a bizarre accident on 10 September 1197. He fell out of a window in the royal palace of Acre, and a servant, trying to pull him back in, fell too, and landed on top of him. The servant was a dwarf named Scarlet, and though he survived for a little while then died of his injuries, Henri was killed on impact. At the time of his death, Henri had been preparing to go to the defence of Jaffa, then being attacked by al-Adil Saif-al-Din after some German Crusaders made incursions into Muslim territory without notifying Henri.[12]

Only a few months later, in January 1198, Queen Isabella married her fourth and last husband, the late Guy de Lusignan's widowed older brother Aiméry de Lusignan, recently crowned the first king of Cyprus and now crowned king of Jerusalem alongside Isabella as well. Very little is known about their joint rule of the much-diminished Latin Kingdom. Isabella had two more daughters with Aiméry who lived into adulthood, Sibilla and Melisende, and they also had a son named Amaurion who would almost certainly have succeeded his mother and become king of Jerusalem, but he died as a young child in early February 1205. The little boy was followed to the grave by both of his parents two months later; the royal couple died within a few days of each other in early April 1205. Isabella was just thirty-two or thirty-three when she died, and was judgementally called 'feckless and weak' though 'beautiful' by historian Steven Runciman.[13] Thirteen-year-old Marie of Montferrat, eldest of Isabella's five living daughters, succeeded her as queen regnant of Jerusalem, with Isabella's Ibelin half-brother John, lord of Beirut, as her regent.

Far away in France, Blanca of Navarre, regent of Champagne for her young son Thibaut (b.1201), did not wish her late brother-in-law Henri's daughters Alice and Philippa to lay claim to their father's county of Champagne, which in 1197 had passed to Henri's younger brother, Blanca's husband (d.1201), then to Henri's nephew Thibaut. She therefore put forward John de Brienne, a nobleman of Champagne whom she trusted, as a husband for Queen Marie of Jerusalem, hoping that he would be able to arrange marriages in the Holy Land for Marie's half-sisters Alice and Philippa and keep them well away from Champagne. Philip II Augustus, king of France, also promoted John de Brienne as Queen Marie's husband.[14] Brienne was a cousin of Gautier de Montbéliard, who at the time was regent for the underage King Hugh I of Cyprus, son and successor of the late Aiméry de Lusignan from his first marriage; another factor in his favour.

The regents of Jerusalem agreed, albeit somewhat reluctantly after a far more impressive marriage for Queen Marie to King Pere II of Aragón in

Spain (r.1196–1213) fell through because Pere was unable to persuade the Pope to annul his existing marriage to Marie of Montpellier.[15] Realpolitik demanded that the young queen marry a strong husband who could defend what was left of the Latin Kingdom from Salah al-Din's Ayyubid dynasty and other external enemies, as Marie's mother Isabella had done in 1192 when she took Corrado of Montferrat as her second husband. The king of France, Philip, and the Pope, Innocent III, each gave John de Brienne a dower of 4,000 silver pounds to make him a more acceptable candidate. John was promised the rule of the Latin Kingdom before he arrived, and landed in Acre to great celebrations, though supposedly when he arrived the Frankish barons were dismayed to find that he was not rich nor even a count, merely the youngest son of a count.[16]

Queen Marie was eighteen at the time of her wedding to John de Brienne in September 1210, and John was in his early or mid-thirties.[17] Marriage to the queen of Jerusalem was a brilliant match for him; he was the landless, penniless son of a minor French nobleman, and now became a king. He thus went one better than his eldest brother Gautier de Brienne, their father's heir, who had married the eldest daughter of Tancredi, king of Sicily (d.1194), but failed to take the Sicilian throne. Queen Marie's father Corrado of Montferrat, though merely a marquis, at least had highly impressive family connections. John de Brienne did not even have that, and, like the marriage of Marie's aunt Queen Sibilla and Guy de Lusignan, younger son of a baron, their marriage was a rather bizarre mismatch. John de Brienne assumed control of the Latin Kingdom of Jerusalem, and Marie of Montferrat's uncle and former regent John d'Ibelin was edged out of power, although there was no open breach between the two men in Marie's lifetime. D'Ibelin made his way to Cyprus instead, where his niece Alice of Champagne, Marie's half-sister, was married to their stepbrother Hugh I de Lusignan.[18]

Marie of Montferrat and John de Brienne's only child, a daughter often called Yolande or Yolanda by historians, though more accurately named Isabella like her maternal grandmother, was born in November 1212, and Marie died soon after giving birth to her, aged twenty.[19] Queen Marie died tragically young and was outlived by her grandmother Maria Komnene, who did not die until 1217, while the infant Yolande de Brienne succeeded as queen of Jerusalem, its fourth queen regnant in a row after her mother, grandmother Isabella and great-aunt Sibilla. John de Brienne became regent of the Latin Kingdom for his infant daughter and was still acknowledged as its king as he had been crowned and anointed alongside Marie, though had Yolande followed her mother to the grave, the rightful rulers of Jerusalem would have been Alice of Champagne, the next eldest daughter of the late Queen Isabella, and Alice's husband the young king of Cyprus.

In 1213, Alice's younger full sister, Philippa, living in John de Brienne's care, 'left the castle of Acre secretly by night' and married Brienne's cousin Érard de Brienne, the lord of Ramerupt in northern France and a man at least a quarter of a century her senior.[20] Blanca of Navarre's plan to keep her late brother-in-law Henri of Champagne's daughters far away in Outremer fell apart, despite her efforts to persuade the papacy to investigate the last three of Queen Isabella's four marriages in the hope of excluding Isabella and Henri's daughters from any chance of inheriting the county of Champagne.[21] Philippa and Érard travelled to France to claim her late father's county, and the War of the Succession to Champagne began in 1216; it lasted for the next few years, as Philippa's sister Queen Alice of Cyprus also tried to claim Champagne in the early 1230s. Alice and Philippa were, unlike their three half-sisters Marie, Sibilla and Melisende, great-granddaughters of the redoubtable Eleanor of Aquitaine, dowager queen consort of both France and England, who was still alive when they were born and did not die until 1204 when she was about eighty. They were also great-granddaughters of Melisende, queen regnant of Jerusalem, and were forces to be reckoned with. The sisters failed, however, to gain control of their late father's county of Champagne, because their cousin Thibaut succeeded his maternal uncle Sancho VII as king of Navarre in 1234 and became far more important and influential, and thus far harder to dislodge, than he had been previously.[22]

Chapter 4

Lords of the Mountains

The widowed John de Brienne married his second wife, whose name appears in contemporary sources as both Stephanie and Rita, in April 1214, a year and a half after Queen Marie's death. Stephanie/Rita was born sometime after 1195 as the elder daughter of Levon, the tenth lord and first king of Armenian Cilicia, a Christian state in modern-day Turkey created by Armenian refugees in the 1000s and sometimes called Little Armenia or Lesser Armenia. Its rulers were rather poetically called Lords of the (Taurus) Mountains, and its largest city was Tarsus, birthplace of Saint Paul the Apostle, known as Saul of Tarsus before his conversion to Christianity.

Levon mostly lived in the ancient, fortified city of Sis, now called Kozan, which was located at the northern end of the Cilician plain and sat on a hill with three peaks. Armenian Cilicia bordered Antioch, a city which lies near the modern city of Antakya in the southernmost region of what is now also Turkey; it was taken by the Crusaders in 1098 and, like the kingdom of Jerusalem, was much weakened by the incursions of Salah al-Din in the late 1180s. Though Levon married a woman from Antioch as his first wife, fighting and power struggles between Armenian Cilicia and Antioch often took place. In 1193, for example, Levon lured Bohemond III, prince of Antioch, to Baghras Castle, then sent him to prison in Sis. Henri of Champagne, king of Jerusalem, had to intervene.[1]

As well as the struggles between Armenian Cilicia and Antioch, the principality of Antioch itself was, like the county of Champagne, plagued by different claimants at the start of the 1200s, and a period called the War of the Antiochene Succession lasted from 1201 to 1219.[2] When Bohemond III, prince of Antioch, brother-in-law of the Byzantine Emperor Manuel I Komnenos, died in April 1201, it was unclear who should succeed him. There were two plausible candidates: Bohemond's younger son Bohemond IV, called 'the One-Eyed', or Bohemond III's toddler grandson Raymond-Roupen, the posthumous son of his late older son Raymond IV, count of

Tripoli. Strict rules of primogeniture had not yet been established, and another contemporary example can be found in England after the death of Richard I Lionheart in 1199. Richard had no children from his marriage to Berengaria of Navarre, and was succeeded as king by his youngest brother John (b.1166) in preference to their adolescent nephew Arthur of Brittany (b.1187), posthumous son of John's older brother Geoffrey (1158–86). Bohemond IV rushed to Antioch on the day of his father's funeral in April 1201 to find that many Antiochene nobles had already taken oaths to his three-year-old nephew Raymond-Roupen, but others feared Armenian influence in the principality, as the boy was the son of Alice of Armenia, niece of King Levon. Raymond-Roupen would be crowned as Levon's junior king of Armenian Cilicia in August 1211 and would also be crowned as prince of Antioch in 1216, though he was ousted by his uncle Bohemond IV in 1219.

Levon succeeded his brother as prince of Armenian Cilicia and Lord of the Mountains in 1187, and in January 1199 was crowned as its first king in the church of Sourp Sophia ('Holy Wisdom') in Tarsus. The Armenian patriarch Grigor VI Pahlavuni and Konrad von Wittelsbach, the nobly born German archbishop of Mainz, who had crowned Aiméry de Lusignan as the first king of Cyprus a year earlier, conducted the coronation. Levon became a vassal of the Holy Roman Empire, and in 1190 had sent an embassy to the Holy Roman Emperor Friedrich Barbarossa, who drowned in Levon's domains shortly afterwards, requesting that Armenian Cilicia should be converted into a kingship. Friedrich's eldest son and heir Heinrich granted this wish in 1196. In 1191, Levon had acted as one of King Richard Lionheart's chief attendants during his wedding to Berengaria of Navarre in Limassol, Cyprus, and took part in the Crusaders' long though ultimately successful siege of Acre. He is often known to history as the Great or the Magnificent, and a contemporary German chronicler called him 'a powerful and distinguished man'.[3]

Levon's first marriage to Isabelle of Antioch, Stephanie/Rita of Armenia's mother, ended badly in 1205 when the archbishop of Sis accused Isabelle of committing adultery. Levon imprisoned Isabelle in Vahka Castle, where she died, supposedly poisoned.[4] Around 1210, Levon married his young second wife, Sibilla of Cyprus and Jerusalem (b. *c.*1198/99), elder of the two daughters of Queen Isabella of Jerusalem and her fourth husband Aiméry de Lusignan, king of Cyprus. An Armenian chronicler described Sibilla as 'a woman of Frankish nationality'.[5] Despite being half a century younger than her husband, Sibilla bore Levon a daughter, Zabel, in 1216 or 1217. Around the same time, probably in 1216, Zabel's half-sister Stephanie gave birth to John de Brienne's son, whose name was most likely also John. John the father and his wife claimed the right to succeed Stephanie's father on the throne of Armenian Cilicia. Before King Levon died in May 1219, however, he stated that he wished his successor to be his infant daughter Zabel rather than her much older half-sister Stephanie or his young de Brienne grandson. Another plausible candidate for the throne was Levon's great-nephew Raymond-Roupen of Antioch, whom Levon himself had once favoured as his successor and whom he had crowned as his co-ruler before Zabel was born.

In the last couple of years of King Levon's life, his son-in-law John de Brienne took part in the Fifth Crusade, which began in 1217 and which aimed, like the two crusades before it, to recapture the city of Jerusalem for Christianity. Also like the previous two crusades, it failed in this objective, though the Crusaders did take the Egyptian port city of Damietta in late 1219 after a long siege. Thirty years later, the French chronicler Jean de Joinville wrote that 'King John of Jerusalem' was the man chiefly responsible for capturing Damietta, which he and his allies did by 'reducing the enemy to starvation'.[6] Following the successful capture of the port, John prepared to travel to Armenian Cilicia, hoping to claim the throne a few months after King Levon's death, but was thwarted by his wife's sudden death. Stephanie of Armenia died in June 1220 shortly before she and her husband could depart from Acre to try to claim the kingdom, and was rumoured to have been killed by John de Brienne after trying to poison her young stepdaughter Queen Yolande of Jerusalem.[7] As, however, little John de Brienne the son, aged about four, died just fifteen days after his mother, it seems far more likely, though less dramatic, that they both died of illness. John de Brienne therefore lost any claim to the throne of Armenian Cilicia and gave up all efforts to try to take the kingdom. Pope Honorius IV declared in 1219/20 that either Stephanie or her de Brienne son should succeed King Levon, and after their deaths he declared for Raymond-Roupen of Antioch, but Raymond-Roupen died in prison in the early 1220s. He and his mother Alice of Armenia had invaded Cilicia hoping to seize the throne, but Raymond-Roupen was captured in Tarsus by Kostandin of Baberon, regent for the toddler Queen Zabel, and imprisoned.[8]

Zabel ruled as queen of Armenian Cilicia until her death in 1252. As a child in 1222, she married Philip of Antioch, a younger son of Bohemond IV 'the One-Eyed' and cousin of Raymond-Roupen, but in 1225 Philip was imprisoned in Sis and subsequently poisoned. He had provoked a revolt in the kingdom by favouring and promoting Latins over Armenians and sending much of Armenia's royal treasure to his native Antioch.[9] A heartbroken young Zabel was forced to marry Hethum of Baberon, son of her regent Kostandin and called 'a physically robust and handsome lad' by a chronicler, in June 1226 (the young queen was only about nine or ten when she married for the second time). For years she refused to live with Hethum and escaped to Silifke Castle to stay with her mother Queen Sibilla for a while, but finally returned to her husband and ultimately gave birth to five sons and three daughters.[10] After Zabel's death, her widower ruled Armenian Cilicia until his own death in 1270. Zabel's grandson Bohemond VII, count of Tripoli and titular prince of Antioch, born in *c.*1260 as the son of Zabel and Hethum's daughter Sibilla of Armenia, married John de Brienne's granddaughter from his third marriage, Marguerite de Brienne, in 1278. According to a chronicler, after Bohemond quarrelled with the lord of Jebail in 1282, he captured him and had him buried up to his neck in sand, and let him starve to death. Bohemond also had some of his other enemies blinded.[11]

The last king of Armenian Cilicia was Levon V de Lusignan, who was born around 1342 as the illegitimate son of the constable of the kingdom and was a member of the Lusignan family who were kings of Cyprus. Levon was the successor and distant cousin of Kostandin IV, who died in 1373 and was known as Richard in western European sources. Kostandin/Richard might have been one of the three kings who acted as godfather to Richard of Bordeaux, the future King Richard II of England, at the beginning of 1367.[12] In 1375, Levon V surrendered his kingdom to the Mamluk forces who had invaded Armenian Cilicia, and spent the rest of his life in exile in Spain and France. Other members of his family were taken to Cairo as prisoners of the Mamluks, who ruled Egypt for centuries.

The dispossessed King Levon visited England in late 1385 and early 1386 and spent time with Richard II and his Prague-born queen, Anne of Bohemia. Richard called him 'our cousin the king of Armenia', *nostre cousin le roy d'Armenye*, and gave Levon a safe conduct to travel to England on 24 October 1385. He also gave the master of Levon's household permission to bring wine to England for Levon's use.[13] Levon arrived in Dover in late 1385 and was met by Richard's uncles the dukes of York and Gloucester, and taken to the palace of Eltham in Kent to meet the eighteen-year-old king of England. At some point during his sojourn, which ended on 3 February 1386, Levon gave the Spanish duchess of York, King Richard's aunt-in-law Isabel of Castile (b.1355), a valuable gift which she mentioned in her will of 1392: 'a tablet of jasper which the king of Armonye gave me'.[14] Levon himself died in Paris in 1393 and was buried at Saint-Denis, where most of the kings of France were buried down the centuries. The kingdom of Armenian Cilicia ultimately became part of the Ottoman Empire. As for the principality of Antioch, the kingdom's neighbour and great rival, it existed only until 1268, when it was captured by the Mamluks under the command of Sultan al-Zahir Baibars (whose last name means 'great panther'), who massacred the Christian population of the city.

Chapter 5
Shot Up Like Lethal Hemlock

In 1206, the year after Queen Isabella of Jerusalem's death, plans were set in motion for the marriage of her second eldest daughter, Alice of Champagne and Jerusalem. Alice landed a husband of much higher rank than her older half-sister Queen Marie did: their stepbrother Hugh I de Lusignan, king of Cyprus, Aiméry's son from his first marriage to Eschiva d'Ibelin. Alice's grandmother the dowager queen Maria Komnene conducted the negotiations for the marriage, while Blanca of Navarre, regent of Champagne, provided the dowry, no doubt delighted that the marriage would keep the elder of the late Henri's two daughters well away from the county of Champagne and her son Thibaut.[1] Alice of Champagne and Hugh de Lusignan were close to the same age – Alice was born around 1194/95, and Hugh came of age in September 1210, suggesting he was born in September 1195 – and their three children were born in the 1210s.

That the Lusignans, a baronial family from western France, ended up ruling the island of Cyprus was thanks to King Richard I Lionheart of England and his defeat of Isaakios Doukas Komnenos, the self-proclaimed emperor of Cyprus, in the early 1190s. Isaakios was a scion of the family who were emperors of Byzantium, and like Queen Maria Komnene of Jerusalem, was a great-grandchild of Emperor Ioannes II Komnenos (d.1143). His maternal grandfather, whose last name he took – his father's family name was Doukas Kamateros – was the *Sebastokrator* Isaakios Komnenos, an older brother of Emperor Manuel I. Isaakios Doukas Komnenos spent many years imprisoned in Armenia after being captured in battle there. Released in *c.*1183 thanks to the intervention of his kinsman and uncle-in-law Andronikos I Komnenos, who had recently had himself crowned Byzantine Emperor, and ransomed by the Knights Templar, Isaakios returned to his native Constantinople. He soon, however, proved himself unwilling to accept Andronikos's authority, because he 'passionately desired to become emperor himself'. Isaakios fled to Cyprus, then part of the Byzantine Empire, and, armed with forged letters, claimed to have been appointed governor of the island. Soon afterwards, on the downfall of his dynasty the Komnenoi in Constantinople in 1185 (see Part 3 below), Isaakios declared himself emperor of Cyprus; the Greek title he used was *Basileus*.

As historian Helena Schrader states, Isaakios then 'began a reign of terror' on the island.[2] He starved the inhabitants, robbed them, murdered them, and reduced them to despair. Supposedly he was an ally of Salah al-Din against his fellow Christians, or so many people at the time believed, and certainly he refused to allow the Crusaders to land in Cyprus on their way to Outremer. A German chronicler states that Richard Lionheart of England 'was unable to suffer the insolence and cruelty that [Isaakios] was said to have exercised against poor pilgrims', while the Byzantine Greek chronicler Niketas Choniatēs (d.1217) called Isaakios an 'inhuman and implacable destroyer' and an 'accursed wretch'. He added, with his usual descriptive turn of phrase, that Isaakios 'shot up like lethal hemlock' in Cyprus.[3]

Isaakios, however, overreached himself and brought about his own downfall in 1191. Berengaria, the eldest daughter of Sancho VI, king of the small realm of Navarre in northern Spain, was on her way to marry Richard Lionheart in the company of Richard's widowed sister Joan of England, the dowager queen of Sicily. During a fierce storm, their ship was driven ashore on the coast of Cyprus, and Isaakios took both ladies hostage. (The unfortunate Queen Joan had already been imprisoned in Palermo by her late husband's illegitimate cousin Tancredi, and had only recently been freed; see Part 4 below.) King Richard responded in typical fashion by attacking and seizing the Cypriot port of Limassol, where he married Berengaria in May 1191. The defeated Isaakios tried to flee, but Niketas Choniatēs says that Richard put him in silver chains and he was imprisoned in Marqab Castle in the principality of Antioch. In 1195, Isaakios's kinswoman Euphrosynē Doukaina Kamatera, wife of the new Byzantine Emperor Alexios III Angelos, did her best to help him and ensured that he was released. Soon afterwards, however, Isaakios was poisoned and 'joined those other tyrants whom the hand of the Lord utterly destroyed'. He left one child, a daughter whose given name is unrecorded and who is known to history as the Damsel of Cyprus; she married the count of Toulouse, and secondly an illegitimate son of the count of Flanders.[4]

Having defeated the self-proclaimed *Basileus*, Richard Lionheart saw an immediate solution to the problem of Guy de Lusignan, who was extremely reluctant at the start of the 1190s to give up the Latin Kingdom of Jerusalem to his sister-in-law Queen Isabella and her husband Corrado of Montferrat. The Lusignans were vassals of Richard, who ruled the duchy of Aquitaine in southwest France as the heir of his mother Eleanor, duchess of Aquitaine in her own right (and the queen consort of France until 1152, then of England from 1154 to 1189). Richard therefore gave Guy the rule of the island of Cyprus instead, 'as though it were his own province' according to a Byzantine chronicler.[5]

Guy de Lusignan's death only a couple of years later in 1194 proved something of a blessing for Cyprus, as it brought his more intelligent and competent older brother Aiméry to the fore.[6] Aiméry had travelled to Outremer from their native Poitou in 1174 or earlier and settled there, and married Eschiva d'Ibelin, whose father was the lord of Ramla and who was a cousin of Queen Maria Komnene's second husband Balian d'Ibelin. In 1197, not long before his unfortunate demise by falling out of a window, Henri of Champagne, king of Jerusalem, visited Aiméry de Lusignan in Cyprus. The men agreed that Henri and Queen Isabella's three daughters would marry Aiméry and Eschiva's three sons. In fact, one of the three Jerusalem daughters died young, as did two of the Cyprus boys; Alice of Champagne and Jerusalem, the elder surviving daughter of Isabella and Henri, married Hugh, the only survivor of the Lusignan brothers, even though her mother had married his father in the meantime. Hugh de Lusignan succeeded his father as king of Cyprus in April 1205, probably not yet ten years old. A chronicler described him, rather unhelpfully, as 'neither large nor small', though added that Hugh had a 'well-proportioned' body, sloping shoulders, pale skin and auburn hair.[7]

During Hugh's minority, Cyprus was ruled by Gautier de Montbéliard, sometimes called Gautier de Montfaucon, yet another French nobleman who was a cousin of John de Brienne and married Aiméry and Eschiva's elder daughter Bourgogne de Lusignan. Bourgogne was, because Aiméry and Eschiva's other sons died young, heir to the Cypriot throne until her brother and Alice of Champagne had children.[8] After Hugh de Lusignan came of age in September 1210, he supposedly had a huge row with his regent and brother-in-law Gautier de Montbéliard, which resulted in Gautier fleeing to Acre to seek refuge with his de Brienne cousin, who had just arrived there to marry Queen Marie.[9]

Alice of Champagne herself, meanwhile, was heir to the throne of Jerusalem until the birth of her niece Yolande de Brienne in 1212. Her wedding to

Hugh de Lusignan, arranged a few years earlier, took place in Cyprus shortly before John de Brienne married her half-sister Marie, and their d'Ibelin uncles John and Philip accompanied Alice to the island. She received the county of Jaffa as dower.[10] Hugh and Alice's children Marie, Isabelle and Henry were born in 1214 or 1215, 1216 and 1217, and their eldest child Marie de Lusignan displaced her aunt Bourgogne as heir to the throne of Cyprus until herself displaced by the birth of her brother Henry in 1217.

In January 1218, an important wedding took place in Tripoli. The groom was the widowed Bohemond IV 'the One-Eyed', then in his early forties and the father of three sons, including Zabel of Armenian Cilicia's first husband Philip of Antioch, from his first marriage to Plaisance of Jebail. Bohemond was the count of Tripoli and became prince of Antioch too in 1219 when he displaced his nephew Raymond-Roupen. The teenage bride was Melisende of Cyprus and Jerusalem, youngest daughter of Queen Isabella of Jerusalem. King András II of Hungary was present, as was King Hugh of Cyprus, Melisende's half-brother (confusingly, Hugh's wife Alice of Champagne was Melisende's half-sister). Hugh was taken ill during the celebrations and died on 10 January 1218 at the age of twenty-two. His and Alice's third child and only son Henry de Lusignan, just eight months old, succeeded as king of Cyprus.

Alice was appointed as her son's regent and selected her uncle Philip d'Ibelin to act with her. A few years later the two quarrelled, and Alice tried to oust Philip from power but ultimately failed, even though she married her half-sister Melisende's stepson Bohemond V of Antioch and did her best to install him as governor of her son's kingdom instead.[11] This marriage was annulled for consanguinity, and in the early 1230s Alice left Cyprus for France and tried to claim her long-dead father Henri's county of Champagne, having also tried unsuccessfully to claim the kingdom of Jerusalem when her niece Yolande de Brienne died in 1228. Queen Alice married the nobly-born Raoul de Nesle, crusader and troubadour, as her third and last husband, and died in 1246 four years before her younger sister Philippa, lady of Ramerupt and wife of Érard de Brienne. Alice's son King Henry I of Cyprus died in early 1253 leaving a son, Hugh II, who, like his father, was just a few months old when he succeeded to the throne and whose mother was Henry's third wife Plaisance of Antioch.[12] In April 1256, a suggestion was made in England that the widowed Queen Plaisance might marry Edmund of Lancaster, younger son of Henry III and Alienor of Provence, and Plaisance sent a man to England to discuss the matter. Ultimately nothing came of it, not least because Plaisance was a decade older than Edmund, who was only eleven in 1256.[13] Hugh II of Cyprus died as a teenager and left no children, and was succeeded as king by his cousin Hugh of Antioch-Lusignan.

A decision made by the king of England in the early 1190s to support one of his vassals meant that the Lusignan family ruled Cyprus for 300 years. One of the last members of the house to rule the island was Queen Charlotte, born in 1444 as the daughter of King John II and his Byzantine wife Helena Palaiologina. Charlotte was crowned queen regnant of Cyprus in 1458, but in 1463 was deposed by her illegitimate half-brother James, King John's son from his relationship with his Greek lover Marietta Patras. She died in exile in Rome in 1487. James reigned in turn as king of Cyprus, and after his death in 1473, his Italian widow Caterina Cornaro acted as regent for their short-lived son then became the island's queen regnant. In 1489, Queen Caterina was forced to cede control of Cyprus to the mighty city-state of Venice, thus ending its 300 years as a Crusader kingdom.

Chapter 6

The Last Crusades

John de Brienne and Queen Marie's daughter Yolande de Brienne, who was born in late 1212 and became queen regnant of Jerusalem shortly after her birth, bore her son Konrad von Hohenstaufen in April 1228. She died a few days later, still only fifteen years old. As he was her only living child, Konrad was Yolande's heir, and the baby boy became rightful king of Jerusalem on his mother's death. His father Friedrich II von Hohenstaufen, Holy Roman Emperor and king of Sicily, pressed his right to act as regent, and captured the city of Jerusalem in 1229. It was held again in Christian hands for another fifteen years, though in 1244 fell once more to the Ayyubids. Konrad himself, however, never set foot in Jerusalem, and when he died in 1254, his heir was his only child Konradin or 'Little Konrad', just two years old and the great-grandson of John de Brienne. Konradin was executed by beheading in 1268 at the age of sixteen (see Part 4 below), and the line of Marie of Montferrat and her daughter Yolande de Brienne became extinct.

Claimants arose to the throne of Jerusalem, and although John de Brienne had plenty of other descendants besides Konradin alive in the late 1260s, none of them had a claim, as they were descended from John's third wife and not from Marie of Montferrat. Hugh of Antioch-Lusignan, also known as Hugh III of Cyprus, had the best claim to Jerusalem by primogeniture, as he was the grandson of Alice of Champagne, second eldest daughter of Queen Isabella of Jerusalem. The other chief claimant to Jerusalem was Maria of Antioch, the only surviving child of Queen Isabella's youngest daughter Melisende, princess of Antioch and countess of Tripoli. Maria claimed as the nearest generation in blood: she was a grandchild of Queen Isabella, whereas Hugh of Antioch-Lusignan was a great-grandchild.[2] In 1269, however, the High Court of Jerusalem turned down Maria's claim in favour of Hugh, who subsequently ruled as king of Jerusalem and Cyprus until his death in 1284. Hugh had to contend with Charles of Anjou (b.1227), the ambitious youngest son of Louis VIII of France and a man who seems to pop up everywhere in the story of Europe and the Mediterranean in the second half of the thirteenth century, as Maria of Antioch sold her claim to the throne of Jerusalem to Charles in 1277. The row between Hugh and Charles over who should hold the title of king of Jerusalem carried on until their deaths in the mid-1280s. Curiously by the standards of the time, Maria of Antioch – who was in her mid or late forties in the late 1260s when she claimed the right to rule the Latin Kingdom, and rather remarkably lived until 1307 – never married. Her kinsman Hugh of Antioch-Lusignan was briefly succeeded as king of both Cyprus and Jerusalem by his eldest and short-lived son John after his death in 1284, then by his second son Henry II of Cyprus, the last crowned Latin king of Jerusalem, in 1285. As Helena Schrader points out, by selling her claim to Jerusalem to Charles of Anjou, Maria of Antioch demonstrated 'a mercenary disregard for the well-being of the kingdom', and there is little doubt that the long era of absentee kings and queens of Jerusalem in the thirteenth century was an important contributing factor to the collapse of the Crusader States at the end of that century.[1]

In the middle of the 1200s, the Mamluks, a caste of elite Muslim warriors who had once been slaves, became the rulers of Egypt by overthrowing the Ayyubid dynasty founded by Salah al-Din. They also defeated the forces of the Mongolian Empire led by Genghis Khan's grandsons at the battle of Ayn Jalut in 1260, by luring the Mongolians into a trap and slaughtering them. This was no mean feat given that the Mongolians had, just two years and seven months earlier in February 1258, besieged and captured the mighty city of Baghdad, and were massively and rapidly expanding into the second largest empire in history. The king of Armenian Cilicia, Queen Zabel's widower Hethum of Baberon, and the prince of Antioch, Hethum's son-in-law Bohemond VI, had submitted to the Mongolians to protect their territories, and their men fought alongside the Mongolians against the Mamluks, but to little avail. The Mamluk leader, Sultan al-Zahir Baibars – the 'great panther' – who had commanded the vanguard in their victory at Ayn Jalut, captured numerous important cities and towns of Outremer including Antioch, Tyre, Beirut and Jaffa in the late 1260s. Henry III of England's sons, the future King Edward I and Edmund of Lancaster, were among the many European men who took part in a crusade against the Mamluks led by Louis IX of France at the start of the 1270s, and Edward's Spanish wife Leonor of Castile accompanied him to the Holy Land. On Edward's thirty-third birthday, 17 June 1272, Sultan Baibars sent an assassin to kill him, but Edward survived and managed to kill his attacker instead. The 'knife with which King Edward was wounded at Acre in the Holy Land' was kept and taken to England, and was still held in the English treasury seventy years later in the early 1340s, during the reign of Edward's grandson.[3] Louis IX himself and his twenty-year-old son Jean Tristan both died in 1270 during this crusade, as did John de Brienne's eldest son from his third marriage, Alphonse de Brienne, count of Eu.

The Mamluks, meanwhile, under the command of Baibars' successor Sultan Qalawun, kept up their attacks on Outremer. Bohemond VII, count of Tripoli and titular prince of Antioch, grandson of Zabel and Hethum of Armenian Cilicia and the husband of John de Brienne's granddaughter Marguerite, died in 1287. As he and Marguerite had no children, Bohemond's heir was his sister Lucia, who travelled from western Europe to take control of Tripoli. Her journey was in vain; Tripoli fell to the Mamluks soon afterwards in April 1289. Two years later in April 1291, the Mamluks began to besiege the vital port of Acre as well. Henry II de Lusignan, the reigning king of Cyprus and the last Latin king of Jerusalem, sent his younger brother Amalric there with troops, and Amalric was created lord of Tyre shortly before the city also fell to the Mamluks.

Amalric's efforts in Acre were, as with all the Christian efforts to maintain control of at least some of Outremer, in vain, and on 18 May 1291, the Mamluks captured the port. Henry II de Lusignan, the crowned king of Jerusalem and the last one who was at least somewhat worthy of the name – not counting those who used the empty title 'king of Jerusalem' after the collapse of the Latin Kingdom in 1291 – reigned as king of Cyprus until his death in 1324, though was ousted from power by his brother Amalric of Tyre in 1306 and lived in exile for a few years. With the loss of Acre in 1291, the Holy Land was lost to the Christians, and the 192-year existence of Outremer came to an end.

Part II

Spain

Dramatis Personae

John de Brienne, king of Jerusalem, b. *c.*1175/78; widower of Queen Marie of Jerusalem and Stephanie of Armenia; marries his third wife Berenguela of León in 1224

Berenguela of León, queen of Jerusalem, b. *c.*1204/05; daughter of Alfonso IX, king of León, and his second wife Berenguela, queen of Castile; ancestor of the Brienne/Beaumont family in England and France

Alfonso IX, king of León, b.1171, r.1188–1230; son of Fernando II; marries firstly Teresa of Portugal and secondly Berenguela of Castile; father-in-law of John de Brienne

Teresa of Portugal, queen consort of León, b.1175/76; eldest daughter of Sancho I, king of Portugal; marries her cousin Alfonso IX, but their marriage is annulled for consanguinity

Sancha (1191–*c.*1240), **Fernando** (1192–1214) and **Dulce** (1193/94–after 1243) **of León;** children of Alfonso IX and Teresa; half-siblings of Berenguela of León

Berenguela of Castile, b.1180, queen of Castile in her own right, queen consort of León; eldest child of Alfonso VIII, king of Castile, and Eleanor of England; marries Alfonso IX of León as his second wife in 1197; mother of Berenguela of León and Fernando III, king of Castile and León; mother-in-law of John de Brienne

Enrique I, king of Castile, b.1204, youngest child of Alfonso VIII of Castile and Eleanor of England; brother of Berenguela of Castile and uncle of Berenguela of León

Fernando III, king of Castile and León, b.1201; son and heir of Alfonso IX of León and Berenguela of Castile; full brother of Berenguela of León, half-brother of Sancha, Fernando and Dulce of León, and nephew of Enrique I; marries firstly Beatriz of Swabia and secondly Jeanne, countess of Ponthieu

Beatriz of Swabia, aka Elisabeth von Hohenstaufen, probably b.1205, queen consort of Castile and León; daughter of Philipp of Swabia, King of the Romans, and Eirene Angelina of Byzantium; marries Fernando III in 1219

Blanche (née Blanca) **of Castile**, b.1188, queen consort of France, married to **Louis VIII** (r.1223–26); sister of Berenguela, queen of Castile and León, and aunt of Berenguela of León, queen of Jerusalem

Louis IX (b.1214, r.1226–70), king of France; eldest son of Blanche of Castile and Louis VIII; married to Marguerite of Provence (b.1221); their second son and ultimate heir is **Philip III** (b.1245, r.1270–85)

Alfonso X, b.1221, king of Castile and León; eldest child of Fernando III and Beatriz of Swabia; marries Yolande of Aragón in 1249

Fadrique, b.1223, **Enrique**, b.1230, **Sancho**, b.1233, archbishop of Toledo, and **Manuel**, b.1234; some of the younger sons of Fernando and Beatriz; brothers of Alfonso X

Leonor of Castile, queen of England and countess of Ponthieu, b.1241; daughter of Fernando III and his second wife Jeanne of Ponthieu; half-sister of Alfonso X; niece of Berenguela of León; marries the future Edward I of England in 1254

Yolande of Aragón, b.1236/37, queen consort of Castile and León; daughter of **Jaume I** and sister of **Pere III**, kings of Aragón; marries Alfonso X in 1249

Alfonso III, king of Aragón, b.1265, and his brother and successor **Jaume II**, b.1267; sons of Pere III, nephews of Yolande

Fernando de la Cerda, b.1255, eldest son of Alfonso X of Castile and Yolande of Aragón; marries Blanche of France, b.1253, daughter of Louis IX, in 1269

Alfonso de la Cerda, b.1270, and **Fernando de la Cerda** the younger, b.1275; sons of Fernando de la Cerda and Blanche of France; rightful heirs to their grandfather Alfonso X's kingdoms of Castile and León after their father dies in 1275

Sancho IV, king of Castile and León, b.1258, second son of Alfonso X and Yolande; his father's successor in 1284 instead of his de la Cerda nephews; ancestor of the later kings of Castile and León

María de Molina, queen consort of Castile and León, b. *c.*late 1250s, daughter of Alfonso of León, lord of Molina, brother of Fernando III and Berenguela of León; marries her cousin Sancho IV in 1282

Fernando IV, king of Castile and León, b.1285, eldest son of Sancho IV and María de Molina; marries **Constança of Portugal** (b.1290), daughter of Diniz, king of Portugal, in 1302

Leonor of Castile, queen consort of Aragón, b.1307; daughter of Fernando IV and Constança of Portugal; second wife of Alfonso IV of Aragón and stepmother of Pere IV

Alfonso IV, king of Aragón, b.1299; son and successor of Jaume II (b.1267); father of **Pere IV** (b.1319), king of Aragón, by his first marriage to Teresa d'Entença

Alfonso XI, king of Castile and León, b.1311; son of Fernando IV and Constança of Portugal; marries his cousin Maria of Portugal (b.1313) in 1328, but has a long-term relationship with Leonor de Guzmán

Leonor de Guzmán, b. *c.*1310, Castilian noblewoman, daughter of Pedro Núñez de Guzmán; mistress of Alfonso XI

Pedro I 'the Cruel', king of Castile and León, b.1334; son of Alfonso XI and Maria of Portugal; marries Blanche de Bourbon in 1353, but his mistress María de Padilla is the mother of his daughters and heirs Costanza (b.1354) and Isabel (b.1355)

Blanche de Bourbon, queen consort of Castile and León, b. mid or late 1330s; daughter of Pierre, duke of Bourbon, and Isabelle de Valois; niece of Philip VI, king of France

María de Padilla, b. *c.*1334, Castilian noblewoman, daughter of Juan García de Padilla; mistress of Pedro the Cruel

Costanza (b.1354), duchess of Lancaster, and **Isabel** (b.1355), duchess of York; daughters of King Pedro and María de Padilla, legitimised in 1362; they marry Edward III of England's sons John of Gaunt (b.1340) and Edmund of Langley (b.1341)

Enrique II of Trastámara, king of Castile and León, b.1334; eldest surviving son of Alfonso XI and Leonor de Guzmán; illegitimate half-brother and usurper of Pedro I; marries Juana Manuel of Peñafiel and Villena

Fadrique, Tello, Sancho, Juan and **Pedro**; younger sons of Alfonso XI and Leonor de Guzmán; full brothers of Enrique of Trastámara and half-brothers of Pedro I

Juan I, king of Castile and León, b.1358; son of Enrique II of Trastámara and Queen Juana Manuel; marries Leonor of Aragón

Enrique III, king of Castile and León, b.1379; son of Juan I and Queen Leonor; marries Catalina of Lancaster in 1388

Catalina of Lancaster, queen consort of Castile and León, b.1372/73; only child and heir of Costanza of Castile, duchess of Lancaster; granddaughter and heir of Pedro I

Juan II, king of Castile and León, b.1405, son of Enrique III and Catalina of Lancaster

Chapter 7

The Kings of León

After taking part in the Fifth Crusade in the late 1210s, failing to gain the kingdom of Armenian Cilicia in 1219/20, and visiting both his native France and England in 1223 (see Part 5 below), John de Brienne, who was now in his mid or late forties, travelled to Spain in the spring of 1224. He undertook a pilgrimage to Santiago de Compostela, and while in Spain also travelled to Toledo, where he married his third and last wife, Infanta Doña Berenguela of León.[1] Medieval Spain was divided into four kingdoms. Navarre lay in the far north, next to and over the Pyrenees – part of its territory lay in modern France – with its capital at Pamplona; León was the part of Spain that lay north and east of Portugal, and its main cities were Zamora and Salamanca plus the great pilgrim site of Santiago; Aragón covered most of eastern Spain, including the cities of Barcelona, Zaragoza and, after it was captured from its Muslim rulers in 1238, Valencia; and Castile was the largest of the kingdoms, covering central Spain and parts of the north, and some of its chief towns were Burgos, Palencia, Toledo and Madrid. By 1250, after a series of military campaigns against the Almohad caliphate, Castile expanded far into the south of Spain and incorporated Seville, Córdoba, Alicante and Jaén as well. In the twelfth and thirteenth century, the kingdoms of Castile and León were sometimes united as one realm, at other times broken apart. From the mid-1100s until 1230, they were separate kingdoms, Castile ruled by Alfonso VIII between 1158 and 1214, and León ruled by Alfonso IX between 1188 and 1230.

Beginning in the year 711, armies of the Umayyad caliphate of North Africa swept through the Iberian Peninsula and conquered much of it. They named the territory they had seized al-Andalus. The Christian rulers of the much-diminished Spanish kingdoms and Portugal waged war against the Muslim settlers, often known to history as the 'Moors', over many centuries and slowly recaptured lost territory, an era called the *Reconquista* or Reconquest of Spain. The Christian kings, though also often enemies and rivals of each other, worked together in 1212, and at the battle of Las

Navas de Tolosa in July that year – four months before the death of John de Brienne's first wife Queen Marie of Jerusalem – inflicted a massive defeat on the Almohad caliphate, successors of the Umayyads.

One of the victors of Las Navas was Alfonso VIII of Castile, who succeeded his father Sancho III as a child in 1158. In 1170, Alfonso married Eleanor of England (b.1161), second daughter of Henry II and Eleanor of Aquitaine.[2] She was a sister of two kings of England, Richard Lionheart and John, and was also a sister of Joan, queen of Sicily, held prisoner in Cyprus by Isaakios Doukas Komnenos in 1191. Between 1180 and 1204, Alfonso VIII of Castile and Eleanor of England had eleven children, of whom the eldest was Berenguela and the youngest was Enrique. Their most famous child was Blanca, born in 1188 and known to posterity as Blanche of Castile, who was to rule France as regent for her son Louis IX. Alfonso VIII's heir for many years was his and Queen Eleanor's eldest surviving son Fernando, who was born in 1189 eighteen months after his sister Blanca/Blanche, but was killed in 1211 fighting against the Almohad rulers of al-Andalus.

King Alfonso died on 5 October 1214, two years after the victory at Las Navas de Tolosa, followed less than a month later on 31 October by his queen Eleanor of England. Theirs had been one of the most successful royal marriages of the European Middle Ages, and of their children, four became queens, one was a king, and one was an abbess. Three of their grandchildren are venerated as saints.[3] Their youngest child and only son still alive in 1214 when they died, ten-year-old Enrique, succeeded as king of Castile, but died just three years later after an unfortunate accident when a roof tile fell on his head in Palencia. Enrique's eldest sister Berenguela, who had acted as his regent and was twenty-four years his senior, succeeded as queen of Castile in her own right, but abdicated her throne to her teenage son Fernando III, who was born in 1201 and was, confusingly, three years older than his uncle Enrique. Queen Berenguela remained her son's chief adviser for many years, and Fernando treated her as his co-ruler, adding her name to his own in all the important documents he issued. Fernando was thirteen when his grandparents Alfonso VIII of Castile and Eleanor of England died in 1214, and according to Fernando's eldest son Alfonso X in a text he wrote called the *Estoria de España*, they had raised the boy and loved him dearly.[4]

In November 1219, Queen Berenguela arranged Fernando's marriage to Beatriz of Swabia, also known as Elisabeth von Hohenstaufen. She was one of the four daughters of the German king Philipp of Swabia and Eirene

Angelina of Byzantium (for whom, see Parts 3 and 4 below). Rodrigo Jiménez de Rada, archbishop of Toledo, described Beatriz as small, blonde and refined in appearance, wise and honest in character, and an examination of her remains in modern times showed that she stood 154cm tall, just over five feet. Beatriz, a granddaughter of two emperors and niece of two more, grew up at the court of another, Otto IV von Welf, and before her wedding lived in the household of yet another, her cousin Friedrich II von Hohenstaufen.[5] Beatriz died in 1235 after bearing ten children, and two years later Berenguela arranged her son's second marriage to the French heiress Jeanne de Dammartin, countess of Ponthieu in her own right. Jeanne gave Fernando another five children. Although Fernando III, with no fewer than seven sons from his first marriage to Beatriz, hardly needed to beget more heirs, supposedly his mother Berenguela was concerned that he might seek 'illicit relations' if he did not remarry, and thus disgrace himself and her.[6] Jeanne de Dammartin, known as Doña Juana in Spain, could not match Beatriz's imperial ancestry, but was a great-granddaughter of Louis VII of France and a great-great-granddaughter of Alfonso VII of Castile and León, hence was of suitably illustrious birth to marry King Fernando. Fernando's aunt Blanche of Castile, dowager queen of France and regent for her son Louis IX, probably had something to do with the match: Jeanne had been betrothed to Henry III of England in 1235, but Blanche was keen to prevent the English king gaining a foothold in the county of Ponthieu, which was situated close to the wealthy duchy of Normandy. Blanche's father-in-law Philip II Augustus had captured Normandy from Henry III's father King John in 1204, and Blanche did not wish Henry to use Jeanne's territories in an attempt to gain it back.

Berenguela of Castile herself had married her father's cousin Alfonso IX of León in 1197, and according to their grandson Alfonso X in his *Estoria de España*, Berenguela's mother Eleanor of England arranged it.[7] They became the parents of Fernando III, and one of their other children was Infanta Doña Berenguela of León, born in *c.*1204/05. Alfonso IX had previously been married to his cousin Teresa of Portugal and had three children with her, Fernando, Sancha and Dulce of León, all born in the early to mid-1190s. Both of Alfonso's marriages were annulled by Pope Innocent III on the grounds of consanguinity, and Innocent thundered about 'nefarious copulation'. He also declared that 'in the East, a woman has been joined incestuously with two men, while in the West one man has dared to join himself with two women through incest'.[8] The man in the West was Alfonso IX, and the woman in the East was Queen Isabella of Jerusalem; two of her four husbands were the brothers of her half-sister Queen Sibilla's two husbands, hence 'incestuous'. Alfonso's second marriage to Berenguela of Castile was forcibly ended by Innocent in 1204, around the time that their daughter, later John de Brienne's third wife, was born, and the year before Brienne's first wife's mother Isabella of Jerusalem died. Pope Innocent did, however, also decree that Alfonso and Berenguela's children should remain legitimate, while Alfonso's children with his first wife Teresa of Portugal were made illegitimate by the annulment of their parents' marriage and remained so. Alfonso went back to live with Teresa after his second marriage ended. Their son Fernando of León, who bore the same given name as his younger half-brother Fernando III of Castile, died as a young man in 1214.

On the look-out for husbands for his and Teresa's daughters Sancha and Dulce a few years later, Alfonso IX settled on John de Brienne as an excellent candidate, and seemingly promised John his kingdom after his own death if he agreed to marry one of the two. Alfonso's estranged second wife Berenguela, however, had other ideas, and like her more famous younger sister Blanche, queen consort and regent of France, Berenguela of Castile was a force to be reckoned with. She persuaded de Brienne to marry her own daughter instead, and the wedding of 'John, the king of Jerusalem, and the lady Berenguela [of León], sister of… Fernando [III], the illustrious king of Castile' took place in Burgos, northern Spain, in May 1224, with the archbishop of Toledo officiating.[9] Rather astonishingly, the man born as the youngest son of a comparatively minor French noble family had now made his third royal marriage.

Although marrying Sancha or Dulce might ultimately have made John de Brienne ruler of the small kingdom of León in northern Spain, his marriage to Berenguela of León brought John and his Brienne/Beaumont descendants other advantages which marriage to one of her older half-sisters would not have. Via her mother, his third wife was a great-granddaughter of Henry II of England and Eleanor of Aquitaine, a niece of Blanche of Castile and her husband Louis VIII of France, and a cousin of Louis IX. Berenguela of León's niece Leonor of Castile, her brother Fernando III's fourth and youngest daughter, would marry Lord Edward of England, heir to his father Henry III's throne, in 1254. This close connection to the English royals was to prove vitally important for the later Brienne/Beaumont family.

John himself must have been highly delighted with his third marriage, given that it was, as his biographer Guy Perry has pointed out, 'an excellent back-door route, more or less the best available, into the French royal family'.[10] As for Sancha and Dulce of León, they both became nuns in Villabuena after the Treaty of Benevente at the end of 1230, three months after their father Alfonso IX's death. This treaty, sealed by Sancha and Dulce's mother Teresa of Portugal and their stepmother Berenguela of Castile, made the sisters' half-brother Fernando III king of León as well as Castile, and 'established peace between don Fernando, king of Castile and Toledo, of León and Galicia, and the *infantas* his sisters, doña Sancha and doña Dulce'. The kingdoms of Castile and León were thus reunited forever.[11]

John's brother-in-law Fernando III and mother-in-law Berenguela of Castile easily set aside the claims of Fernando's older half-sisters to their late father's kingdom, and Brienne would have had to defeat Fernando to have stood any chance of making himself king of León. Given that Fernando is famous for his vital role in the *Reconquista* and for capturing much of al-Andalus from its Muslim rulers between the early 1220s and the late 1240s, this would not have been easy. John surely, therefore, realised that marrying Fernando's sister rather than one of his half-sisters in 1224 had been the correct decision.

Chapter 8
The Learned King

John de Brienne and Berenguela of León's first child, Marie, was born in Capua in Italy in April 1225, eleven months after their wedding in Burgos.[1] They perhaps named their daughter in honour of John's first wife, the queen regnant of Jerusalem. Marie de Brienne was followed by three brothers: Alphonse, John the younger, and Louis. The four siblings and their offspring lived lives that were, like their father's, international. Marie spent her life in Constantinople, France, Italy, and Cyprus; Alphonse went on two crusades to Egypt and Outremer, and visited England; and three of Louis de Brienne's children and one of John the younger's children were to settle in England, while John the younger himself lived in Scotland for a while. The three de Brienne brothers are also known to have spent much time in their mother Berenguela's homeland and were probably fluent in her native Castilian as well as their native French. The siblings lost their parents early; both John de Brienne and Berenguela of León died in 1237 when their four children were aged between about five and twelve.

Berenguela's brother Fernando III of Castile and León died in Seville – which he had captured in late 1248 after more than 500 years of Muslim rule over the city – on 30 May 1252, and was buried in Seville Cathedral on 1 June. His French widow Jeanne and all of his ten living children were present at his deathbed and interment with the exception of Don Sancho, his sixth son, later archbishop of Toledo.[2] Fernando was succeeded in his two kingdoms by Alfonso X, the eldest of his seven sons and three daughters from his first marriage to Beatriz of Swabia (he had another four sons and one daughter from his second marriage to Jeanne of Ponthieu). Centuries later in 1671, Fernando III was canonised as a saint of the Catholic Church with his feast day as 30 May, the date of his death, and is known as San Fernando or Fernando *el Santo*, 'the Saint'. The valley and city of San Fernando in California are named after him. His eldest son Alfonso X is known to posterity as *el Sabio*, 'the Wise' or 'the Learned', and was a polymath: a lawgiver, composer, translator, writer and amateur scientist who took a particular interest in astronomy. The Alphonsus Crater on the Moon is named after him. He is still well known today for his composition of more than 400 poems with musical notation which he called the Cantigas of Santa Maria, and he wrote, edited and sponsored books including the *Estoria de España* or History of Spain, and had Arabic works on astronomy translated into Castilian, a language he promoted industriously. Last but by no means least, Alfonso devised a massive and influential law code called the *Siete Partidas*, which Spanish explorers introduced to the New World centuries later.

The three de Brienne brothers, evidently keen to forge good relations with their Spanish cousin, witnessed many of Alfonso X's documents and charters from the early 1250s to the early 1270s. The long list of witnesses to royal documents was written in order of rank, and the Briennes always appeared near the top of the list, after the king's brothers and sons and any archbishops who acted as witnesses, but before everyone else.[3] As well as spending time in his mother's homeland, Alphonse de Brienne visited England: Henry III gave him a safe-conduct in May 1252, the month of Fernando III's death and Alfonso X's accession to the joint throne of Castile-León, to travel there. Alphonse wished to visit the shrine of St Thomas Becket (d.1170) in Canterbury Cathedral, as his father had done thirty years earlier when he spent time with King Henry. The Brienne brothers' older sister Empress Marie was also in Castile sometime in the late 1250s or early 1260s. She had come to ask King Alfonso to ask him to give her money for the ransom of her son Philippe de Courtenay, held captive in Venice as surety for the enormous debts of Marie's husband (see Chapter 17).[4]

Alfonso X laid claim to the duchy of Aquitaine in south-west France in 1253, not long after his accession, stating that it had been the dower which his great-grandmother Eleanor of England had brought with her on marriage to Alfonso VIII of Castile in 1170. The duke of Aquitaine in 1253 was Henry III of England, who was the son of King John, nephew of Eleanor of England, and grandson and heir of Eleanor of Aquitaine. To avoid going to war against the powerful Spanish monarch, and keen to avert the possibility of losing his French territory, King Henry proposed a marriage between his son and heir Lord Edward (b. June 1239) and Alfonso's half-sister Doña Leonor (b. *c.* November 1241). Alfonso agreed, and in early November 1254 the young couple duly married in Burgos, where Leonor's aunt Berenguela of León had married John de Brienne thirty years earlier.

Alfonso X knighted Edward before the wedding, and for several months afterwards dated his documents as 'the year that Don Odoart, first son and heir of King Henrrich of England [*Anglatierra*], received knighthood in Burgos from King Don Alfonso'. One of these documents was witnessed by the three de Brienne brothers, who were then all in their twenties.[5] They had surely attended the royal wedding of the king of England's son to their Spanish cousin Leonor. Edward and Leonor succeeded as king and queen in November 1272 on Henry III's death, and the close family connection to the English royal family took several of John de Brienne and Berenguela of León's grandchildren to England in and after the late 1270s. Leonor was the mother of one king of England and grandmother of another, and an ancestor of all the later English royals.[6]

King Alfonso had a rather tense relationship with his stepmother Queen Jeanne, and by the time of her daughter's wedding to the heir to the English throne in late 1254, Jeanne had already left Castile and returned to her native northern France. Alfonso also had stressful relations with two of his many younger brothers, Fadrique and Enrique, and after they rebelled against him in the 1250s, Enrique fled to England and spent several years at the court of his half-sister Leonor's father-in-law Henry III. Despite his annoyance with his English allies for hosting his brother and enemy Enrique – and there were even rumours that Enrique had become their stepmother Queen Jeanne's lover when she sheltered him in her county of Ponthieu – Alfonso X kept in touch with Leonor and Edward for many years. He travelled to Bayonne just over the border into France in November 1273 to meet them. Leonor gave birth to her third son in Bayonne that month, and Alfonso X was his godfather and gave the child his name. After the death of his six-year-old brother Henry of Windsor in October 1274, the partly Castilian Alfonso of Bayonne became heir to the English throne and remained so until his own death a decade later; had he lived long enough to become king of England when his father died, 'Alfonso', or a variant of it, would have become a common English name.

After the deaths of Friedrich II von Hohenstaufen, Holy Roman Emperor, in 1250, and his two legitimate sons Heinrich (Henry III of England's nephew) and Konrad (John de Brienne's grandson from his first marriage to Queen Marie of Jerusalem) in 1253 and 1254, it was not clear who should succeed as King of the Romans and ultimately as Holy Roman Emperor. Konrad's son Konradin, born in 1252, was only a young child, and the partly English Heinrich died in his teens and left no children. Willem, count of Holland and Zeeland, had been elected by the *Kurfürsten* or 'Prince-Electors' as King of the Romans in 1248 in opposition to the excommunicated Emperor Friedrich, but was killed in early 1256 while putting down a rebellion in his territories. The seven *Kurfürsten* subsequently put forward two possible candidates for King of the Romans and could not decide between them: Henry III of England's brother Richard, earl of Cornwall (b.1209), was chosen by three Electors, and Alfonso X of Castile-León was chosen by four. Alfonso surely thought he had a better chance of election as he was a great-grandson of the Holy Roman Emperor Friedrich Barbarossa, Friedrich II's grandfather, while Richard was merely Friedrich II's brother-in-law and had only distant blood ties to the imperial Hohenstaufen dynasty. It was the wealthy Richard, however, who was crowned in Aachen in May 1257, though Alfonso used the title King of the Romans for the next few years as well. Neither man managed to achieve much, if any, control and authority in Germany. Alfonso X was highly ambitious and hoped to become the most powerful king in Europe, and though ultimately he did not succeed in this endeavour, his brother-in-law and Richard of Cornwall's nephew Edward I of England always addressed him as 'King of the Romans and Castile' in letters.[7]

Chapter 9

Poisoned Cherries

In 1249, the future Alfonso X had married Yolande, eldest daughter of King Jaume I of Aragón and Violante of Hungary. Alfonso's father Fernando III was not able to attend the wedding, though his wife Queen Jeanne did.[1] As Yolande of Aragón was a decade and a half her husband's junior and barely thirteen when they wed, their first child was not born until late 1253, eighteen months after Alfonso X acceded to the throne. This was Berenguela, who was treated as heir to the throne of Castile-León until her brother Fernando de la Cerda was born in October 1255. 'De la Cerda' means 'of the bristle', as Fernando was supposedly born with hair, and his descendants used the moniker as their family name. When he was fourteen, Fernando de la Cerda married Blanche of France, daughter of Louis IX and a granddaughter of Blanche of Castile. She was almost three years older than he, born in the Outremer city of Jaffa in early 1253 during her father's long first crusade in Egypt and the Holy Land. This important royal wedding took place in Burgos, northern Spain, on 30 November 1269, fifty years to the day after Fernando's grandparents Fernando III and Beatriz of Swabia married there, and Fernando de la Cerda's other grandfather, the mighty and long-lived Aragónese king Jaume I, attended. The three de Brienne brothers, Alphonse, John and Louis, were perhaps also there given that they continued to witness their cousin Alfonso X's documents in the late 1260s and, in John and Louis's case, the early 1270s.[2]

Fernando and Blanche's first son, Alfonso de la Cerda, was born in 1270 when Fernando was still only fourteen or perhaps recently fifteen, in the year that Blanche's father Louis IX died. Fernando de la Cerda died in the summer of 1275 some months before his twentieth birthday. Blanche of France was pregnant with a second son at the time, whom she named Fernando after her late husband, and, having expected to become queen consort of Castile-León, now faced an uncertain future.[3] She outlived her husband by almost half a century and never remarried, and died in Paris in 1323 when she was seventy years old. In 1290, her elder son Alfonso de la Cerda married Mathilde (also sometimes called Mahaut) de Brienne, a great-granddaughter of John de Brienne and Berenguela of León.

As the elder son of Alfonso X's eldest son, Alfonso de la Cerda was the rightful heir to Castile and León by primogeniture. King Alfonso, however, was unwilling to risk a long minority in his kingdom after his death, and after his eldest son died unexpectedly, he named his and Yolande of Aragón's second son Sancho (b. May 1258) as his successor instead of his grandson Alfonso de la Cerda. In early 1278, for reasons which are not entirely clear, Queen Yolande fled to her native Aragón and the protection of her brother Pere III, Jaume I's successor, taking her daughter-in-law Blanche of France and her two young de la Cerda grandsons with her. The reasons perhaps had something to do with Alfonso X and Queen Yolande's rather unhappy marriage and with Alfonso's decision regarding the succession, or perhaps with Alfonso's ongoing ill-health and consequent irritability. In a rather cloak-and-dagger move, Pere III came over the Castilian border by night and took his sister, her daughter-in-law and her grandsons back to Aragón with him. By the summer of 1278, Blanche had returned to her native France and the court of her brother Philip III, though this was perhaps not a voluntary move on her part, as her children remained in Aragón.[4]

Something of Queen Yolande's personality, or at least what contemporaries might have thought was her personality, is revealed by a rumour, which is certainly untrue but was current in her own lifetime, that she killed her sister Costanza in 1269 by sending her poisoned cherries out of envy for Costanza's beauty and happiness. Yolande's second son Sancho told one of his cousins on his deathbed that he believed his grandfather Jaume I of Aragón did not love his daughter Yolande because he suspected her of killing another of his daughters, and that Jaume cursed Yolande before he died.[5] Later, when Alfonso X changed his mind and supported the rights of his grandson Alfonso de la Cerda to his throne rather than his son Sancho's, Queen Yolande changed her mind as well and supported Sancho instead of her grandson; this perhaps also reveals something of her contrarian personality, or of her unhappy marriage. Alfonso yielded to pressure from the French by promoting the rights of his grandsons, as the two de la Cerda brothers were partly French and were Louis IX's grandchildren, and the French wished to see Blanche of France's son on the throne of Castile-León.[6]

In the late 1270s and early 1280s, before Alfonso X changed his mind in favour of his de la Cerda grandson, France and Castile almost went to war over the succession to the throne of Castile-León. The maternal uncle of the de la Cerda boys was Philip III of France, who prepared to march into Castile to protect his nephews' rights. Before doing so, and accompanied by a cousin named Charles of Salerno, Philip met the two boys' paternal uncles Pere III of Aragón and his brother the king of Majorca in Toulouse in December 1280 to discuss what should become of the boys, but was shocked when Pere treated Charles of Salerno with icy disdain (see Part 4 below; as well as the conflict between Aragón and Castile, Aragón was sliding into war against Philip III's uncle the king of Sicily, Charles of Salerno's father). The discussions stalled completely when Pere III refused to allow his de la Cerda nephews to leave Aragón, as having them under his control gave him leverage over two other kings: Alfonso X of Castile-León and Philip III of France.[7]

In late 1281, Alfonso X quarrelled bitterly with his eldest living son Sancho, who in the summer of 1282 launched a rebellion against his father with the support of his younger brothers Pedro and Juan and his sister Violante. A two-year power struggle between Alfonso and Sancho ensued.[8] Alfonso X died in his early sixties on 4 April 1284, three weeks before his half-sister Leonor gave birth to her youngest child in distant Wales: Edward of Caernarfon, future king of England (Edward became heir to the throne when his ten-year-old brother Alfonso of Bayonne, Alfonso X's godson, died in August 1284). Alfonso X's second son, known as *el Bravo* or 'the Brave' and a volatile and temperamental man, was crowned as King Sancho IV by four bishops in Toledo Cathedral. It was the first coronation in Castile since 1111, and was intended to strengthen Sancho's legitimacy.[9] At the time of his accession, and until he fathered sons, Sancho IV's heir was his only living child, Infanta Doña Isabel (b.1283). Sancho's nephew Alfonso de la Cerda, in Aragón and barely into his teens, was unable to prevent Sancho's accession to his late grandfather's throne, and though both he and his brother Fernando de la Cerda the younger married and had descendants, this branch of the Castilian royal family was never able to claim the joint kingdoms of Castile-León.

Philip III of France and Pere III of Aragón both died in 1285, the year after Alfonso X, and there was a sudden rush of new young kings in western Europe.[10] Seventeen-year-old Philip IV succeeded his father as king of France, and twenty-year-old Alfonso III succeeded his father as king of Aragón; both young men were cousins of the de la Cerda brothers, and Alfonso III took over custody of them from his father. Their existence continued to cause problems in Castile-León, as did the struggle among Castilian nobles regarding the kingdom's alliance with either Aragón or France. Lope Díaz de Haro, lord of Biscay, a brother-in-law of Sancho IV's wife Queen María, preferred the alliance with Aragón; Sancho turned against him, as he himself preferred an alliance with France, hoping to eliminate the threat of the de la Cerdas and ongoing papal disapproval of his and María's marriage. In 1288, Lope made to attack Sancho and was stabbed to death by some of the crossbowmen and knights who formed the king's bodyguard.

In the late 1280s, Castile-León and France came to an agreement: Sancho IV promised to give his de la Cerda nephews the rule of Murcia and Cuidad Real if they gave up their claims to his kingdom. At this point, Alfonso III of Aragón freed them and declared Alfonso, the elder de la Cerda brother, to be the rightful king of Castile-León. Border warfare between Castile and Aragón continued until 1291, when Alfonso III died suddenly and his brother Jaume II (b.1267) succeeded and married Sancho IV's eldest child Isabel to seal peace between the kingdoms. And in 1290, Philip IV of France promised Sancho IV that he would not support the claims of the de la Cerda brothers against Sancho.[11]

Chapter 10

An Extraordinary Queen

Sancho IV died in Toledo on 25 April 1295, only in his thirties, and was buried in the Catedral Primada Santa María de Toledo, where he had been crowned eleven years earlier. His mother Yolande of Aragón outlived him, and his eldest son Fernando IV succeeded him as king of Castile and León. Fernando was not yet ten years old; he was born in Seville on 6 December 1285, and baptised in the city's cathedral by the archbishop of Seville, Remondo Losana.[1] Fernando's mother was María de Molina, a close relative of her husband Sancho IV: her father Infante Don Alfonso, lord of Molina, was the brother of Fernando III of Castile and León and Berenguela of León, queen of Jerusalem. Although Queen María de Molina was 'a woman of extraordinary abilities, character, and resourcefulness', her marriage to Sancho was to cause problems for their son Fernando after his accession to the throne, as they had not received a papal dispensation for consanguinity. Sancho had also been betrothed to another woman when he married María, which created another difficulty, and in the words of historian Peter Linehan, Sancho and María's marriage was 'extravagantly uncanonical'. Despite the difficulties, Sancho was determined to remain married to María, and it was surely a love match. Finally, on 6 December 1301, Fernando IV's sixteenth birthday, he and his descendants were legitimised by Pope Boniface VIII.[2]

On the other hand, at the outset of Fernando's reign Castile was once again beset by foreign enemies and torn apart internally, and without María de Molina and her steady guiding hand, her son's kingship might not have survived. The queen's biographer Paulette Lynn Pepin draws attention to María's 'intellectual and political astuteness' and points out that her skilful use of her own regal authority to 'repulse predatory nobles, sullen prelates, resolute townsmen and voracious foreign monarchs' secured the throne not only for her son, but in later years for her grandson as well. María was cast in the mould of her grandmother, the great Berenguela of Castile, queen of Castile and León (who was also her husband's great-grandmother), and her great-aunt Blanche of Castile, queen of France. She had married Sancho in July 1282 during his rebellion against his father Alfonso X, and a chronicler makes clear that she supported her new husband against the king. After Sancho's accession, María continued to support him to the point of taking an active role in the governance of the two kingdoms.[3]

As well as Queen María, the other powerful figures during Fernando IV's minority were his long-lived great-uncle Infante Don Enrique (1230–1304), the fourth son of Fernando III and brother of Alfonso X, who had spent part of the 1250s in England and subsequently spent decades in a Naples prison (see Part 4 below); Don Gonzalo, archbishop of Toledo; Don Nuño González de Lara, a high-ranking nobleman; and Don Diego López de Haro, lord of Biscay and Fernando IV's uncle by marriage. Although Philip IV of France had promised not to support the de la Cerdas, the crisis in Castile in the 1290s worsened when Infante Don Juan, a younger brother of Sancho IV, supported the rights of his de la Cerda nephews in preference to his nephew Fernando IV.[4] In addition to the internal crisis, the joint kingdoms of Castile and León were threatened by outsiders and by possible invasion, and on Sancho IV's death, Jaume II of Aragón had his marriage to Infanta Doña Isabel, Sancho and María de Molina's eldest child, annulled. As Isabel was still only eleven or twelve years old in 1295, it seems likely that the marriage was never consummated.[5]

Fernando IV married Constança of Portugal, daughter of Diniz, king of Portugal (r.1279–1325) in 1302.[6] Their marriage remained childless for a few years, and oddly, there is evidence that the Castilian magnates considered the possibility of Fernando's English cousin Edward of Caernarfon (b.1284), prince of Wales, succeeding him if he never had children. This seems hard to believe, because although Edward was a grandson of Fernando III *el Santo* via his late mother Leonor of Castile, Fernando *el Santo* had other male descendants via his many sons who had a superior claim. According to a contemporary newsletter, however, a Spanish cardinal who visited England in 1306/07, Petrus Hispanus, told Edward I and his son that the magnates of Castile had decided on this.[7] The Spanish kingdoms were growing in power and confidence, and after Edward of Caernarfon succeeded his father as Edward II in 1307, an English chronicler asserted that his being the cousin of the king of Castile was one of his greatest assets as king of England. His father Edward I commented to Pope Clement V in early 1307 that Cardinal Petrus Hispanus 'should especially love Edward, our dear son, who is of the blood of Spain'.[8] In the end, Edward of Caernarfon's possible accession to the throne of Castile-León never came about as Fernando IV and Constança of Portugal had a daughter named Leonor in or not long before December 1307, and finally, in Salamanca on 13 August 1311, the longed-for son, Alfonso.[9]

Also in 1311, Fernando IV asked Edward II to fulfil clauses of the treaty in 1254 made between Edward's grandfather Henry III of England and Alfonso X, who was Fernando's grandfather and Edward's uncle. Fernando also asked Edward to lend him money to help him fight people whom he called the 'Saracens', i.e., the Muslim rulers of Granada, an emirate in the far south of Spain that was technically a vassal state of Castile but was influential and prosperous. Edward replied in October 1311 that he was always ready to help Fernando, but was sorely pressed by the ongoing war in Scotland and what he described as other hindrances, meaning his struggles with some of his barons over their reforms of his household and government (called the Ordinances). The following year, Edward requested a favour for a Spanish widow living in England, and a few years later sent an English nobleman, Hugh Despenser the Elder, to Castile with letters for infantes Juan and Pedro and Andres Perez, a merchant of Burgos. This reveals that the king of England and his advisers had a good knowledge of Castilian affairs, as the infantes were then co-regents of the kingdom with Queen María de Molina, while Perez was someone known at the English court who could provide aid and support to Despenser during his journey.[10]

In September 1312, the year after the birth of his son, Fernando IV died of tuberculosis at the age of just twenty-six.[11] Castile was thrown into another minority, this one much longer than Fernando IV's own minority had been given that the new king, Alfonso XI, was just thirteen months old. Fernando's Portuguese widow Constança died in 1313, and his mother María de Molina stepped into the breach and ruled the two kingdoms for her infant grandson Alfonso XI, as she had for Fernando himself. Once again, however, there were other regents battling for power, the two most important being Infante Don Juan (b. *c.*1262), lord of Biscay, son of Alfonso X, brother of Sancho IV and great-uncle of Alfonso XI, and Infante Don Pedro (b.1290), one of the younger sons of Sancho IV and María de Molina, and Alfonso XI's uncle. In 1315, the two infantes finally agreed to share the regency with Queen María, with Pedro taking control in the south of Spain and Juan in the north. The squabbling over power left Castile and León vulnerable not only to invasion by their neighbours, but also to possible renewed attacks by the Nasrid rulers of Granada. The Nasrids defeated the two infantes at the battle of Vega de Granada in June 1319, and both men were killed.

Fernando IV's daughter Leonor of Castile, now aged twelve or almost, married Jaume II of Aragón's eldest son and heir, Jaume the younger (b.1296), in October 1319. The wedding took place in Tortosa and was celebrated by the archbishop of Tarragona. Shortly afterwards, however, the young Jaume renounced both his wedding vows and his rights to his father's throne, and announced his intention of becoming a monk instead. Jaume II was instead succeeded on his death in 1327 by his second son Alfonso IV, who in February 1329, in order to repair the Castilian-Aragónese alliance broken a decade earlier, married his former sister-in-law Leonor of Castile as his second wife.[12] His son and heir, the future King Pere IV of Aragón, had been born in 1319. Thirty years after marrying Alfonso IV of Aragón, Leonor would be assassinated by her nephew the king of Castile, as would one of her two sons, while her other son was killed by his half-brother Pere IV; see below.

At the end of June or beginning of July 1321, two years after losing her son Pedro at the battle of Vega de Granada, Queen María de Molina passed away, leaving a will in which she left some of her lands and castles, including Guadalajara in central Spain, to her eldest child Infanta Doña Isabel, briefly married as a child to Jaume II of Aragón and now duchess of Brittany.[13] Her death was a great loss for the joint kingdoms of Castile and León and for her grandson Alfonso XI, then coming up to ten years old. As had happened in the 1290s, in 1312 and in 1319, for a while chaos reigned in Castile-León after Queen María's death, and yet again a number of potential regents jockeyed for power: chief among them were Don Juan Manuel (b.1282), duke of Peñafiel, a nephew of Alfonso X and one of the most famous Spanish writers of the Middle Ages; Infante Don Felipe (b.1292), another younger brother of Fernando IV and uncle of Alfonso XI; María Diaz de Haro (b. *c.*1270), lady of Biscay, widow of Infante Juan who fell at Vega de Granada; and Juan *el Tuerto*, 'the One-Eyed', son of María Diaz de Haro and Juan.

Chapter 11

Natural and Gracious Good Qualities

In 1324/25, Alfonso XI was betrothed to Eleanor of Woodstock (b. June 1318), elder of the two daughters of the partly Castilian king of England, Edward II, and his French queen Isabella, daughter of Philip IV and great-granddaughter of Louis IX. Alfonso XI's older sister Leonor, a few years after her husband Jaume of Aragón renounced both her and his future throne, was betrothed at the same time to Edward II and Isabella's son and heir Edward of Windsor (b. November 1312), the future Edward III of England. Ultimately neither marriage went ahead as Edward II was deposed in 1327 and the political climate changed, despite the English king's enthusiasm for both the joint marriage of two of his children into his mother Queen Leonor's homeland, and for Alfonso XI personally. In early 1325, Edward talked of the adolescent king's many 'virtues and natural and gracious good qualities', and of the 'joy' he felt at being in contact with the Castilian royal family. Edward's letters again reveal his and his advisers' detailed knowledge of who the regents of Castile and the king's guardians were, and how they were related to each other and to him.[1] Alfonso XI married Maria of Portugal in 1328 instead. Maria was her husband's first cousin on both sides of the family: his father and her mother were siblings, and his mother and her father were siblings.[2] A possible alternative marriage for the young king was suggested, to Costanza, daughter of the duke of Peñafiel, Juan Manuel, but Alfonso was determined to break the power of his squabbling regents and rejected her.

Alfonso assumed his majority when he turned fourteen in August 1325, and the following year had his kinsman and co-regent Juan *el Tuerto* of Biscay killed in Toro. Ultimately, Alfonso XI was to prove an effective leader of Castile-León, and restored peace to the joint kingdoms, which had become lawless and ungoverned during the previous few years. During the quarter of a century in which he ruled Castile-León, Alfonso captured and held a number of fortresses from the emirate of Granada, though he also lost control of Gibraltar to the emirate in 1333. In 1340 he and Afonso IV of Portugal, aided by a fleet sent by Pere IV of Aragón, defeated the forces of Granada at the battle of Tarifa, also called the battle of Río (River) Salado. And the threat of the two de la Cerdas, Alfonso and his younger brother Fernando, was finally ended in the early 1330s when Alfonso de la Cerda gave up all claims to the throne, and pledged his allegiance to his kinsman Alfonso XI.

Perhaps because he had little sexual attraction to his wife Maria of Portugal, to whom he was so closely related, Alfonso XI had a long-term passionate relationship with another woman: a Castilian noble widow called Doña Leonor de Guzmán. With Queen Maria, Alfonso had only one child who survived infancy, Pedro, born in August 1334; with Leonor, he had ten or eleven children, though several of them died young. Their eldest living sons were twins, Enrique and Fadrique, born in January 1334 and seven months older than their legitimate half-brother and Alfonso's heir, Infante Don Pedro. Enrique and Fadrique, and their younger brothers Tello, Sancho, Juan and Pedro, were known by the last name Trastámara. King Alfonso's neglect and mistreatment of his queen, whom he kept almost as a prisoner, almost led to war between Castile and Portugal when Afonso IV of Portugal, who was both Alfonso XI's father-in-law and uncle and had formerly been his close ally, threatened to invade Castile in 1336 to avenge the insult to his daughter Maria. The following year, Alfonso XI prepared a retaliatory invasion of Portugal, and war was only averted when Pope Benedict XII persuaded the two kings to come to terms and to launch a joint invasion of the emirate of Granada instead.[3]

Infante Don Pedro was betrothed to Joan of Woodstock (b. *c.* January 1334), daughter of Edward III of England and granddaughter of the late Edward II. Edward III had, in 1337, claimed the throne of France, currently occupied by his mother Queen Isabella's cousin Philip VI, the first French king of the house of Valois. The mighty joint kingdom of Castile-León was a very useful ally for the king of England against his French enemies, and as his father had a few years earlier, Edward III and his advisers showed that they understood the Castilian situation very well by sending letters to Alfonso XI's powerful lover Doña Leonor de Guzmán as well as to Queen Maria. Edward thanked Leonor, whom he addressed in Latin as *domina Alianore Gusman*, for promoting the marriage of her lover's son Infante Don Pedro to his daughter. He invited one of her and King Alfonso's sons to come and live in England for a while as a companion for his son and heir Edward of Woodstock, prince of Wales (b.1330).[4] Sadly, however, the planned Anglo-Castilian marriage alliance did not come to pass, because fourteen-year-old Joan of Woodstock became one of the many victims of the Black Death, the terrible pandemic of plague that scythed its way through Europe in the late 1340s. She died in her father's city of Bordeaux in the summer of 1348, on her way to her wedding to Pedro.

Unluckily for Castile-León, Alfonso XI died in March 1350 at the age of only thirty-eight, while he was besieging Gibraltar. Like the young English girl who should have become his daughter-in-law in 1348, Alfonso died of plague, and his only legitimate child Pedro, aged fifteen, became king (and a few months later became seriously ill, perhaps also of the plague, though recovered). Leonor de Guzmán, formerly highly influential at court, lost her protector, and Maria of Portugal accused her rival of inciting a rebellion among the Castilian nobility against her son the young king and had her imprisoned in Talavera in central Spain. The dowager queen's rage and bitterness over her years of ill-treatment at the hands of her husband and his lover resulted in her ordering Leonor's death in the summer of 1351, with King Pedro's knowledge and consent. This, in turn, was to make Pedro a mortal enemy in the person of his eldest half-brother, Leonor de Guzmán's son Enrique of Trastámara.[5] Alfonso XI's preference for his mistress Leonor and his favouring her and their children over his neglected Portuguese queen and their son was ultimately to reap a bitter harvest: the deaths of four of his offspring. Three of his and Leonor's sons were killed by his legitimate son Pedro, and Pedro would be killed by his half-brother Enrique.

Having lost his English fiancée Joan to the Black Death, in 1353 King Pedro married the French noblewoman Blanche de Bourbon, a niece of Philip VI of France (d.1350) and sister-in-law of the man who would become king of France in 1364, Charles V. Earlier that same year, however, Pedro's mistress Doña María de Padilla had borne their first child, Beatriz, in Córdoba in southern Spain, and Pedro abandoned the unfortunate Blanche mere days after their wedding and went off with María. Their second child, Costanza, future duchess of Lancaster, was born in Castrojeriz near Burgos in the north of Castile in July 1354, and hence was conceived about four months after her father's wedding to another woman. Costanza married Edward III of England's son John of Gaunt, younger brother of her father's late fiancée Joan of Woodstock, in 1371. Pedro and María's third child was Isabel, born in 1355 in Tordesillas in central Spain, and the future duchess of York; she married John of Gaunt's brother Edmund of Langley in 1372, and was the great-grandmother of two English kings, Edward IV (r.1461–83) and Richard III (r.1483–85). Finally, Pedro and María de Padilla also had a son named Alfonso, born in Tordesillas in 1359. The three-year-old boy died in Seville in October 1362, and his eldest sister Beatriz died as a teenager sometime after the autumn of 1366. Had Beatriz lived some years longer and outlived her father, she would have been his heir.

King Pedro and María had met during a series of peregrinations the seventeen-year-old king made through Castile in the spring and summer of 1352, which were, in part, a campaign against his illegitimate half-brother Enrique of Trastámara. Enrique had rebelled against his hated half-brother the king with his younger twin Fadrique, master of the military and religious Order of Santiago, and their next oldest brother, Tello. In 1354, King Pedro also became involved with his kinswoman Doña Juana de Castro, who, like Pedro himself, was a great-grandchild of Sancho IV. Pedro claimed to have wed Juana in Cuéllar near Valladolid in early April 1354, even though he had already married Blanche de Bourbon ten months earlier and even though he was also involved in an intense relationship with María de Padilla; their second child Costanza was born about three months after her father's wedding ceremony with Juana. The king, who made a habit of abandoning women just after he married them, left Juana the day after their wedding and never saw her again, though their brief relationship resulted in a son named Juan born nine months later in January 1355, who was a few months younger than his half-sister Costanza and a few months older than his half-sister Isabel.

Having claimed in 1354 to have wed Juana de Castro, Pedro was to claim in 1362 that he had married María de Padilla in Seville in 1352 before his official wedding to Blanche de Bourbon the following year. In the interests of political expediency, several biased witnesses confirmed his tale, including Doña María's brother Don Diego García de Padilla and their uncle Don Juan Fernández de Henestrosa. The Castilian *Cortes* duly legitimised their daughters Beatriz, Costanza and Isabel. In his will of November 1362, made a month after the death of his and María de Padilla's three-year-old son Alfonso, Pedro named their three daughters as his heirs in birth order, followed by his and Juana de Castro's seven-year-old son Juan – whom he always acknowledged as his child despite the brevity of his and Juana's relationship – in case his daughters died and left no legitimate children.[6] After Pedro's eldest daughter Beatriz died sometime in the late 1360s, his and María de Padilla's second daughter Costanza became her father's heir, and carried her claim to the throne of Castile-León to her English husband John of Gaunt, duke of Lancaster, and their daughter.

María de Padilla died in July 1361, still only in her twenties. For all his complicated associations with other women, King Pedro deeply loved María and grieved for her sincerely. He held a state funeral for her as though she were his wife and the rightful queen of Castile – in his will of November 1362, he referred to her repeatedly as 'the queen, Doña María, my wife' – and buried her in the monastery of Santa Clara de Astudillo. In his will, Pedro left a 'French crown' which had belonged to Blanche de Bourbon to his and María de Padilla's third daughter, Isabel. He refused to acknowledge Blanche as his wife and queen, and referred to her instead as 'Doña Blanca, daughter of the duke of Bourbon'.[7]

Blanche de Bourbon herself, meanwhile, died in prison in the same year as María de Padilla, and was buried in Jerez; she was also only in her twenties when she passed away. Pedro had not set eyes on his French wife since he abandoned her for María shortly after their wedding in 1353. Whether the king had a hand in the death of the unfortunate and tragic Blanche, who had done nothing wrong yet whom he kept in captivity for eight years, is still debated, though as she was the sister of the queen consort of France, Pedro's harsh treatment of Blanche played an important role in his downfall when the French supported Enrique of Trastámara against him in the late 1360s.[8] Pedro's father sowed the seeds of his only legitimate son's destruction by his neglect of Pedro's mother and his infatuation with a mistress; Pedro failed to learn the vital lesson.

Chapter 12

The Cruel King

Enrique of Trastámara's younger twin Fadrique was, despite his extreme youth, appointed as the grand master of the religious-military organisation the Order of Santiago as early as 1342. A propaganda tale created later to blacken King Pedro's name stated that Fadrique was murdered by Pedro in the Alcázar in Seville on 29 May 1358; supposedly, Pedro invited his half-brother to dine with him, and after Fadrique sat down, one of Pedro's men smashed in his head with a mace. Noticing he was still alive, Pedro administered the coup de grace with a dagger, then ate his meal next to Fadrique's body. And according to the chronicler, historian and statesman Don Pedro López de Ayala (1332–1407), whose niece Teresa de Ayala was one of King Pedro's mistresses in the 1360s and bore him a daughter, ordered the deaths of two of his other half-brothers, Alfonso XI and Leonor de Guzmán's sons Juan and Pedro, who were murdered in Carmona in late 1359. Pedro, who was Alfonso and Leonor's youngest child, was only fourteen years old when he died, and Juan was nineteen.[1] King Alfonso and Leonor de Guzmán's other sons who lived into adulthood, Tello and Sancho, survived their half-brother's reign, as did Fadrique's twin Enrique.

Other relatives killed by King Pedro in the late 1350s were his aunt Leonor of Castile, the dowager queen of Aragón and the daughter of Fernando IV of Castile, and her younger son Infante Don Juan. Leonor, who had made herself an enemy of her stepson Pere IV by promoting the interests of her two sons, Pere's half-brothers, over the king himself, plotted against Pedro of Castile after she returned to her homeland, and was killed in the castle of Castrojeriz in March or April 1359. Her son Don Juan himself had been murdered in Bilbao in June 1358, and in 1363 her other son, Don Fernando, was killed by his half-brother Pere IV, who as a seventeen-year-old in 1336 had succeeded their father Alfonso IV as king of Aragón.

In his will of November 1362, Pedro left a large number of items to his and María de Padilla's three daughters, whom he loved dearly, and to his and Juana de Castro's son Juan. The items he bequeathed to Costanza included a crown which had once belonged to his father Alfonso XI, another crown decorated with eagles which had once belonged to the aunt Pedro had had assassinated some years earlier, Leonor of Castile, and a third crown which Pedro had had made in Seville. This last crown was set with a large balas ruby which had once been in the possession of 'King Bermejo', the name given by Pedro and other Christians to Abu Abdullah Muhammad VI, emir of Granada. A chronicler says that in April 1362, Pedro invited the emir and thirty-six members of his entourage to Seville, where, after dining with them, he had them killed and stripped of their valuables. Whether the story of the assassination is completely accurate or not, it is certainly true that Pedro took possession of the emir's valuables: another of Bermejo's large balas rubies was set into a decorative eagle which Pedro bequeathed to his eldest daughter Beatriz in his will.[2]

Whatever happened between King Pedro of Castile and Abu Abdullah Muhammad VI, Pedro allied himself with the emirate of Granada against Pere IV of Aragón, and from 1356 to 1366 border warfare took place between the two Christian kingdoms in what is sometimes called the War of the Two Peters (*la Guerra de los Dos Pedros*). Pedro's appalling treatment of his wife Blanche de Bourbon brought him the enmity of the French, who supported his half-brother and deadliest enemy Enrique of Trastámara against him. Pedro did, however, enjoy the support of Edward III of England and his sons, and at the battle of Nájera in April 1367, Pedro defeated Enrique with the aid of the eldest of Edward's sons, Edward of Woodstock, prince of Wales, and the prince's brother John of Gaunt, duke of Lancaster, who would marry Pedro's daughter in 1371. Jaume IV, titular king of Majorca and the third of the four husbands of Giovanna I, queen regnant of Naples, also fought at Nájera for Pedro.

Enrique of Trastámara returned to Castile with a force of Spanish and French soldiers and turned the tables on the king, defeating him at the battle of Montiel in March 1369. Enrique subsequently stabbed Pedro to death, and made himself King Enrique II of Castile-León. Born in August 1334, Pedro was only thirty-four years old when he died. He has an atrocious reputation, much of which is deserved, though it was in the interests of the usurping Trastámara dynasty to blacken his name as much as possible. Unlike his half-brother Enrique, who carried out several massacres of the Jewish population of his kingdom, Pedro showed a tolerance and friendliness to his Jewish and Muslim subjects that was remarkable by the standards of medieval Europe. His and María de Padilla's daughters Costanza and Isabel moved to England in the early 1370s when they married into the English royal family, and Costanza's, and therefore also Pedro's, heir was her only child Katherine or Catalina of Lancaster, born sometime between early June 1372 and the end of March 1373. King Pedro's illegitimate sons, including Juana de Castro's son Juan and several other boys whom Pedro fathered after María de Padilla's death, did not fare so well, and were imprisoned for many years by their Trastámara kin.

John of Gaunt, duke of Lancaster, claimed the Castilian throne as Costanza's husband and called himself king of Castile and León from the early 1370s onwards, but was not able to lead a military expedition there until 1386. By then, Enrique of Trastámara had been dead for seven years; he was succeeded on his death in 1379 by his son Juan I (b.1358). Gaunt was never able to make his and Costanza's claim to Castile-León more than merely titular, and in the Treaty of Bayonne of 1388, he and Juan I came to an agreement which involved Gaunt being handsomely paid off to give up his and Costanza's claims. Instead, their daughter Catalina, aged fifteen or sixteen, married Juan I's son Enrique, prince of Asturias, born in October 1379 and not yet nine years old, in September 1388. The young couple united the rival branches of the Castilian royal family.

Catalina of Lancaster and Enrique III succeeded as king and queen on the death of Juan I in 1390, and were the parents of Juan II, who himself became king of Castile-León as an infant in 1406 when Enrique died in his twenties. Catalina, who had acted as her husband's regent for a while after he became king at the age of eleven, acted as her son's regent as well until her death in 1418. By his second marriage, Juan II was the father of the great Isabel la Católica (1451–1504), queen regnant of Castile, who married Fernando or Ferdinand, king of Aragón; they are known to history as the Catholic Monarchs. During their joint reign, they created the Spanish Inquisition, brought down the emirate of Granada, and sponsored Christopher Columbus's voyages across the Atlantic. Their youngest child Katherine of Aragón (b.1485), presumably named after her English-born great-grandmother Catalina of Lancaster, married Henry VIII of England in 1509, and her daughter Queen Mary I (r.1553–58) was, after Edward II, only the second English monarch in history with a Spanish parent.

Part III

Constantinople

Dramatis Personae

John de Brienne, b. *c.*1175/78, widower of Queen Marie of Jerusalem and Stephanie of Armenia; marries Berenguela of León in 1224; elected fifth Latin Emperor of Constantinople for life in 1228

Berenguela of León, b. *c.*1204/05, Latin Empress of Constantinople; mother of Marie, Alphonse, John and Louis de Brienne; daughter of Alfonso IX, king of León, and Berenguela of Castile

Manuel I Komnenos, *Porphyrogennetos*, b.1118, Byzantine Emperor 1143 to 1180; son of Emperor Ioannes II Komnenos and grandson of Emperor Alexios I; marries 1) Bertha von Sulzbach (renamed Eirene, d.1159/60) in 1146 and 2) Maria of Antioch in 1161

Maria of Antioch, b. *c.*1145, Byzantine Empress; daughter of Constance, princess of Antioch, and Raymond of Poitiers; sister of Bohemond III, prince of Antioch, and aunt of Bohemond IV 'the One-Eyed'; marries Emperor Manuel in 1161; regent during the minority of her son Alexios II Komnenos

Maria Komnene, *Porphyrogennete* and *Kaisarissa*, b.1152/53, only child of Emperor Manuel and Bertha/Eirene von Sulzbach; stepdaughter of Maria of Antioch; marries Ranieri of Montferrat in 1180

Ranieri of Montferrat, b. *c.* early 1160s, youngest brother of Corrado of Montferrat (d.1192), king of Jerusalem; renamed Ioannes in Constantinople and given the title *Kaisar*

Alexios II Komnenos, *Porphyrogennetos*, b.1169, Byzantine Emperor 1180 to 1183; only child of Emperor Manuel and Maria of Antioch; half-brother of the *Porphyrogennete* Maria Komnene; marries Agnès of France in 1180

Agnès of France, b.1170/71, Byzantine Empress; daughter of Louis VII, king of France, and sister of Philip II Augustus; renamed Anna in Constantinople

Andronikos I Komnenos, b. late 1110s, Byzantine Emperor 1183 to 1185; grandson of Emperor Alexios I and cousin of Emperor Manuel; marries Alexios II's widow Agnès/Anna

Theodora Komnene, b. mid-1140s, queen consort of Jerusalem; niece of Emperor Manuel, and widow of Baldwin III of Jerusalem (d.1163); lover and perhaps wife of her kinsman Andronikos

Isaakios II Angelos, b. mid-1150s, Byzantine Emperor 1185 to 1195 and again 1203 to 1204; great-grandson of Emperor Alexios I; the identity of his first wife is unknown; his second is Margit of Hungary

Alexios III Angelos, b. early 1150s, Byzantine Emperor 1195 to 1203; older brother and usurper of Isaakios II; married to Euphrosynē Doukaina Kamatera

Theodora Angelina, b. *c.*1160, sister of Isaakios II and Alexios III; marries Corrado of Montferrat, later king of Jerusalem, in 1187

Alexios IV Angelos, b. *c.* early 1180s, co-Byzantine Emperor 1203 to 1204; son of Isaakios II from his first marriage; nephew of Alexios III

Eirene Angelina, b. *c.* early 1180s, daughter of Isaakios II from his first marriage, sister of Alexios IV; marries Philipp of Swabia, son of the Holy Roman Emperor Friedrich Barbarossa, in 1197

Alexios V Doukas, Byzantine Emperor 1204, son-in-law of Alexios III Angelos and Euphrosynē

Bonifacio of Montferrat, b. *c.*1150, brother of Corrado, king of Jerusalem, and *Kaisar* Ranieri/Ioannes; king of Thessaloniki 1204 to 1207; his second wife is Margit of Hungary, widow of Isaakios II

Béla III, b. *c.* late 1140s, king of Hungary 1172 to 1196, son of Géza II; long-term fiancé of the *Porphyrogennete* Maria Komnene; later marries Agnes of Antioch, daughter of Constance of Antioch and Raynald de Châtillon, and half-sister of Maria of Antioch, Byzantine Empress

Margit of Hungary, b. *c.*1175, Byzantine Empress and queen of Thessaloniki; eldest daughter of Béla III and Agnes of Antioch; marries Isaakios II Angelos in 1185 and secondly Bonifacio of Montferrat in 1204

Baudouin I of Flanders, b.1172, first Latin Emperor of Constantinople 1204 to 1205; son of the count of Hainault and the countess of Flanders, and his parents' heir; married to Marie of Champagne; his sister Isabelle (b.1170) marries Philip II Augustus of France and is the mother of Louis VIII

Hendrik of Flanders, b. mid or late 1170s, second Latin Emperor of Constantinople from 1205 to 1216; brother and successor of Baudouin

Yolanda of Flanders, b. mid-1170s, sister of Baudouin and Hendrik; third Latin Empress of Constantinople 1216 to 1219; married to **Pierre de Courtenay,** nephew of Louis VII of France, and succeeded by her son **Robert de Courtenay,** fourth Latin Emperor 1219 to 1228

Baudouin II de Courtenay, *Porphyrogennetos,* b.1217, sixth Latin Emperor of Constantinople; son of Yolanda of Flanders and Pierre de Courtenay; younger brother of Robert de Courtenay; marries Marie de Brienne, and son-in-law of John de Brienne and Berenguela of León

Marie de Brienne, b.1225, Latin Empress of Constantinople; eldest child of Emperor John de Brienne and Berenguela of León; half-sister of Yolande de Brienne (b.1212), queen regnant of Jerusalem

Philippe de Courtenay, b.1243, titular seventh Latin Emperor of Constantinople; son and heir of Baudouin II de Courtenay and Marie de Brienne; grandson of John de Brienne; married to Beatrice of Sicily

Alphonse de Brienne, b. *c.*1228, second child and eldest son of Emperor John de Brienne and Berenguela of León

John de Brienne the younger, b. *c.* early 1230s, almost certainly a *Porphyrogennetos*; second or third son of Emperor John de Brienne and Berenguela of León

Louis de Brienne, b. *c.* early 1230s, almost certainly a *Porphyrogennetos*; second or third son of John de Brienne and Berenguela of León; ancestor of the Beaumont family in England via his son Henry de Beaumont

Alexios I Megas Komnenos and his brother **David Komnenos,** b. early to mid-1180s; grandsons of the Byzantine Emperor Andronikos I Komnenos; founders of the Empire of Trebizond

Tamar, b. *c.*1160, queen regnant of Georgia 1184 to 1213; daughter and heir of King Giorgi III; relative and protector of Alexios and David Komnenos

Chapter 13

The Sack of Constantinople

The remarkable career of John de Brienne, king of Jerusalem, reached a pinnacle in 1228, when he was elected Latin Emperor of Constantinople for life. The man born with few prospects as the youngest son of a minor French noble family had now reached the highest secular rank any man possibly could.

The Latin Empire was founded in April 1204, when the streets of Constantinople, the largest and wealthiest city in Europe, ran with blood as it was sacked by Crusaders during the Fourth Crusade. This Crusade was called in 1198 and its original objective was, like the Third's, to recapture the city of Jerusalem from the Ayyubid dynasty, though the plan later evolved to attacking Egypt. As it turned out, the participants did not travel anywhere near either the Holy Land or Egypt, but arrived outside Constantinople in June 1203 instead. The reasons for the Crusaders' violent assault on a Christian city are complex but have much to do with the turbulent political situation in Constantinople and the mutual hostility between the western Latin and eastern Orthodox Christian faiths, which grew ever worse after the sack of Constantinople. The Byzantines, or rather the Greeks, believed the western Europeans, or Latins, to be bloodthirsty, supercilious, overweening and boastful; the Latins for their part believed the Greeks to be cowardly and 'devoted to servile luxuries', while William of Tyre sniped at 'false and perfidious Greece' and claimed that all Greeks were 'completely given over to the lustful sins of the flesh'. He also poured scorn on their 'boundless arrogance' at having 'insolently' separated from the Roman Church to follow their own 'foolish traditions' instead.[1]

In the early 1200s, the young Byzantine nobleman Alexios Angelos begged the participants of the Fourth Crusade to come to Constantinople and help him and his father, the deposed, imprisoned and blinded Byzantine Emperor Isaakios II Angelos. In return, Alexios promised to 'place the entire empire of Byzantium in obedience to Rome' and to fund the Crusade to the tune of 200,000 marks of silver.[2] The Crusaders rampaged through the streets for three days after capturing the city of Constantinople on 12 April 1204, massacring the inhabitants, tearing down buildings, and destroying or looting numerous priceless works of art. Even the great sixth-century Hagia Sophia, the Church of Holy Wisdom, was not spared, and though the building itself remained intact – and survives to the present day as a mosque and museum – its treasures was ransacked and carried off to western Europe. The desecration and sacrilege, and the 'licentious and wanton behaviour' of the Latins, shocked chronicler Niketas Choniatēs and others who witnessed it profoundly.[3]

After the sack of Constantinople, the Byzantine Empire fragmented into various territories as ambitious men from western Europe saw the potential for gaining new fiefs in this part of the world: in modern times, some of these territories are known as the Latin Empire of Constantinople, the empire of Nicaea, the empire of Trebizond, the despotate of Epirus, the kingdom of Thessaloniki, the lordship of Athens, and the principality of Achaea.[4] The period of their existence was known to contemporaries as the *Frankokratia* or *Latinokratia*, the 'rule of the Franks' or the Latins, and the treaty signed among the Crusaders dividing them all up in 1204 was called the *Partitio Terrarum Imperii Romaniae*, 'Partition of the Lands of the Empire of *Romania*' (meaning the Eastern Roman Empire, not the country of Romania).

The first Christian Roman emperor, Constantine the Great, renamed the city of Constantinople, originally called Byzantium (or Byzantion) and later called Istanbul, in his own honour in the year 330. It was the capital of what is known nowadays as the Byzantine Empire, though it would be more correct to call it the Eastern Roman Empire. After the Roman Empire collapsed in western Europe in the 400s, the eastern part of the empire survived for another 1,000 years, and the Byzantines referred to themselves, rather confusingly, as 'Romans', while western Europeans were 'Latins' or 'Franks'. The Eastern Roman Empire reached its zenith and its greatest territorial extension under Emperor Justinian in the 500s and was restored to some of its former glories by the Komnenoi dynasty, who ruled the empire from the accession of Alexios I Komnenos in 1081 until the downfall of his grandson in 1185. We know much about Emperor Alexios I and his reign thanks to the (very biased) *Alexiad* written about him by his eldest child, the highly educated and erudite *Porphyrogennete* and *Kaisarissa* Anna Komnene, though the historian William of Tyre was not impressed, calling Alexios a 'wicked and crafty man' who 'detested the whole Latin race'.

Anna's younger brother and their father's successor, Emperor Ioannes II Komnenos, reigned from 1118 to 1143 and was said by William of Tyre to be 'generous and pious, kind and merciful… with black hair and swarthy skin, and for this reason is called the Moor'. In her *Alexiad*, Anna Komnene also described her brother Ioannes as 'swarthy' with 'very black eyes'. Ioannes was the father of Emperor Manuel I, his youngest son but the only one who was a *Porphyrogennetos*; Manuel was born in November 1118 three months into his father's reign. According to Niketas Choniatēs, Manuel had, like his father, dark skin, so that a group of Venetians who wished to mock him dressed an Ethiopian man in imperial robes and crown and 'led him about in procession'. Manuel succeeded Ioannes in 1143 in preference to his elder brother the *Sebastokrator* Isaakios, grandfather of the man who was to proclaim himself *Basileus* of Cyprus in 1185, because he was 'wiser, more valiant in arms, and more affable' than his brother.[5] By the 1170s, however, Emperor Manuel's star was somewhat on the wane. In 1176, he led a huge army to defeat against the Seljuk Sultanate of Rûm at the battle of Myriokephalon – near Lake Beyşehir in modern-day Turkey – at which his brother-in-law Baldwin of Antioch, his nephew Andronikos Vatatzes and his nephew-in-law Ioannes Kantakouzenos were killed. Another nephew, Ioannes Doukas Komnenos, the maternal grandfather of Queen Isabella of Jerusalem, fought in the battle and died shortly afterwards, presumably of his wounds.

Chapter 14

A Lively Form of Air and Crystal

William of Tyre spent seven months in Constantinople in 1179/80 and met Manuel I Komnenos for the last time; the emperor was to die a few months later. William attended the weddings of Manuel's two children in February and March 1180. The emperor had one child from his first marriage to the Bavarian noblewoman Bertha von Sulzbach, who was renamed Eirene in Constantinople.[1] This was the *Porphyrogennete* Maria Komnene, who was born *c.*1152 and was a couple of years older than her namesake cousin who married Amalric, king of Jerusalem, in 1167. In February 1180, the *Porphyrogennete* Maria wed Ranieri of Montferrat, whose eldest brother Guglielmo had died three years earlier only a few months after marrying Amalric's daughter Sibilla. Ranieri was renamed Ioannes in Constantinople – as this was the name of his wife's grandfather Emperor Ioannes II, it was intended as an honour – and was granted a large territory in Thessaloniki as a wedding gift and given the title *Kaisar*. That the second-oldest Montferrat brother, Corrado, was already married to a wife whose identity is unknown, as stated by Niketas Choniatēs, is strongly suggested by the fact that it was Ranieri who married the *Porphyrogennete* even though he was a few years her junior, implying that Corrado was unavailable in 1180 as a husband for her. Niketas states that Emperor Manuel was particularly fond of Corrado, 'as one graced with good fortune, acute intelligence, and strength of arm', so would surely have chosen him as a son-in-law had he been unmarried.[2]

The youngest son of an Italian marquis was, for all the Montferrats' excellent connections, a rather poor match for an emperor's only daughter, though as one historian has pointed out, Ranieri's family was 'the cornerstone of surviving Byzantine interests in Italy'. The *Porphyrogennete* Maria had previously been suggested as a bride for Friedrich Barbarossa's eldest son Heinrich, future Holy Roman Emperor, King Guglielmo II of Sicily, the future King John of England, and the future King Béla III of Hungary. Béla's betrothal to her advanced so far that he lived in Constantinople for a few years and was treated as Emperor Manuel's heir apparent with the new name Alexios and the title *Despot*.[3] The betrothal was finally broken, and Maria married very late by the standards of medieval royal and imperial families. Niketas Choniatēs claimed that by 1180, she had 'rav[ed] long in the palace… and long[ed] for the marriage bed'. He also wrote that *Kaisar* Ranieri/Ioannes of Montferrat was 'fair of face and pleasant to look at; his well-groomed hair shone like the sun', while his new wife the *Porphyrogennete* 'was as strong as a man' and 'masculine in her resolution'.[4] William of Tyre says that Ranieri/Ioannes was only about seventeen when he wed in 1180 and was therefore a decade younger than his wife, which seems rather unlikely given the ages of Ranieri's mother and siblings; his brothers Guglielmo and Corrado are believed to have been born in the early to mid-1140s, and their parents married in or before 1133. As William attended the wedding, however, his testimony cannot be entirely discounted, and Niketas Choniatēs agrees and says that Ranieri was 'too young to grow a beard'.[5]

Emperor Manuel's second wife, whom he married in 1161, was Maria of Antioch, then about sixteen and a cousin of Eleanor of Aquitaine, queen consort firstly of France and later of England, via her father Raymond of Poitiers. She was the sister of Bohemond III (d.1201), prince of Antioch.[6] Raymond of Poitiers was killed at the battle of Inab in modern-day Syria in June 1149 during the Second Crusade, leaving Maria, Bohemond and several other small children, and his head was sent to the Caliph of Baghdad in a silver box. His widow Constance, princess of Antioch in her own right, subsequently married the French adventurer Raynald de Châtillon, Maria's stepfather, who showed appalling brutality to Muslims on many occasions and was personally executed by Salah al-Din in 1187 after Guy de Lusignan led the Christian forces to defeat at the battle of Hattin.[7]

After the death of his first wife Bertha/Eirene von Sulzbach, Manuel Komnenos sought a second bride in Outremer, and sent an envoy to Jerusalem to treat with his nephew-in-law Baldwin III (who had married Manuel's niece Theodora Komnene in 1158). Offered a choice between Melisende of Tripoli, a cousin of Baldwin III and his brother Amalric, and Maria of Antioch, he – eventually – plumped for the latter.[8] This decision was perhaps partly based on hearing a description of Maria's physical beauty; a contemporary talked of 'the radiance of her appearance, her pearly countenance, her even disposition, candour, and charm of speech'. Another wrote that Maria 'was fair in form and exceedingly beautiful; her beauty was incomparable' and that she was 'the sweet light and a vision of beauty unto men'. Manuel had, however, originally chosen Melisende of Tripoli as his future wife, and her mother Hodierna and aunt Queen Melisende of Jerusalem purchased numerous expensive ornaments and jewellery for her trip to Constantinople, but Manuel changed his mind and selected her cousin instead. This must have been deeply humiliating for Melisende, especially as the Byzantine envoys had 'pried further into the morals of the girl by examining the state of the secret hidden parts of her body'. Her brother the count of Tripoli was furious that she had been rejected 'like the daughter of a common person'.[9]

Emperor Manuel and his young Antiochene wife Maria struggled to conceive, and in 1165 Manuel designated his adolescent daughter the *Porphyrogennete* and her Hungarian fiancé *Despot* Béla/Alexios as his heirs.[10] Finally, in September 1169, eight years after their wedding and when the emperor was almost fifty-one, Manuel and Maria of Antioch produced a son, Alexios Komnenos, *Porphyrogennetos*. Béla's betrothal to the *Porphyrogennete* was subsequently broken now that she was no longer heir apparent to the imperial throne. He returned to his native Hungary, where he succeeded his father as king in 1172 and married Maria of Antioch's half-sister Agnes, daughter of Constance, princess of Antioch, and Raynald de Châtillon.[11] Empress Maria gave birth to her son in the porphyry chamber of the great imperial palace in Constantinople, which had been adorned in readiness for her labour: the roof was covered with thick purple textiles woven by the palace weavers and the outside walls were hung with silken cloths. Maria lay in a four-poster bed draped with curtains embroidered with gold, and after her son Alexios was born, the happy event was signalled to the outside world by means of a red slipper embroidered with pearls being suspended outside the main entrance to the palace. The residents of the city hung cloths and lamps in the streets and listened to Ethiopian and European trumpeters playing a fanfare on the steps of the palace.

At the age of ten, on 2 March 1180, Alexios the *Porphyrogennetos* married Agnès of France, renamed Anna in Constantinople, who was slightly younger than her new husband. Agnès/Anna was the youngest daughter of Louis VII of France, who died six months after her wedding and was succeeded by her brother Philip II Augustus. A poet who witnessed the two imperial wedding celebrations of 1180 compared Agnès/Anna and her sister-in-law the *Porphyrogennete* Maria Komnene to the meeting of two stars. He told Agnès, who was only eight or nine years old, that 'One of these [brides] was the glory of the whole West, your own lively form of air and crystal, while the other, the second, *Augusta*, unable to bear comparison with your beauty, was your sister-in-law, the *Porphyrogennete*'.[12]

Manuel I Komnenos died in September 1180, six days after Louis VII of France, having achieved the comparatively rare, by the standards of Byzantine Emperors, feat of dying from natural causes. William of Tyre mourned Manuel as 'the illustrious emperor of Constantinople, of immortal memory, the most munificent of all the princes of the land', and called him a 'great-souled man of incomparable energy'.[13] The long period of political stability in the Byzantine Empire, which had only three rulers between the accession of Manuel's grandfather Alexios I in 1081 and his own death a century later, was about to come to an end.

Chapter 15

He Who Stank of the Dark Ages

Manuel's only legitimate son, Alexios II Komnenos, who had just turned eleven, succeeded to the Byzantine throne in September 1180 under the regency of his deeply unpopular mother the dowager empress, Maria of Antioch. Maria was known in Constantinople as *Xenē* or 'Foreigner' and was widely rumoured to have taken her late husband's nephew, a *Protosebastos* who was her chief adviser, as her lover.[1] Her son Emperor Alexios was said by Niketas Choniatēs to have a character 'imprinted with the worst qualities' and to pay no attention to his duties, as he had been 'nurtured on soft airs'. Like Baldwin IV of Jerusalem, who was eight years his senior, Alexios had a stammer, and had 'yellowish brown hair', which Choniatēs calls 'the colour of summer'.[2]

Only a couple of years into the reign of the young emperor, his much older half-sister the *Porphyrogennete* and *Kaisarissa* Maria Komnene incited a rebellion, and invited her late father's infamous and dangerous cousin Andronikos Komnenos to Constantinople as part of it. Her revolt was aimed mostly at her stepmother Empress Maria and her chief adviser the *Protosebastos*, but also at Emperor Alexios himself. Perhaps Maria Komnene had the example of her great-aunt the *Porphyrogennete* Anna Komnene of *Alexiad* fame in mind: after the death of her father Emperor Alexios I in 1118, there is evidence that Anna tried unsuccessfully to depose her brother Ioannes II Komnenos. Anna claimed that she, as her father's eldest child, had been crowned and acclaimed as Byzantine Empress shortly after her birth, and was unfairly displaced by her younger brother.[3] According to Choniatēs, in the early 1180s the *Porphyrogennete* Maria 'dispatched letters to Andronikos Komnenos prodding him like a horse at the starting gate anxious to run the race, delighting in the evil joy of her own making and bringing on her own ruin'. Over the years Manuel I Komnenos had made repeated attempts to capture and imprison his cousin, long a thorn in the emperor's side, but Andronikos was adroit at 'leaping nimbly over the many traps set to ensnare him' and remained at large.[4]

During the chaos which followed Andronikos's arrival in Constantinople in 1182, Maria of Antioch and her son Emperor Alexios II were murdered at Andronikos's command. Alexios, barely into his teens, was forced to sign his mother's death warrant, and they were both strangled by Andronikos's chief henchman Stephanos Hagiochristophoritēs, the *hetairiarch* (imperial bodyguard) Konstantin Tripsychos, and a eunuch named Pterygeonitēs. A desperate Empress Maria tried to summon help from her brother-in-law Béla III, formerly the *Porphyrogennete*'s fiancé and now king of Hungary, but her attempt failed. She was incarcerated in a 'cramped dungeon' before her murder and allowed no food or water, and after her strangulation her body was buried in an unmarked grave. A few months later, her adolescent son's body was thrown into the Bosporus in a lead coffin, though Alexios II was decapitated after death and his head was buried somewhere in the city of Constantinople. Andronikos Komnenos showed deliberate disrespect to the emperor by kicking his body when it was brought before him and hanging a wax impression of his own signet ring from it.[5] It was a tragic and violent end for the young Emperor Alexios, who was born in the purple to a father who was himself also born in the purple. Empress Maria's adviser and probable lover the *Protosebastos* suffered too; he was imprisoned, tormented and finally blinded.

After having the adolescent Alexios II killed, Andronikos was himself proclaimed and crowned Byzantine Emperor in 1183. In an act of stunning ingratitude, he had the *Porphyrogennete* Maria Komnene and her Italian husband Ranieri/Ioannes of Montferrat killed with a slow-acting poison that 'lulled its victims little by little and drained their lives unhurriedly'.[6] If chroniclers were correct as to *Kaisar* Ranieri's age, he cannot have been much more than twenty when he died. Andronikos also ordered the massacre of the Latin inhabitants of Constantinople as part of a fierce backlash in the empire against the pro-western policies followed by the late Emperor Manuel, whose death in 1180 marked the end of strong Byzantine support of Outremer.[7] Andronikos's attitude towards foreigners can be seen in his reluctance in 1165 to swear an oath of loyalty to the *Porphyrogennete* and her then fiancé *Despot* Béla of Hungary as Manuel's heirs, exclaiming 'What madness is this of the emperor… to choose before all others this foreigner and interloper to be emperor of the Romans?' (i.e., the Byzantines or Greeks).[8]

Emperor Andronikos I Komnenos, about sixty-five years old in 1183, married Alexios II's barely pubescent widow Agnès/Anna of France, who was forced to wed the man who had killed her husband and mother-in-law. Andronikos had previously had sexual relationships with Maria of Antioch's sister Philippa in 1166 and with his own kinswomen Eudokia Komnene and Theodora Komnene, both of whom were Emperor Manuel's nieces. Theodora, aunt of the self-proclaimed *Basileus* Isaakios Doukas Komnenos of Cyprus, was the widow of Baldwin III, king of Jerusalem (d.1163). She and Andronikos, both Orthodox Christians, made the highly unconventional, by the standards of the time, decision to live in the Muslim city of Damascus, where they had two children together. Andronikos's decades-long wanderings also took him to the kingdom of Georgia and the court of King Giorgi III, and to the protection of Kilij Arslan II, whose name means 'Sword Lion' and who was the Seljuk sultan of Rûm who defeated Emperor Manuel at the battle of Myriokephalon in 1176.[9] Queen Theodora is assumed to have died before her partner, or husband, returned to their native Constantinople. Andronikos's subsequent marriage to a girl more than half a century his junior excited much scandalised comment among Greek and French chroniclers alike, and Niketas Choniatēs talks in disgust about how 'he who stank of the dark ages was not ashamed to lie unlawfully with his nephew's [*sic*] red-cheeked and tender spouse… the overripe suitor embracing the unripe maiden'. Andronikos comes across as a deeply unpleasant and lecherous figure as well as a violently murderous one, though Choniatēs does concede that in his youth, he was 'endowed with a wondrous comeliness' and was 'the handsomest of men'.[10]

In 1185, barely two years after his coronation – and in the same year as the death of the Leper King, Baldwin IV of Jerusalem – Andronikos was himself overthrown by a kinsman. This was Isaakios II Angelos, several of whose brothers had been blinded during a deadly campaign against Byzantine aristocrats carried out by Emperor Andronikos.[11] The emperor fled from Constantinople with his teenage French wife and his favourite mistress, Maraptikē, in the direction of Russia, but was captured by a mob and tortured for several days until he died, his torments related in considerable stomach-churning detail by Niketas Choniatēs. His sons Manuel and Ioannes were almost certainly also executed, even though at least one of them, Manuel, had opposed his father and refused to have anything to do with Andronikos's murders of Maria of Antioch and her son Emperor Alexios II. During his coup, Isaakios II Angelos used an axe to split open the head of Andronikos's henchman Stephanos Hagiochristophoritēs, one of the killers of Empress

Maria.[12] The chaos in Constantinople and the downfall of the Komnenoi dynasty in 1185 had further consequences when Isaakios Doukas Komnenos, yet another imperial kinsman, made himself *Basileus* of Cyprus that same year. Also in 1185, the Byzantine city of Thessaloniki was sacked by a Sicilian force under the command of Tancredi, count of Lecce, who was to make himself king of Sicily several years later (see Part 4 below).

Agnès/Anna of France, widowed from two emperors by the age of fourteen or fifteen, spent the remaining decades of her life in Constantinople rather than returning to her homeland, where her brother Philip II Augustus reigned as king until his death in 1223. In the early 1200s she married her third husband, Theodoros Branas, son of a *Protosebastos*, after they had lived together for many years. Robert Clari, one of the French Crusaders who arrived in Constantinople in the early 1200s, wrote that when some of his compatriots, including Agnès/Anna's own nephew the count of Blois, went to greet the dowager empress, she treated them 'with very bad grace' and claimed via an interpreter to have forgotten her native French entirely. As she left France as a child in 1179, was now in her thirties and had presumably only spoken Greek all that time, her claim was perhaps not wholly untrue.[13]

Isaakios II Angelos's reign as Byzantine Emperor lasted for a decade, and was a troubled one, plagued by several pretenders to the throne including a young man who claimed to be Alexios II Komnenos.[14] In early 1187, Emperor Isaakios arranged the marriage of his sister Theodora Angelina to Corrado of Montferrat, who was the older brother of the poisoned Ranieri/Ioannes and was presumably now widowed from his unknown first wife, to rebuild the Byzantine-Montferrat connection. His efforts would be in vain, however, as Corrado abandoned Theodora within months of their wedding when he set off for Outremer, saving the port of Tyre from Salah al-Din later in 1187, and ultimately marrying Queen Isabella. During Isaakios's reign in Constantinople, momentous events took place in Outremer: Guy de Lusignan lost the battle of Hattin and most of the Latin Kingdom of Jerusalem was lost, the Third Crusade began, Emperor Friedrich Barbarossa drowned in Armenian Cilicia, and Corrado of Montferrat was assassinated while his wife Isabella was pregnant with the daughter who would marry John de Brienne eighteen years later.

Isaakios was deposed in turn in 1195 by his and Theodora Angelina's older brother the *Sebastokrator* Alexios III Angelos, whose coup d'état was aided by his wife Euphrosynē Doukaina Kamatera. Niketas Choniatēs railed contemptuously at the 'stupid men' in Constantinople who 'prostrated themselves before the supposed emperor's wife… like fawning puppies… with their bellies stroked and their ears tickled'. He wrote that the powerful and intelligent Euphrosynē 'gave orders with equal authority' to those of her husband, often nullifying decrees Alexios had made and replacing them with her own commands.[15] Alexios III had his brother Isaakios imprisoned and blinded, a tragically all too common mutilation inflicted on former emperors of Byzantium and numerous other unfortunates. Emperor Isaakios, despite the loss of his eyes, survived deposition and imprisonment and lived until 1204.

Alexios III, however, proved no better a ruler than Isaakios had been, and a despairing Choniatēs wrote in the early 1200s of the 'common calamities which this queen of cities endured during the reign of the terrestrial angels', i.e., the two Angeloi brothers.[16] At the end of the 1100s, Alexios III sent gifts and a gold crown to Levon, the first king of Armenian Cilicia, whose coronation had recently taken place with a crown sent to him by the Holy Roman Emperor, Friedrich Barbarossa's eldest son Heinrich von Hohenstaufen (d. September 1197). Supposedly Alexios told Levon, somewhat jealously, that he should not accept the 'crown of the Franks' as he and his kingdom were closer to Constantinople than to Rome. Alexios's own relations with Emperor Heinrich were not happy: he had to raise a tax called *Alamanikon* or 'German tax' to pay the tribute demanded of him by Heinrich, and was forced to strip imperial tombs of their treasures to gather enough cash.[17]

Emperor Isaakios II's adolescent son, also named Alexios Angelos, was imprisoned by his namesake uncle in 1195 and held in captivity with his father, though was not blinded. At the start of the 1200s, Alexios managed to escape, supposedly by cutting his hair short and wearing 'Latin raiment', i.e., western-style clothes. He sought refuge with Philipp of Swabia, Barbarossa's youngest son and Heinrich von Hohenstaufen's brother, and met some of the leaders of the impending Fourth Crusade. Niketas Choniatēs ascribes Philipp's willingness to aid Alexios, whom he calls a 'witless lad', to the entreaties of his wife Eirene Angelina, Alexios's sister, who was concerned that her brother had lost his country and 'wandered about like the planets'. It was agreed that the crusading forces would divert to Constantinople to attempt to overthrow Alexios III and replace him with his brother Isaakios and his nephew the young Alexios.[18]

The leaders of the Fourth Crusade included Bonifacio of Montferrat, brother of the assassinated Corrado and the poisoned Ranieri/Ioannes; Baudouin of Flanders, count of Flanders and Hainault, brother-in-law both of Henri of Champagne, late king of Jerusalem, and Philip II Augustus, king of France; Louis, count of Blois, Philip II's nephew; and the *Doge* of Venice, Enrico Dandalo, whom Niketas Choniatēs described as 'a man maimed in sight and along in years, a creature most treacherous... a sly cheat'.[19] Dandalo was indeed aged, born around 1107, and therefore in his late nineties when he died in 1205; his father had also lived into his nineties.

In 1203 Alexios III and his wife Euphrosynē fled from Constantinople and from the Crusaders, and the blinded Isaakios II Angelos was restored to his lost throne with his son Alexios IV Angelos crowned alongside him as co-emperor. Isaakios died in early 1204 – whether by poison or of natural causes is unclear – around the time that his son Emperor Alexios IV was deposed and strangled by yet another pretender, Alexios V Doukas, son-in-law of the exiled Alexios III and Euphrosynē. Doukas reigned as emperor for only a few weeks, then was, almost inevitably, captured, blinded and executed in his turn. This was achieved by hurling him from 'the lofty column standing in the Forum of the Bull', i.e., the triumphal column of Emperor Theodosius I (d.395) in what is now Beyazit Square in Istanbul, so that he 'was all broken to pieces'.[20] To make the whole dizzying affair even more confusing, an obscure young nobleman named Nikolaos Kannavos had also been anointed emperor at the beginning of 1204 apparently against his own will, 'reigned' for several days, then was imprisoned by Alexios V Doukas and probably decapitated; and another nobleman named Constantine Laskaris appears also to have been elected emperor for a day or two in April 1204 just before Constantinople was sacked.[21] Such was the state of affairs in the Byzantine Empire in the early 1200s.

Chapter 16

The Incendiary Angel of Evil

A few weeks after the deaths of Isaakios II and Alexios IV, the Crusaders sacked Constantinople. The historian and writer Niketas Choniatēs was one of the many inhabitants who voluntarily left the city in April 1204; Niketas carried his infant son out of the city, while his wife walked alongside him, her pregnancy almost at full term. The family did eventually return to Constantinople in 1206, though Niketas left again some months later, unable to bear 'the Latins and their drivelling' (a word he used on several occasions in his works to talk about western Europeans). Utterly horrified to witness the destruction of his beloved Constantinople in 1204, and by the way Isaakios II Angelos and his son Alexios IV 'prayed for the end of all things' and gloried in destruction, Niketas called the two men 'these firebrands of the country, flaming in visage, thus personifying the incendiary angel of evil', in another play on the Angeloi name.[1]

In 1204, the Crusaders divided the city of Constantinople and the empire into eight parts, though as most of the empire was still held by the Byzantines, a man assigned a territory still had to fight for and capture it. The Latin Emperor was assigned a quarter of Constantinople and a quarter of the empire, including Thrace, which was vital to the defence of the city. Venice, a city-state growing ever wealthier and more influential, acquired another quarter of the city and three-eighths of the empire, including most of Epirus. The rest was divided into fiefs and assigned to the leading Crusader knights, while six Venetians and six Frenchmen were chosen to elect an emperor of Constantinople.[2] Their choice landed on Baudouin of Flanders (b.1172), count of Flanders and Hainault and brother-in-law of the king of France, and he was crowned Latin Emperor in the church of Hagia Sophia on 16 May 1204 with the regalia of the Byzantine emperors. Baudouin's clothes were as splendid as the regalia: hose of the finest red samite, shoes studded with gemstones, a coat with gold buttons, and a cloak and gown both also studded with precious stones. His wife Marie of Champagne, sister of Henri, king of Jerusalem, who had died falling out of a window in Acre seven years earlier, also died in Acre on her way to be crowned alongside her husband; she fell victim to an epidemic of plague then raging through Outremer.[3]

Like John de Brienne, the Montferrat brothers, sons of the marquis of Montferrat (d.1191) and his Austrian wife Judith von Babenberg, loom large in the history of Europe and the Mediterranean in the late twelfth and early thirteenth century. Guglielmo, the eldest, was the first husband of Sibilla of Jerusalem and died in 1177 while she was pregnant with the future Baldwin V, and Corrado, the second brother, married Sibilla's half-sister Queen Isabella; when he was assassinated in 1192, he also left his wife pregnant, with John de Brienne's first wife Queen Marie. The youngest brother was *Kaisar* Ranieri/Ioannes, poisoned in 1182 or 1183 during the maelstrom stirred up by his wife the *Porphyrogennete* Maria Komnene in Constantinople. And the third Montferrat brother was Bonifacio, a leader of the Fourth Crusade and one of the men who carved up the Byzantine Empire after the sack of Constantinople in 1204. According to the French crusader and chronicler Geoffroi de Villehardouin, marshal of Champagne, who must have known him well, Bonifacio was 'one of the most highly esteemed knights in the whole world, and one whom his fellow knights loved most, since no one was more open-handed and generous than he'.[4] After the assassination of Corrado in 1192, Bonifacio succeeded him as marquis of Montferrat; Queen Marie of Jerusalem never claimed her father's Italian lands. Bonifacio also considered himself the heir of his younger brother Ranieri/Ioannes, who had been given a large territory in Thessaloniki by his father-in-law Emperor Manuel.[5] In pursuit of his hopes of becoming Latin Emperor of Constantinople, Bonifacio married Margit of Hungary, who was the widow of the blinded emperor Isaakios II Angelos and niece of the strangled empress Maria of Antioch. Margit was raised from the age of about ten in Byzantine customs and the rites of the eastern Orthodox faith.[6] Her father, *Despot* Béla III, had also spent many years of his youth living in Constantinople.

Bonifacio, however, lost out to Baudouin of Flanders in the struggle to become emperor, and instead claimed the right to carve out his own kingdom in Thessaloniki as his younger brother's heir. He duly did so, and Margit, an empress by her first marriage as Isaakios II's child-bride in 1185 and about twelve when her maternal grandfather Raynald de Châtillon was beheaded by Salah al-Din after the battle of Hattin two years later, now became a queen by her second. Geoffroi de Villehardouin met her in the early 1200s

– she and Empress Agnès/Anna had sought refuge in the Boukoleon Palace during the assault on Constantinople – and described her as 'a good and beautiful lady who was the king of Hungary's sister' (her father Béla had died in 1196 and was succeeded by her brother Imre). Margit proved to be a real asset to her husband during his creation of his own kingdom: Villehardouin states that 'because his wife, the former Empress, was known to them, the Greeks began to rally to his side'.[7] The reign of Margit's husband as king of Thessaloniki was, however, short. In September 1207, Bonifacio of Montferrat was killed in an ambush set for him by the Emperor or *Tsar* of Bulgaria, Kaloyan – also often called Ioannitsa or 'Little Ivan' – and his head was sent to Kaloyan. Margit subsequently ruled Thessaloniki as regent for their infant son Demetrios, and Bonifacio's niece Queen Marie of Jerusalem married John de Brienne three years after his death. The kingdom he had created only outlived him by a few years: Thessaloniki was absorbed into the despotate of Epirus in the mid-1220s.

Baudouin of Flanders did not reign for long as Latin Emperor of Constantinople either. He was captured by Kaloyan/Ioannitsa, a ferocious opponent of the Byzantine Empire and its successor Latin Empire, after a fiercely fought battle at Adrianople in April 1205 during which the count of Blois, nephew of Philip II Augustus of France and Empress Agnès/Anna, was killed. Kaloyan/Ioannitsa had in his army a large force of Cumans, a nomadic tribe of the Eurasian steppes who practised shamanism.[8] Emperor Baudouin died not long after the battle of Adrianople, though the date of his death is uncertain. Niketas Choniatēs says that his arms were cut off at the elbows and his legs at the knees and that he was thrown into a ravine, where he lived for three days, though this seems unlikely to be true. He left no children from his marriage to the late Marie of Champagne and was succeeded by his younger brother Hendrik, whose coronation did not take place until August 1206 when it finally became widely accepted that Baudouin must by now be dead.[9] As a result of the mystery surrounding the date and circumstances of his death, a pretender claiming to be Baudouin appeared in western Europe in 1224 and was believed and supported by many. The game, however, was soon up when 'Baudouin' met his nephew Louis VIII of France and it transpired that he could not remember any details of his wedding to Marie of Champagne, nor his performing homage to Louis's father Philip II Augustus. Nor could he speak French correctly.[10]

Chapter 17

The Latin Emperors

In the period from 1203 to 1205/06, Constantinople had no fewer than seven and perhaps even eight emperors: Alexios III Angelos, deposed in 1203, though he lived until 1211 in exile; his brother Isaakios II, restored to his lost throne, and Isaakios's son and co-emperor Alexios IV; the obscure youth Nikolaos Kannavos for a few days at the start of 1204; the pretender Alexios V Doukas for a few weeks in 1204; possibly Constantine Laskaris for a day or two in 1204; Baudouin of Flanders, first Latin Emperor; and Hendrik of Flanders, second Latin Emperor. Hendrik, who married twice but had no surviving legitimate children, was succeeded in 1216 by his and Baudouin's sister Yolanda of Flanders and her husband Pierre de Courtenay (their eldest sister, by now long dead, was Isabelle, the first wife of Philip II Augustus and mother of Louis VIII). Pierre de Courtenay was captured in the newly created despotate of Epirus in 1217 and held in prison there until his death in 1219, and Yolanda also died in 1219. As had happened with Yolanda's brother Emperor Baudouin in 1205, Pierre's fate remained unknown for some years, and their son Robert de Courtenay was not crowned as Latin Emperor until 1221 when it became clear that Pierre must be dead. Robert reigned until his death in 1228, at which point John de Brienne entered the story.

Robert's younger brother Baudouin de Courtenay was a *Porphyrogennetos*, born the year after his parents Yolanda and Pierre succeeded her brother Hendrik as Emperor and Empress of Constantinople, and shortly after his mother arrived in the city. He was just eleven when his brother died in 1228, and the barons of Constantinople decided that the boy would marry John de Brienne and Berenguela of León's daughter Marie, who was then three years old. They rejected an offer by the Bulgarian *Tsar* Ivan Asen II, nephew of Kaloyan/Ioannitsa, for Baudouin to marry his daughter Elena Asenina.[1] At first, John de Brienne was chosen as regent for his daughter and son-in-law until Baudouin was old enough to rule in person, but he managed to manipulate matters so that he was elected Latin Emperor for life.[2] Despite John's elevation to Emperor, the year 1228 was not a complete success for him, as his fifteen-year-old daughter Yolande de Brienne, queen of Jerusalem and Sicily and Holy Roman Empress, died shortly after giving birth to her son that April; see Part 4 below.

John de Brienne's election as emperor was confirmed in a treaty made in Perugia, Italy, in April 1229, which also stipulated that his and Berenguela's daughter Marie would marry Baudouin de Courtenay. John was crowned emperor in the Hagia Sophia in the autumn of 1231, shortly after he finally arrived in the city. Pope Gregory IX sent a letter to Brienne in August 1231, not long before his coronation, addressing him as 'emperor of the Romans, king of Jerusalem and Sicily'.[3] Marie de Brienne, future Latin Empress, was the oldest of John and Berenguela of León's children. As her youngest brothers John and Louis de Brienne were almost certainly born after their father's election as an emperor in Constantinople, they would, like their de Courtenay brother-in-law, have had the right to the title *Porphyrogennetos*.[4] When the three de Brienne brothers witnessed documents issued by their cousin Alfonso X of Castile-León, they were named as the 'son of King Don John of Acre, Emperor of Constantinople, and Empress Doña Berenguela' (*fijo del Rey D. Johan Dacre Emperador de Constantinopla et de la Emperadriz Doña Berenguela*).[5] Louis de Brienne was a great-great-grandfather of King Henry IV of England (b.1367) via his son Henry de Beaumont, and his brother John de Brienne was, via his only child Blanche de Brienne, a great-great-great-grandfather of King Richard II of England (b.1367), who was deposed by Henry IV in 1399. The brothers' six-year-old sister Marie married fourteen-year-old Baudouin de Courtenay in the summer or early autumn of 1231, around the same time as their father's coronation in Hagia Sophia; Baudouin rendered homage to his father-in-law John as his co-emperor.[6]

As John de Brienne's biographer Guy Perry has pointed out, creating a narrative of John's reign as Latin Emperor of Constantinople is very difficult thanks to the 'extreme paucity of the surviving source material'. Not one single text issued by John as emperor, nor even one addressed to him as emperor, exists. Nor did the empire over which he presided have much going for it, and John managed to leave it in an even worse state than he found it. Christopher Tyerman does not mince his words when he states that 'the Latin empire was a failure, politically, financially, culturally and dynastically' and that its centre, Constantinople itself, 'soon degenerated into a bankrupt husk' and a 'shabby outpost, increasingly irrelevant as well as impotent'.

John himself was described by contemporaries as a 'pauper'. And Jonathan Phillips points out the numerous issues that distracted attention and led to a general waning of interest and support in western Europe for the Latin Empire: the Albigensian Crusade against the Cathars in southern France; the failing relations between the papacy and John de Brienne's son-in-law, the Holy Roman Emperor Friedrich II; the Christianisation of Lithuania; the ongoing Christian campaigns between the 1210s and 1240s against the large territories in Spain still ruled by Muslims; the danger from the rapidly advancing Mongolian Empire led by Genghis Khan (d.1227) and his sons; and the endless struggles by Christians to hold onto their territories in Outremer.[7]

Another issue was the number of adversaries John de Brienne had to face during his reign, not only the resurgent empire of Bulgaria, but also the hostile rulers of several of the other territories created during the *Frankokratia*. John's greatest enemy was Ioannes III Doukas Vatatzes, emperor of Nicaea, and in 1235 Vatatzes joined forces with Ivan Asen II, *Tsar* of Bulgaria. They laid siege to the city of Constantinople in what Guy Perry has called 'the war of the three Johns'. Brienne received aid from Venice, Genoa and Pisa, and managed to hold off the siege.[8] Pope Gregory IX called for crusading forces to divert from the Holy Land and go to Constantinople's aid. One of the leaders of this crusade, which took place at the end of the 1230s and was called the Barons' Crusade, was Thibaut of Champagne (b.1201), king of Navarre, cousin and rival of Alice and Philippa of Champagne and Jerusalem; and another was Richard of Cornwall (b.1209), son of King John of England and younger brother of Henry III. Although John de Brienne's nephew Gautier de Brienne also took part, Pope Gregory's efforts to divert the Crusaders from the Holy Land to Constantinople to help John were mostly unsuccessful.[9]

In 1236, de Brienne's son-in-law Baudouin de Courtenay set off on a long tour of western Europe to plead for more aid and support for the beleaguered Latin Empire, accompanied by his three young brothers-in-law Alphonse, John and Louis de Brienne. The Latin Emperor and Empress of Constantinople never saw their sons again.[10] The remarkable career of Emperor John de Brienne came to an end when he died sometime between 19 and 27 March 1237, at the age of about sixty or sixty-two, and he was probably, though not certainly, buried in Hagia Sophia. Philip of Novara, a thirteenth-century historian from Italy, declared that John had been a good knight who 'by the fame of his valour and by his effort, has frequently come into great riches and acquisitions'.[11] John's Spanish wife Berenguela of León seems to have died mere weeks later on 12 April, although this is uncertain; the exact date of her death is recorded, but not the year. If she did die in 1237, this was the year when her brother Fernando III of Castile and León married his second wife Jeanne, countess of Ponthieu. On John de Brienne's death Baudouin de Courtenay became sole Latin Emperor, and Marie de Brienne, barely even twelve years old, became an empress by marriage, as her late half-sister Queen Yolande of Jerusalem had at a similar age in 1225. One of Baudouin de Courtenay's sisters, who herself was empress of Nicaea by marriage, acted as her younger brother's regent until her own death a few months later.

Marie de Brienne and Baudouin de Courtenay had one child, a son Philippe, *Porphyrogennetos*, born in 1243. Little is known otherwise of Marie and Baudouin's personal relationship. Baudouin as an adult did not cut much of an impressive figure, appearing immature as he travelled around western Europe trying to drum up financial aid and support for the perpetually impoverished Latin Empire. He toured around the west from 1236 to 1239 and again from 1244 to 1248, yet received little in exchange except empty promises and small gifts. A rather scornful contemporary wrote that he was ineffectual and had 'nothing except the shadow of a great name'. Venetian creditors even demanded that Philippe de Courtenay, John de Brienne's teenage grandson, be left with them as surety for the Latin Emperor's enormous debts.[12] The city of Constantinople was recaptured for the Byzantine Empire in 1261, and Philippe and Marie were destined to spend much of their lives in exile. Marie de Brienne met her kinsman Louis IX of France in Limassol, Cyprus, in 1249, during his first crusade; accompanied by her brother the *Porphyrogennetos* John de Brienne the younger, she was met by the very long-lived historian and chronicler Jean de Joinville (1224–1317) at Paphos and he took her to meet Louis and his queen, Marguerite of Provence. Empress Marie suffered a misfortune on her way to Cyprus when the ship containing her wardrobe was destroyed in a storm, and Joinville gave her fabric to attire herself properly when meeting the French king. Joinville and many others were impressed by the Empress of Constantinople and spoke to Louis in her support, though ultimately the king did not provide any aid to Marie and her husband.[13] Enthusiasm in western Europe for the Latin Empire of Constantinople had long since passed.

Chapter 18

Nicaea, Trebizond and Epirus

The Latin Empire's greatest rival, the empire of Nicaea, was founded in 1204 by Theodoros I Laskaris, who was a son-in-law of the Byzantine Emperor and Empress Alexios III Angelos and Euphrosynē Doukaina Kamatera and was made *Despot* by his father-in-law. Nicaea was a rump state of the Byzantine Empire ruled by Greeks rather than Latins. Its chief town was Nicaea, once a Greek city in northwest Anatolia and now the Turkish city of İznik, famous as the site of the First Ecumenical Council held by Constantine the Great in the year 325 which established the Nicene Creed. Theodoros I Laskaris was followed on his death in 1221 by his son-in-law Ioannes III Doukas Vatatzes, who a few years later would become the main enemy of the Latin Emperor John de Brienne.[1]

Another successor state of the Byzantine Empire was the empire of Trebizond, which covered the far northeast corner of Anatolia and part of the southern Crimea and was centred on the city now called Trabzon, on the coast of the Black Sea. Another of the successor states ruled by Byzantines/Greeks rather than Latins, the empire of Trebizond was established by two grandsons of the Byzantine Emperor who 'stank of the Dark Ages' and was tortured to death by a mob in 1185, Andronikos I Komnenos. The two were Alexios I Megas Komnenos and his younger brother David, and their father Manuel had been blinded and almost certainly murdered in 1185, shortly after his father the emperor was killed. Born around the early 1180s, the Komnenoi were young children when their father and grandfather died.

A relative of the two brothers was another queen regnant of the era: Tamar, queen of Georgia, who was born *c.*1160, succeeded her father Giorgi III on the throne in 1184, and passed away in early 1213 a couple of months after Marie of Montferrat, queen regnant of Jerusalem, died after giving birth to her daughter Yolande de Brienne. The empire of Trebizond was founded during Tamar's reign, and she protected the two Komnenoi. The precise familial connection between Queen Tamar and the brothers is uncertain, though it may be that Emperor Andronikos's first wife was a member of the

Georgian royal family, or that the brothers' mother, Andronikos's daughter-in-law, was Tamar's sister Rusudan. Andronikos was in Georgia when his cousin Emperor Manuel I Komnenos died in 1180, having been appointed governor of Pontos, the area later known as the empire of Trebizond.[2] With Tamar's help, Alexios and David successfully invaded Trebizond in 1204, and Alexios, the elder brother, still only twenty-two, made himself the first emperor of the territory formerly ruled by their grandfather.

Mikhael VIII Palaiologos, a great-grandson of Emperor Alexios III Angelos and Euphrosynē Doukaina Kamatera, became emperor of Nicaea in 1259 and in the same year defeated two other successor states of the Byzantine Empire, the despotate of Epirus and the principality of Achaea, at the battle of Pelagonia. In July 1261, following an unsuccessful attempt in 1260, Mikhael's victorious army captured the city of Constantinople. Mikhael was crowned in Hagia Sophia in August 1261, and ruled as Byzantine Emperor until his death on 11 December 1282 (fans of British history might note that he died on the same day as Llywelyn ap Gruffudd, last of the native Princes of Wales, who was killed in an ambush close to the village of Cilmeri in mid-Wales). John de Brienne's displaced daughter Marie and son-in-law Baudouin de Courtenay, and his grandson Philippe de Courtenay, spent the rest of their lives in exile, first in France and later in Italy at the court of their French kinsman Charles of Anjou, king of Sicily. In late 1263 and early 1264, Marie de Brienne also spent time in Seville, southern Spain, as the guest of her kinswoman Yolande of Aragón, queen of Alfonso X of Castile-León.[3] Between Mikhael's death in 1282 and 1453, the Byzantine Empire was ruled by his descendants the Palaiologoi.

Beginning in the late 1200s, the Ottoman dynasty of Anatolia began expanding their territories and growing in importance. In 1389, Bayezid I succeeded his father Murad as sultan of the Ottoman Empire, and in 1394 began an unsuccessful siege of Constantinople which lasted until 1402. Making his intentions and his attitudes clear, Bayezid threatened to feed his horses on the altar of St Peter's Basilica in Rome.[4] This was considered a dire insult to the whole of Christendom, and Pope Boniface IX called for a crusade against the Ottomans. At the battle of Nicopolis on the banks of the River Danube in Bulgaria in September 1396, the Christian forces against Bayezid were led by Zikmund or Sigismund (b.1368), king of Hungary and Croatia and brother-in-law of Richard II, king of England. Bayezid won the battle and routed his opponents, and though Zikmund himself managed to flee the battlefield unharmed, a large number of western European noblemen were captured and subjected to harsh treatment, which killed some of them. One was Enguerrand, Lord de Coucy, son-in-law of the late Edward III of England (d.1377), and another was Enguerrand's son-in-law Henri de Bar.

In 1402, six years after his victory at Nicopolis, however, Sultan Bayezid was himself defeated and imprisoned by the great Mongolian war leader and conqueror Timur, aka Tamerlane – who had captured cities as far apart as Delhi, Damascus and Baghdad between 1398 and 1401 – at the battle of Ankara.[5] Bayezid's contemporary Manuel II Palaiologos (b.1350) succeeded as Byzantine Emperor in 1391 and spent the period from 1399 to 1403 traipsing around western Europe, as Baudouin de Courtenay had done a few decades earlier, trying to drum up support against the Ottomans. In 1400, he visited England and spent time with Henry IV, a descendant of Emperor John de Brienne. The two men met on Blackheath outside London shortly before Christmas 1400.[6]

The Byzantine Empire struggled on for two more centuries after 1261, but it was merely a shadow of its former great self. As historian John Fine has pointed out, the empire was now just another petty regional state, consisting merely of Constantinople, western Anatolia, Thrace, Macedonia and Thessaloniki.[6] On 6 April 1453, the Ottomans under the command of Bayezid's great-grandson Sultan Mehmed or Mehmet II began besieging Constantinople. The city fell on 29 May 1453 and the inhabitants were raped and killed or enslaved, and Emperor Constantine IX Dragases Palaiologos was killed during the fighting for the city. In 1460/61, Sultan Mehmed also besieged Trebizond, and its last emperor, David Megas Komnenos, surrendered in August 1461; he and his three sons and nephew were executed. The ancient Byzantine Empire passed into history, and the Ottomans would rule Constantinople for almost 500 years until 1922, when their own empire was finally abolished.

Part IV

Holy Roman Empire

Dramatis Personae

John de Brienne, b. *c.*1175/78, king of Jerusalem by his first marriage to Marie of Montferrat in 1210; elected Latin Emperor of Constantinople in 1228

Marie of Montferrat and Jerusalem, b.1192, queen regnant of Jerusalem 1205 to 1212; eldest of the five daughters of Isabella, queen regnant of Jerusalem (d.1205), and the only child of Corrado of Montferrat (d.1192)

Yolande de Brienne, b.1212, queen regnant of Jerusalem, Holy Roman Empress and queen of Sicily by marriage; only child of John de Brienne and Marie of Montferrat; marries Friedrich II von Hohenstaufen as his second wife in 1225

Friedrich II von Hohenstaufen, b.1194, Holy Roman Emperor and king of Sicily; widower of Costanza of Aragón (*c.*1179–1222); son and heir of Costanza de Hauteville and Heinrich von Hohenstaufen; grandson of Friedrich Barbarossa (d.1190), Holy Roman Emperor

Costanza de Hauteville, b.1154, queen regnant of Sicily 1194 to 1198; posthumous daughter of Roger II, king of Sicily; aunt and heir of Guglielmo II de Hauteville; mother of Emperor Friedrich II

Guglielmo II de Hauteville, b.1153, king of Sicily 1166 to 1189; son of Guglielmo I and grandson of Roger II; married to Joan, third and youngest daughter of Henry II, king of England

Tancredi of Lecce, b.1138, illegitimate cousin of Guglielmo II and nephew of Costanza; seizes the throne of Sicily after Guglielmo's death in 1189; his son **Ruggero III** then his younger son **Guglielmo** are crowned as his co-rulers

Heinrich von Hohenstaufen, b.1165, Holy Roman Emperor, king of Germany and Italy, and king of Sicily by marriage to Costanza de Hauteville; eldest son of Friedrich Barbarossa; father of Friedrich II

Philipp (von Hohenstaufen) of Swabia, b.1177, youngest son of Barbarossa and brother of Heinrich; King of the Romans from 1198; father-in-law of Fernando III, king of Castile and León

Eirene Angelina, b. *c.* early 1180s, queen of Sicily and Germany; daughter of Isaakios II Angelos (d.1204), Byzantine Emperor, and sister of Alexios IV Angelos; marries firstly Ruggero III of Sicily and secondly Philipp of Swabia in 1197

Otto IV von Welf, b.1175, Holy Roman Emperor 1209 to 1218; son of Heinrich 'the Lion', duke of Saxony and Bavaria, and Matilda, eldest daughter of Henry II, king of England

Konrad von Hohenstaufen, b.1228; king of Germany, Italy and Sicily, titular king of Jerusalem, duke of Swabia; only surviving child of Queen Yolande of Jerusalem and Emperor Friedrich II; grandson of Emperor John de Brienne; marries Elisabeth of Bavaria

Konradin ('Little Konrad') **von Hohenstaufen,** b.1252, son and heir of Konrad and Elisabeth; great-grandson of John de Brienne; titular king of Jerusalem and Sicily

Manfredi von Hohenstaufen, b.1232, illegitimate son of Emperor Friedrich II and Bianca Lancia; half-brother of Konrad and uncle of Konradin; king of Sicily from 1258; marries firstly Beatrice of Savoy and secondly Helena Angelina Doukaina, daughter of Mikhael II Komnenos Doukas, despot of Epirus

Costanza von Hohenstaufen, b. *c.*1230; illegitimate daughter of Friedrich and Bianca; half-sister of Konrad and full sister of Manfredi; marries Ioannes III Doukas Vatatzes (b. *c.*1192), emperor of Nicaea, and renamed Anna

Louis IX, b.1214, king of France 1226 to 1270; son of Louis VIII (d.1226) and grandson of Philip II Augustus (d.1223); marries Marguerite of Provence in 1234

Charles of Anjou, b.1227, posthumous son of Louis VIII, and youngest brother of Louis IX; count of Anjou and Provence, king of Sicily, titular king of Albania and Jerusalem; marries Beatrice, countess of Provence, in 1246, and secondly Marguerite of Burgundy, countess of Tonnerre, in 1268

Beatrice of Provence, b. *c.* late 1220s, queen consort of Sicily; youngest of the four daughters of Ramon-Berenger (d.1245), count of Provence, and his sole heir; sister of Marguerite, queen of Louis IX, and Alienor, queen of Henry III of England

Charles of Salerno, b.1254, eldest son and heir of Charles of Anjou and Beatrice of Provence; king of Naples, count of Anjou, Maine and Provence; marries Marie of Hungary

Henry III, b.1207, king of England 1216 to 1272; son of King John (d.1216) and Isabelle of Angoulême, and grandson of Henry II; marries Alienor of Provence in 1236; their sons are Edward I (b.1239) and Edmund of Lancaster (b.1245)

Richard, earl of Cornwall, b.1209, second son of King John and brother of Henry III; King of the Romans from 1257; his second wife is Sancha of Provence, sister of Marguerite, Alienor and Beatrice

Isabella of England, b. *c.*1214, Holy Roman Empress, queen of Sicily; second daughter of King John; sister of Henry III and Richard of Cornwall; marries Emperor Friedrich II in 1235

Costanza of Sicily, queen of Aragón and Sicily, b.1248/49; only child of Manfredi von Hohenstaufen, king of Sicily, and his first wife Beatrice of Savoy; granddaughter of Emperor Friedrich II; married to Pere III, king of Aragón

Pere III, king of Aragón, b.1239/40; eldest son of Jaume I, king of Aragón (d.1276); king of Sicily 1282 to 1285

Alfonso III, king of Aragón and Majorca, b.1265; eldest son of Pere and Costanza; grandson of Manfredi, king of Sicily; betrothed to Eleanor (b.1269), eldest daughter of Edward I of England and granddaughter of Henry III

Jaume II, king of Aragón, Sicily and Majorca, b.1267; second son of Pere and Costanza; brother and successor of Alfonso III

Frederic III, king of Sicily, b.1272; third son of Pere and Costanza

Chapter 19

The Wonder of the World

In 1225, the year after he travelled to Spain and married his third wife Berenguela of León, John de Brienne went to Apulia in southern Italy to arrange the wedding of his daughter Queen Yolande of Jerusalem, who was not yet thirteen, to Friedrich II von Hohenstaufen, Holy Roman Emperor and king of Sicily. Hermann von Salza, Grand Master of the Order of Teutonic Knights, helped to negotiate and arrange the marriage. Friedrich sent the archbishop of Capua to Acre in Outremer to wed Yolande on his behalf by proxy, and the archbishop's party sailed from Brindisi in fourteen galleys. The archbishop put a wedding ring on Yolande's finger in the church of the Holy Cross in Acre, and she subsequently went to Tyre to be crowned as queen regnant of Jerusalem in the cathedral, the ceremony conducted by Raoul de Merencourt, patriarch of Jerusalem. Her aunt Alice of Champagne and Jerusalem, dowager queen of Cyprus, was among those who attended her coronation.

The young queen of Jerusalem then sailed to Italy and married Emperor Friedrich in person in Brindisi Cathedral on 9 November 1225. John de Brienne was present at the wedding though Yolande's Spanish stepmother Berenguela – who had given birth to Yolande's half-sister Marie earlier that year – was not, and John stayed beforehand with his son-in-law at the castle of Oria.[1] Yolande turned thirteen in the month of her wedding, and Friedrich was almost thirty-one and was the widower of Costanza of Aragón (d.1222). His and Costanza's son Heinrich was rather older than his new wife. Supposedly, Queen Yolande wept to her father that her husband had seduced her cousin, the daughter of John de Brienne's eldest brother Gautier and his Sicilian wife Elvira, on their wedding day.[2] Whether this is true is unclear, though it is far from implausible; Friedrich is known to have fathered a number of illegitimate children, kept a harem and was accused of neglecting his young wife, though his biographer points out that he and Yolande frequently travelled together.[3]

Friedrich II von Hohenstaufen inherited the kingdom of Sicily from his mother Costanza de Hauteville, and vast territories in Germany and elsewhere in northern Europe from his father Heinrich von Hohenstaufen, Holy Roman Emperor and the eldest son of Emperor Friedrich Barbarossa, who drowned in 1190. The Holy Roman Empire had existed since the year 800, when Charlemagne or 'Charles the Great' was crowned emperor in the cathedral of Aachen on Christmas Day. The reasons for his promotion to emperor had much to do with the Byzantine noblewoman Eirene of Athens, also known as Eirene Sarantapechaina. She deposed her son, the Byzantine Emperor Constantine VI (b.771), in 797 and subsequently ordered him to be blinded, and made herself the first Byzantine Empress. The Eastern Roman Empire, or the Byzantine Empire as we now call it, was held to be in direct descent from the Caesars of ancient Rome, but Pope Leo III (r.795–816) claimed that the imperial office was vacant because a woman was currently occupying it, and a woman did not count. He therefore crowned Charlemagne, who was born into the Carolingian dynasty which ruled massive territories in western Europe and was already king of the Franks and the Lombards, as the first emperor in the west since the collapse of Rome's western empire in the 400s. The 'Holy Roman Empire' thus created in western Europe was deemed to be 'a direct continuation of the ancient Roman one', with Pope Leo transferring the title from the rulers of Byzantium to Charlemagne and his successors.[4]

Though the imperial throne did often pass from father to son, the succession of Holy Roman Emperors down the centuries was not always strictly hereditary, and between Charlemagne's death in 814 and the 1100s there were many years when no emperor existed at all. By the 1100s, a system had evolved whereby a group of *Kurfürsten* or Prince-Electors, consisting of a number of archbishops and secular rulers, chose the emperors. The nominee was first elected as King of the Romans, then usually, albeit not on every occasion, crowned by the Pope as Holy Roman Emperor. Confusingly, the Byzantine Emperors continued to call themselves Emperors of the Romans as well.

Friedrich Barbarossa of the Hohenstaufen dynasty was elected as emperor in 1155, succeeding Lothar von Supplinburg, and was followed by his eldest surviving son Heinrich in 1191, the year after his drowning, as an example of hereditary succession in the empire. When Heinrich von Hohenstaufen died in September 1197, however, his son Friedrich II was not yet three years old. The Hohenstaufens' greatest rivals were the Welf dynasty and in particular Heinrich the Lion (d.1195), duke of Saxony and Bavaria and the founder of the cities of Munich and Lübeck. Heinrich married Matilda (1156–89), eldest daughter of Henry II of England and Eleanor of Aquitaine, and their son Otto IV von Welf was chosen as King of the Romans in 1198. In opposition to him, however, stood Philipp of Swabia, youngest son of Barbarossa and uncle of the toddler Friedrich II, who was elected king by another faction. A decade of civil war ended in 1208 with Philipp's murder, while Otto himself was deposed as emperor after he, aided and supported by his maternal uncle King John of England, lost the battle of Bouvines to Philip II Augustus of France in July 1214. Otto had no children and Philipp of Swabia had only daughters, leaving the way clear for Philipp's nephew Friedrich II von Hohenstaufen to be crowned King of the Romans and subsequently Holy Roman Emperor in 1220.

The English chronicler Matthew Paris called Friedrich II *Stupor Mundi*, 'the Wonder of the World'. He was born in the Italian town of Jesi on 26 December 1194, the day after his father Heinrich von Hohenstaufen was crowned king of Sicily in Palermo Cathedral. According to some reports, Friedrich was born in public. The story goes that Heinrich's wife Costanza de Hauteville had a huge tent erected in the middle of the market square in Jesi and gave orders that any lady of the town was to have free entry during the birth, and nineteen cardinals and bishops were also present. A day or two after giving birth, Costanza returned to the square and publicly breastfed her son.[5] Costanza was forty, had never given birth before and had already been married to Heinrich for nine years, and perhaps feared that her child would be seen as an impostor or a changeling unless she took this highly unconventional, and possibly deeply embarrassing, step.

Costanza de Hauteville herself was born posthumously on 2 November 1254, more than eight months after the death of her fifty-eight-year-old father Roger II, king of Sicily. Roger's successor was Costanza's decades-older half-brother Guglielmo I, who in turn was succeeded by his son Guglielmo II in 1166. Though he was Costanza's nephew, Guglielmo II was in fact a year older than her. Guglielmo died in late 1189 and had been married since 1177 to Joan of England, who was the youngest daughter of Henry II, the aunt of Emperor Otto von Welf, and one of the women taken captive in Cyprus in 1191 by *Basileus* Isaakios Doukas Komnenos until rescued by her brother Richard Lionheart. Guglielmo and Joan had no surviving children, and Costanza was her nephew's rightful heir, but their kinsman Tancredi of Lecce, an illegitimate son of Guglielmo's uncle the late duke of Apulia, seized the throne instead (confusingly, Tancredi was sixteen years older than his aunt Costanza, the duke of Apulia's much younger half-sister). Costanza's marriage to the German Heinrich von Hohenstaufen, arranged by her nephew in 1184, was hugely unpopular in Sicily, and numerous Sicilians feared German influence over their kingdom if Costanza became their queen. Their fears came to pass.

In the summer of 1192, King Tancredi crowned his young son Ruggero III as his co-ruler, and Ruggero married Eirene Angelina, daughter of the reigning Byzantine Emperor Isaakios II Angelos by his unknown first wife. Ruggero died just before Christmas 1193, and Tancredi had his second son Guglielmo – who was well under ten years old – crowned in his place, but himself died in February 1194. Costanza de Hauteville's powerful German husband saw his chance and invaded Sicily. Meeting with little resistance, Heinrich was crowned king of Sicily on Christmas Day 1194, while Costanza remained in Jesi on the Italian mainland to give birth to their son. Little is known of the subsequent fate of the unfortunate Guglielmo, but it is likely that the child was killed, or blinded, castrated and imprisoned until he died. His sister Elvira, King Tancredi's eldest daughter, was married to John de Brienne's eldest brother Gautier, but Gautier was no match for Heinrich and Costanza, and failed to take the Sicilian throne. As for Joan of England, widow of Guglielmo II, in 1196 she became the fourth of the many wives of Raymond VI, count of Toulouse, and was the mother of his son and heir. In 1199 or 1200, shortly after Joan died, Raymond married his next wife, the Damsel of Cyprus, only surviving child of *Basileus* Isaakios Doukas Komnenos.

During his conquest of Sicily at the end of 1194, Heinrich von Hohenstaufen captured Ruggero III's widow Eirene Angelina, whose father Isaakios II Angelos would be overthrown and blinded by her uncle Alexios III a few months later. In May 1197, Heinrich married her to his youngest brother Philipp of Swabia.[6] Philipp was then twenty, Eirene probably still a teenager. She bore five daughters, of whom the youngest died soon after birth and the eldest, very briefly married to the Holy Roman Emperor Otto von Welf, died in her early teens. The second youngest daughter of Philipp and Eirene was Beatriz (née Elisabeth) of Swabia, who married Fernando III of Castile in

The remains of the Crusader Cathedral in the ancient port of Tyre, now in Lebanon, where John de Brienne and his first wife Marie de Montferrat were crowned king and queen of Jerusalem in 1210. (*Flickr*)

The port of Tyre. (*Wikimedia Commons*)

The coronation of John de Brienne and Queen Marie from a thirteenth-century manuscript. (*Public domain*)

The port of Acre, now in Israel, where John de Brienne married Queen Marie in 1210. (*Wikimedia Commons*)

The wedding of Queen Marie's parents Queen Isabella of Jerusalem and Corrado of Montferrat in 1190. (*Public domain*)

Brienne's sister-in-law Alice of Champagne and Jerusalem, queen consort of Cyprus (c.1194–1246). (*Public domain*)

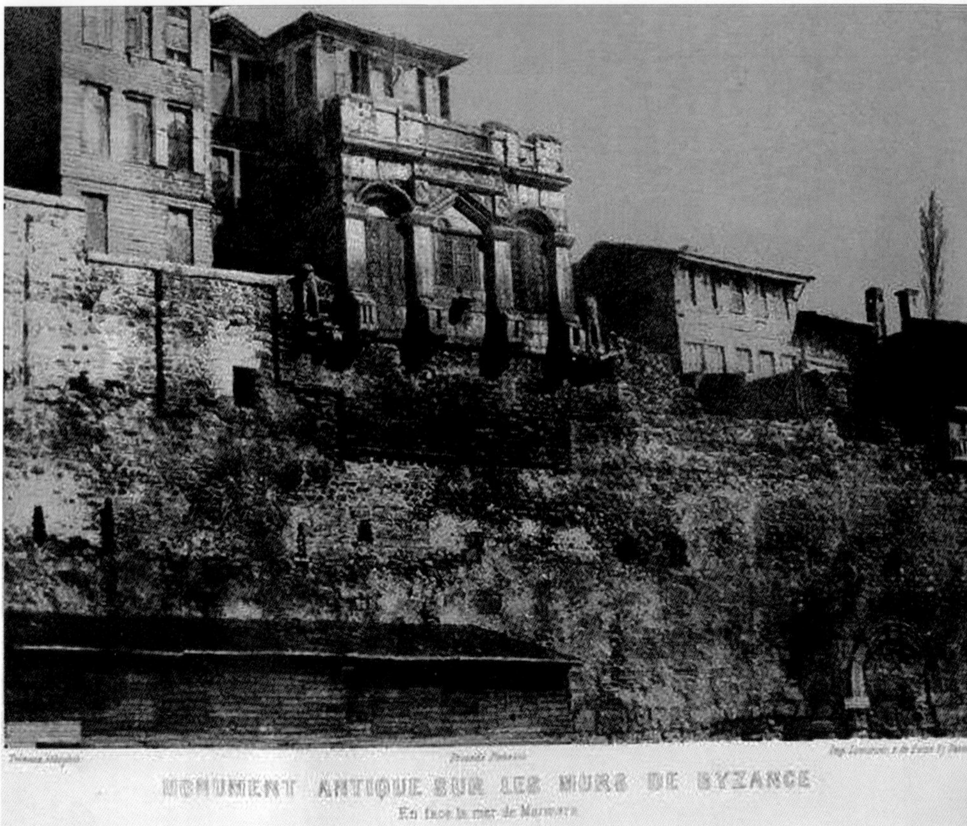

Ruins of the Boukoleon Palace, Istanbul, in c.1850; one of John de Brienne's residences as Latin Emperor of Constantinople. (*Public domain*)

The Hagia Sophia in Istanbul, now a mosque and museum, formerly a cathedral. John de Brienne was crowned Latin Emperor of Constantinople here in 1231 and may have been buried here six years later. (*Wikimedia Commons*)

Kozan in Turkey, formerly called Sis, capital of the kingdom of Armenian Cilicia and ruled from 1187 to 1219 by John de Brienne's father-in-law from his second marriage, Levon I. Brienne tried unsuccessfully to gain control of Armenian Cilicia in 1219/20. (*Wikimedia Commons*)

Toledo Cathedral in Spain, where John de Brienne married his third wife, Berenguela of León, in 1224. (*Wikimedia Commons*)

Rheims Cathedral, where de Brienne attended the coronation of Louis VIII as king of France in August 1223. (*Wikimedia Commons*)

Brindisi Cathedral, Italy. John de Brienne's adolescent daughter Yolande, queen regnant of Jerusalem, married the Holy Roman Emperor Friedrich II here in 1225. (*Wikimedia Commons*)

The wedding of Queen Yolande and Emperor Friedrich. (*Public domain*)

John de Brienne and Berenguela of León's daughter Marie, Latin Empress of Constantinople, was born in Capua near Naples in 1225. Her brother-in-law Friedrich II, Holy Roman Emperor, rebuilt the city gate. (*Flickr*)

Brienne's great-grandson Konradin von Hohenstaufen, titular king of Jerusalem and Sicily, and heir of Queen Marie. (*Public domain*)

The Piazza Mercato in Naples, where sixteen-year-old Konradin was beheaded in 1268. (*Wikimedia Commons*)

Konradin's execution from a fourteenth-century manuscript. (*Public domain*)

John de Brienne's mother-in-law from his third marriage, the great Berenguela of Castile (1180–1246). (*Public domain*)

Brienne's daughter Marie de Brienne, Latin Empress of Constantinople (1225–75). (*Wikimedia Commons*)

Marie's granddaughter and heir Catherine de Courtenay, titular Latin Empress of Constantinople in her own right (1274–1307). (*Public domain*)

Catherine's daughter and heir Catherine de Valois, also titular Latin Empress of Constantinople in her own right (1303–46). (*Wikimedia Commons*)

The monument in Kinghorn, Fife, which commemorates King Alexander III of Scotland (r.1249–86), stepson of John de Brienne the younger (d.1296). (*Wikimedia Commons*)

Bamburgh Castle, Northumberland: Louis de Brienne's daughter Isabelle de Beaumont, Lady Vescy, was appointed its custodian in 1307. (*Wikimedia Commons*)

1219 and was the sister-in-law of Berenguela of León, later queen consort of Jerusalem and Latin Empress of Constantinople.

Heinrich von Hohenstaufen, Holy Roman Emperor, died on 28 September 1197 after a reign of less than three years as king of Sicily, and eighteen days after Henri of Champagne, king of Jerusalem, fell to his death in Acre. Heinrich had brutally suppressed a revolt in his kingdom earlier that year, and at the time of his death was preparing to lead a German crusade to Outremer. Niketas Choniatēs, who took an interest in the matter because Heinrich was the brother-in-law of the Byzantine noblewoman Eirene Angelina, reported that the death of the man he called an 'intractable evildoer' was 'received with great satisfaction' by everyone, especially the Sicilians, on whom he had 'inflicted a host of evils' and subjected to 'such excruciating tortures that death was preferable to life'. Niketas's descriptions of the cruel tortures Heinrich inflicted on his Sicilian enemies have a luridly hyper-violent, *Game of Thrones* quality.[7] Richard Lionheart, king of England, must also have rejoiced at news of Heinrich's death, as Heinrich had imprisoned him on his way back to northern Europe from the Third Crusade and forced Richard's subjects to pay him a massive ransom.

Queen Costanza de Hauteville, who had aided the Sicilian rebellion against her husband, did not long outlive Heinrich and died in November 1198. Their son Friedrich von Hohenstaufen, whom Costanza had crowned king of Sicily earlier in 1198, was left an orphan at not yet four years old, and Pope Innocent III became his guardian. Around this time, Innocent called the Fourth Crusade, and the Crusaders arrived outside Constantinople in 1203 after meeting Eirene Angelina's brother Alexios IV Angelos.

Chapter 20

A Terrifying Marvel

In August 1209, the year before John de Brienne married his first wife Queen Marie of Jerusalem, John's future son-in-law Friedrich von Hohenstaufen also married his first wife. There was an age gap of eleven years between Heinrich von Hohenstaufen (b.1165) and his wife Costanza de Hauteville (b.1154) and one of about a decade and a half between their only child Friedrich, born at the end of 1194, and Costanza of Aragón, born *c.*1179 as the eldest daughter of Alfonso II, king of Aragón. She was the widow of Imre (d.1204), king of Hungary.[1] They married when Friedrich was fourteen and Costanza thirty or close to it, and their only child, named Heinrich after his paternal grandfather, was born in 1211. Costanza was crowned Holy Roman Empress by Pope Honorius III in St Peter's Basilica in Rome in November 1220, but died not long afterwards in June 1222.

Steven Runciman once pointed out that as a ruler in Constantinople or Cairo, Friedrich II would have fitted in, but as a ruler in western Europe he was a 'terrifying marvel' who, in the words of another modern author, 'grew up in the culture of an eastern sultan'. On his father's side he was German, and his mother's family the Hautevilles, who ruled Sicily from 1130 onwards, were of Norman origin, though Friedrich was raised in the 'half-Greek and half-Arab' melting-pot environment of the island of Sicily, where 'Byzantine, Norman Sicilian and Islamic influences overlapped to glorious and, usually, harmonious effect'. Most of the inhabitants of the island of Sicily spoke Greek, though the mainland part of the kingdom mostly used a dialect of Italian; the royal court spoke Norman-French; and the sizeable Muslim population spoke Arabic. There was a small Jewish population as well and both they and the Muslims of Sicily were allowed to practise their religion freely, while the Christian population adhered to Greek rites rather than to the Latin church.[2]

Friedrich II spoke six languages (Arabic, Latin, Greek, French, German and Italian) and was, like his younger kinsman Alfonso X of Castile-León, a polymath: a mathematician, poet, linguist, astrologer and philosopher.

Historian Jonathan Phillips has called him a 'renaissance man', centuries before the Renaissance, and Friedrich also wrote a definitive treatise on falconry in Latin called 'The Art of Hunting with Birds'. His appearance was unprepossessing, bald and short-sighted with 'red skin', but his extraordinary charisma is apparent even 800 years later.[3] He was cast in the mould of his paternal grandfather Friedrich Barbarossa, whose larger-than-life personality also blazes down the centuries.

John de Brienne discussed his daughter Queen Yolande's possible marriage to Friedrich with Pope Honorius III in the autumn of 1222, just months after the death of Friedrich's Aragónese wife Costanza.[4] The wedding finally took place three years later. John was astonished when Emperor Friedrich told him, on the very day of his wedding to Yolande, that John should grant him possession of the kingdom of Jerusalem, as he, Friedrich, was now husband of the reigning queen and therefore took precedence over the widower of the late queen. With little other option besides complaining to Honorius, which achieved nothing but a reprimand to Friedrich which the latter duly ignored, Brienne ceded control of Jerusalem to the powerful emperor. Friedrich and Yolande left Brindisi the day after their wedding there and travelled to Foggia without informing John, who was upset and insulted. One chronicler stated that there was ill will between the two men because John 'corrected and reproved [Friedrich] too often'. After saying farewell to his daughter, John returned to Rome to be reunited with Berenguela, while Friedrich was accepted as regent of Jerusalem by the barons of the Latin Kingdom.[5]

On 29 September 1227, the new pope, Gregory IX, excommunicated Friedrich II, accusing him of violating his sacred oath to go on the Fifth Crusade (1217–21) and of causing the illness and death of many Crusaders who had travelled to Brindisi to sail from there to the Holy Land. A few months later, Friedrich set off for Outremer, though he turned his supposed crusade, otherwise known as the Sixth Crusade, into an imperial expedition. The sentence of excommunication was finally lifted in August 1230, though Friedrich's ongoing conflict with the papacy was to cause huge problems for his sons in later decades.[6]

When Friedrich departed for Outremer, he had recently become a widower. Queen Yolande de Brienne of Jerusalem died on 4 May 1228 a few days after giving birth to her son Konrad von Hohenstaufen on 25 April, when she was fifteen years old. She perhaps named her son in honour of her maternal grandfather, Corrado of Montferrat, though Konrad was also a common name in the Hohenstaufen dynasty. Like her mother Marie of Montferrat and Jerusalem, Queen Yolande died at a young age after giving birth and did not live long enough to see her child, and is hardly likely to have had a particularly happy existence as the emperor's wife; Friedrich kept her in seclusion in Palermo, and at age fourteen she had already borne a child who did not live long.[7] Friedrich's third, English-born wife Empress Isabella was also fated to die in childbirth in 1241.

Konrad von Hohenstaufen was now the rightful king of Jerusalem, though never set foot in his kingdom. When he was born, he was heir to his mother but not to his father, who had a teenage son, Konrad's half-brother Heinrich, from his first marriage. Summoned to Friedrich's court in 1242 after years of imprisonment following an unsuccessful rebellion against his father, the now thirty-year-old Heinrich came to believe that his father would have him put to death on his arrival. During an attempt to escape from his guards, he rode his horse down a precipice and was killed.[8] At that point, John de Brienne's grandson Konrad became Emperor Friedrich's primary heir. Friedrich did not remarry for another seven years after Yolande de Brienne's death in 1228, though he had other interests. He had a long-term mistress named Bianca Lancia, an Italian noblewoman, with whom he had a son, Manfredi, probably born in 1232. Another child of Friedrich and Bianca was Costanza, who married Ioannes III Doukas Vatatzes, emperor of Nicaea, as his second wife in 1244 and was renamed Anna in her new home. Vatatzes was one of the men who besieged the city of Constantinople and the Latin Emperor John de Brienne during the 'War of the Three Johns' in 1235/36. In a situation all too sadly reminiscent of the aftermath of her father's marriage to his second wife Yolande de Brienne in 1225, Costanza/Anna discovered that her decades-older husband (b. *c.*1192) preferred one of her ladies-in-waiting to her.[9]

Chapter 21

Taking Hold of the Moon

In 1235, Emperor Friedrich II married his third wife, Isabella of England, fourth child of King John and Isabelle of Angoulême, and one of the three younger sisters of Henry III. She had previously been suggested as the bride of Friedrich's son Heinrich, but the emperor married her himself.[1] King Henry promised to pay 30,000 marks (£20,000) as Isabella's dowry, and provided her with a magnificent trousseau. In February 1235 he wrote to inform their sister Joan, queen of Scotland, of Isabella's impending imperial marriage, and told her that the archbishop of Cologne and the dukes of Lorraine and Limburg would travel to England to conduct her to Germany.[2] Isabella married Friedrich in the German city of Worms in July 1235 – the celebrations lasted for four days – and was subsequently crowned Holy Roman Empress by the archbishop of Mainz.[3] Isabella bore the emperor four children, of whom two died young and another, Heinrich the younger, died as a teenager; her daughter Margarethe von Hohenstaufen was her only child who lived into adulthood.

As Holy Roman Empress and queen of Sicily, Isabella of England lived a life of the utmost seclusion. She was constantly guarded by eunuchs and not allowed visitors except once, as a great concession, when her brother Richard of Cornwall visited Friedrich II on his way back from crusade. Despite this, her marriage to Friedrich seems to have been a reasonably successful one, and as had been the case with Friedrich and his previous wife Yolande de Brienne, the couple often travelled together. The two apparently enjoyed each other's company.[4] Empress Isabella died in late 1241 after giving birth to her fourth child. Her stepson Heinrich the elder, from Friedrich's first marriage, died a few months later, and her other stepson Konrad came of age at fifteen in 1243. At this point, Konrad should have been allowed to take over the governance of his kingdom of Jerusalem, but his father refused to cede control of it to him.[5]

Emperor Friedrich made his will on 7 December 1250 and left his enormous territories to his and the late Queen Yolande de Brienne's son

Konrad, with his illegitimate son Manfredi appointed as regent of Sicily during Konrad's absences in Germany. Friedrich's partly English son Heinrich the younger was named as Konrad's successor if Konrad died without heirs, and was promised either the kingdom of Burgundy or, surprisingly given that he was not descended from Marie of Montferrat or her and John de Brienne's daughter Yolande, the kingdom of Jerusalem. Manfredi was named as heir to all his father's territories if both Konrad and Heinrich died without children, and was highly favoured by Friedrich, who had at least four or five other illegitimate sons as well but did not name them as potential heirs. The emperor might have married Manfredi's mother Bianca Lancia on her deathbed as his fourth and last wife, and the provisions of his will might indicate that he considered their son legitimate.[6]

Friedrich died on 13 December 1250, a few days before his fifty-sixth birthday. Konrad succeeded as king of Germany, Italy and Sicily and titular king of Jerusalem, but was never elected as Holy Roman Emperor, and the role was not filled again until Henry of Luxembourg briefly reigned many decades later in 1312/13, after a long series of 'little kings' in Germany. Konrad wed Elisabeth of Bavaria in 1246, a marriage intended to help strengthen the Hohenstaufen dynasty's grip on Germany, and they had one child, Konradin or 'little Konrad', in 1252.[7] The following year, Konrad's half-brother Heinrich died in his teens, leaving his sister Margarethe as the only surviving child of Isabella of England, Holy Roman Empress, and as the only living legitimate child of Emperor Friedrich besides Konrad. In 1255, Margarethe married the German nobleman who was margrave of Meissen, landgrave of Thuringia and count palatine of Saxony and who bore the unpromising name of Albrecht the Degenerate.

Rather belatedly, in May 1254, Konrad wrote to Henry III of England announcing the 'sad death' (*lugubrem obitum*) of Henry's nephew Heinrich. He talked at length, and rather movingly, of the bitterness of their shared grief, though he reminded Henry that they could both take comfort in the fact that Margarethe was alive and thriving.[8] Konrad himself died of dysentery on the 21st of that month, aged only twenty-six, whereupon his two-year-old son Konradin became the titular king of Jerusalem and Sicily. Plaisance of Antioch, dowager queen consort of Cyprus, whose son Hugh II of Cyprus was Konradin's heir male to the Latin Kingdom of Jerusalem and was the same age as Konradin, acted as his regent in the kingdom until her death in 1261. Konradin's half-uncle Manfredi at first acted as his regent in

Sicily, but in August 1258 usurped his nephew's position and had himself crowned king of Sicily in Palermo Cathedral.

Over the years, Manfredi was – as his father the emperor had also been – excommunicated by several popes, and Innocent IV offered the Sicilian throne in his stead to the late Emperor Friedrich's English brother-in-law Richard of Cornwall. Always a pragmatist, however, Richard declared that he had more chance of reaching up into the sky and taking hold of the moon than dislodging Manfredi. Undeterred, the Pope landed on Richard's young nephew Edmund (b. January 1245), the younger son of Henry III and his queen Alienor of Provence, as a possible candidate, and offered him the crown instead. Thrilled at the thought of his son ruling in Sicily, and less of a realist than his younger brother, King Henry eagerly accepted. On 25 May 1254, just days after Konrad's death, Henry had a seal made for Edmund as king of Sicily; eighteen months later the papal nuncio in England formally invested the boy with the kingdom by putting a ring on his finger, and in 1257 the king paraded his son before parliament dressed in Apulian clothes. Unfortunately for Henry's ambitions, the English magnates refused to fight a campaign on the far side of Europe merely to put a child on the throne of Sicily, and the matter came to nothing, as did King Henry and Queen Alienor's attempts at this time to marry their son to Plaisance of Antioch.[9] Edmund had to settle for becoming earl of Lancaster, Leicester and Derby, though he did ultimately marry a queen after all: his second wife and the mother of his children was Louis IX of France's niece Blanche of Artois, widow of the king of Navarre.[10] And Richard of Cornwall, though he never sat on the throne of Sicily, was crowned King of the Romans in 1257, one of the early 'little kings' who ruled Germany from the 1250s to the 1310s.

Chapter 22

The Putrid Corpse of That Pestilential Man

Pope Innocent IV's successor Alexander IV was determined to dislodge the detested Manfredi as king of Sicily, and, the English candidates having proved untenable, turned to another man, Charles of Anjou. Charles was born in 1227 as the youngest of Blanche of Castile and Louis VIII of France's sons and was the brother of Louis IX, and was a highly able and ambitious man who seems to pop up everywhere in the history of Europe and the Mediterranean in the second half of the thirteenth century. In 1246, Charles of Anjou had married Beatrice of Provence, youngest of the four daughters of Ramon-Berenger, count of Provence, and sister of Marguerite and Alienor, queens of France and England; the third sister, Sancha, also became a queen in 1257 when her husband Richard of Cornwall was elected King of the Romans. Ramon-Berenger had, in a rare example of ultimogeniture, left Provence in its entirety to Beatrice on his death in 1245 and excluded her three older sisters, to their utter fury. As a result, Queen Marguerite remained bitterly hostile to Beatrice's husband Charles of Anjou for the rest of his life, and as late as the 1360s and 1370s, 125 years after Ramon-Berenger's death, his second daughter Queen Alienor's English descendants were still trying to claim a share of the county.[1]

The Anjou-Provence couple, both the youngest children of their parents, well and truly made their mark on thirteenth-century Europe. With the wealth of Provence behind him, Charles was well placed to invade Sicily and attack King Manfredi. Beatrice, too, had ambitions: when she had last met her three older sisters, they allegedly forced her to sit at a lower table during banquets as they were all queens, while she was a mere countess.[2] Assuming that the three older sisters' hostility towards Beatrice truly existed, the fact that her father had left all of Provence to her surely had much to do with it as well.

Charles of Anjou invaded Italy in 1265. He and Beatrice were crowned king and queen of Sicily by five cardinals in Saint Peter's Basilica in Rome at the beginning of 1266, and Beatrice was thus raised to the same rank as her older sisters. A few weeks later, in February 1266, Charles defeated Manfredi at the battle of Benevento. Manfredi was killed during the battle, though his fate remained unclear for several days until a soldier found his body and placed it on the back of an ass, parading it around and crying out 'Who wants to buy Manfredi?' The delighted Pope, Clement IV, informed his legate in England that Charles of Anjou was in possession of the entire kingdom of Sicily, and had also taken possession of 'the putrid corpse of that pestilential man', Manfredi. Another man who fought at Benevento on Manfredi's side was Don Fadrique (b.1223), brother and enemy of Alfonso X of Castile-León, who managed to flee from the battlefield unharmed – though a few years later he was executed by his brother King Alfonso.[3] Charles of Anjou thus acquired the kingdom of Sicily in more than name only. He enjoyed several other titles as well: as of 1272, he styled himself king of Albania; he bought Maria of Antioch's rights to the Latin Kingdom of Jerusalem in 1277; and in 1278 he also became prince of Achaea, one of the successor states of the Byzantine Empire.

Manfredi's sister Costanza/Anna, dowager empress of Nicaea as the widow of Ioannes III Doukas Vatatzes, and the daughter of Friedrich II and his noble mistress Bianca Lancia, had returned to Sicily in widowhood. After her brother's defeat and death – and after the Byzantine Emperor Mikhael VIII Palaiologos tried unsuccessfully to marry her – she fled to Aragón in Spain, as her niece and namesake, Manfredi's eldest child Costanza from his first marriage, was married to Pere, the heir to the Aragónese throne. Empress Costanza/Anna became a nun in Valencia and was one of the very long-lived ladies of the era: she died in 1307 in her mid or late seventies. Maria of Antioch, daughter of Bohemond IV 'the One-Eyed' of Antioch and Tripoli, and a granddaughter of Queen Isabella of Jerusalem, died in the same year three decades after selling her claim to Jerusalem to Charles of Anjou, and was about eight or ten years older than Costanza/Anna.

From his second marriage to Helena Angelina Doukaina, daughter of the despot of Epirus, King Manfredi had another four children, all under ten or twelve years old in 1266 when he was killed at Benevento. Helena was imprisoned by Charles of Anjou until her death in 1271, and her daughter Beatrice was imprisoned for eighteen years then finally released in 1284, whereupon she married the *marchese* of Saluzzo and had children. A crueller fate awaited Manfredi and Helena's three young sons: they were not only imprisoned in chains, but blinded. At least two and possibly all of them lived into the 1300s, one until as late as 1318, more than half a century later. Manfredi's teenage German nephew Konradin, the little boys' cousin and John de Brienne's great-grandson, marched from Germany to Italy with an army after Manfredi's defeat and death, but he and his friend Friedrich von Baden were captured by Charles of Anjou after losing the battle of Tagliacozzo in August 1268. Don Enrique of Castile, another of the many younger brothers of Alfonso X, fought on Konradin's side against Charles of Anjou, and subsequently spent decades in a Naples prison. His half-sister Leonor and her husband Edward I of England did what they could to secure his release, but to no avail.

Konradin von Hohenstaufen and Friedrich von Baden were publicly beheaded in central Naples in October 1268, on a hastily erected scaffold where the Piazza Mercato is now located. Even Charles of Anjou's own supporters were dismayed by the young men's deaths, especially Konradin's.[4] Konradin, unmarried and childless, and just sixteen years old when he was killed, was the last direct, legitimate male heir of the Hohenstaufen dynasty; although his grandfather Emperor Friedrich II fathered numerous children, he had only three legitimate sons who survived infancy, and of the three, only Konrad had a son of his own who outlived him. Of the eight legitimate sons fathered by Friedrich II's grandfather Friedrich Barbarossa, three died in childhood, Philipp of Swabia had only daughters, Emperor Heinrich had one son, and the other three died childless. Konradin was also the last descendant of Corrado of Montferrat and his daughter Marie, queen of Jerusalem, who had one child, one grandchild and one great-grandchild. Like his father, Konradin never saw the Latin Kingdom of Jerusalem of which he was titular ruler, and nine years after his death, as if to add insult to injury, his long-lived kinswoman Maria of Antioch sold her claim to his kingdom to none other than Charles of Anjou.

Beatrice of Provence died in September 1267 only twenty months after her coronation as queen of Sicily. Just days after the public execution of the teenaged Konradin von Hohenstaufen and his loyal friend Friedrich von Baden thirteen months after Beatrice passed away, the widowed Charles of Anjou, evidently untroubled by conscience, married his second wife Marguerite of Burgundy. Although she was not so great an heiress as Beatrice had been, Marguerite was countess of Tonnerre in her own right, while her sisters were the countess of Nevers and the countess of Auxerre; their mother's inheritance was divided among the three of them. Konradin's kinswoman

Marie de Brienne, with her husband Baudouin de Courtenay and their son Philippe, lived at Charles of Anjou and Marguerite of Burgundy's court until Baudouin died in 1273 and Marie two years later. They both died and were buried in Italy. They had little other choice, having been treated with distant coldness at the court of Charles's brother Louis IX of France, who had met Empress Marie in Cyprus many years earlier but who now, despite his close blood ties to both Marie and Baudouin, had no interest in the couple or in their lost empire.[5] In the 1267 Treaty of Viterbo, Baudouin transferred most of his rights to the Latin Empire of Constantinople to Charles of Anjou, and his and Marie's son Philippe de Courtenay married Beatrice of Sicily, daughter of Charles and Beatrice of Provence; the couple's only child was Catherine de Courtenay, born in November 1274. Catherine, Baudouin de Courtenay and Charles of Anjou's mutual granddaughter and John de Brienne's great-granddaughter, inherited the rights to Constantinople and became titular Latin Empress as a nine-year-old in December 1283 when her father Philippe died.[6]

Chapter 23

Death to the French

During Charles of Anjou's reign over Sicily, having acquired the Brienne/Courtenays' rights to the Latin Empire of Constantinople, he tried to make good on the claims by devoting much effort to his attempts to take the city of Constantinople from the Byzantine Emperor Mikhael VIII Palaiologos. Mikhael had once approached King Manfredi with a view to taking Manfredi's widowed sister Costanza/Anna, dowager empress of Nicaea, as his second wife, so was hardly likely to get on well with Charles. Charles of Anjou's harsh rule over Sicily, his heavy taxes and his foreignness led to a rebellion there in 1282 after his subjects grew sick of being ruled by an 'alien tyrant' whose French officials never bothered to learn the local language or to respect Sicilian customs. Although Charles himself was an 'able and conscientious' man, he never ruled personally on the island of Sicily, which was to prove a great error that resulted in his flight from his kingdom.[1]

The rebellion that began at Easter 1282 is known as the Sicilian Vespers, because it began at the time of Vespers, the prayer held at sunset, on Easter Monday, 30 March. It was fomented by the late King Manfredi's daughter Costanza from his first marriage and her husband, who had now succeeded his father Jaume I as King Pere III of Aragón.[2] Costanza was born not long before 1250 when her father was still a teenager and not long before her grandfather Emperor Friedrich II died, and had been betrothed to Pere of Aragón as a child in 1258. After the death of her father Manfredi in 1266, Pere considered his wife the rightful heir to the kingdom of Sicily.

Byzantine agents also helped to fan the flames of Sicilian resentment in order to prevent Charles of Anjou's planned invasion of the Byzantine Empire ruled by Mikhael Palaiologos (who died later that same year, 1282). In March 1282, a large Aragónese fleet sailed to Sicily, and the French were massacred in Palermo during the evening and night of Easter Monday after armed men tore through the streets shouting *Moranu li Franchiski* or 'Death to the French' in the local dialect. As many as 2,000 French people were killed in a single night.[3] The rebellion soon spread to the rest of the island, and by the autumn of that year, Costanza of Sicily and Pere III of Aragón had captured the island and Pere was crowned king of Sicily.[4] Charles of Anjou had little choice but to flee from his kingdom. The late Manfredi's daughter Beatrice was finally freed after eighteen years of captivity, but it was too late for her brothers, Queen Costanza's young half-brothers, who had been blinded on Anjou's orders.

Charles of Anjou and the late Beatrice of Provence's son and heir was Charles of Salerno. As a sixteen-year-old in 1270, Charles had married Marie of Hungary, one of the daughters of István V, king of Hungary, and Erzésbet the Cuman. Marie's brother Ladislaus, their father's heir, married Charles of Salerno's sister Elisabeth of Sicily at the same time in a double Anjou-Hungary marriage alliance.[5] Ladislaus and Marie's mother Erzésbet was born into a nomadic, shamanistic tribe of the Eurasian steppes, the Cumans, who fled into Hungary in the 1230s and 1240s to escape the incursion of Genghis Khan's sons into their territories. Erzésbet was the daughter of the Cumans' *khan* or chieftain, and married the heir to the Hungarian throne after converting to Christianity. Via her daughter Marie, Queen Erzésbet became an ancestor of several royal families of western Europe, and in the 1330s and 1340s the mitochondrial DNA of a shamanistic people of the steppes was carried by the king of France, Philip VI, and the children of the king of England, Edward III.

In June 1284, Charles of Salerno was captured by Roger of Lauria in the naval battle of Castellammare in the Gulf of Naples. Lauria came originally from the kingdom of Sicily, and his father had served Manfredi. After the execution of Konradin von Hohenstaufen in 1268, the Lauria family – like many others – fled to Aragón and to the protection of Pere and Costanza. After his success in the battle, Roger of Lauria took Charles of Salerno to a prison in Aragón, where he would remain for several years.

Three western European kings died in 1285: Charles of Anjou, at the start of that year and while his son and heir was in captivity; his nephew Philip III of France; and his adversary Pere III of Aragón. Anjou's widow Marguerite of Burgundy, countess of Tonnerre, subsequently lived with the Latin Emperor John de Brienne's widowed granddaughter Marguerite de Brienne, dowager countess of Tripoli, and Brienne's great-granddaughter Catherine de Courtenay, titular Latin Empress of Constantinople. The three women lived lives of prayer and charity at Marguerite of Burgundy's castle of Tonnerre southeast of Paris, and Marguerite founded the *Hospice des Fontenilles* in Tonnerre.[6] Catherine de Courtenay married late by the standards of medieval royalty, and at the age of twenty-six in early 1301 wed Philip IV of France's widowed brother Charles, count of Valois, the younger son of Philip III and his first wife Isabel of Aragón.[7] The heir to her titular empire was the eldest of their three daughters, Catherine de Valois, born in 1303.

Edward I, now fifty years old, king of England since the death of his father Henry III in November 1272, and a respected elder statesman, negotiated with the kingdom of Aragón for Charles of Salerno's release. He was ideally placed to help as he was close to both sides of the conflict: Salerno was his cousin via their Provençal mothers Alienor and Beatrice, while Edward and Leonor of Castile's eldest surviving daughter Eleanor (b. June 1269) was betrothed to Alfonso III of Aragón (b. November 1265), the eldest son of Pere III and Costanza of Sicily, and grandson of King Manfredi. The admiring Catalan chronicler Ramon Muntaner called Alfonso III and his younger brothers 'the wisest, the most skilful in the world both at feats of arms and at everything else, the most courteous, and the best brought up'.[8] Pere III of Aragón had already met Charles of Salerno in Toulouse in 1280 (see Part 2 above) and treated him with disdainful hostility, as Charles was the son of the man who had killed Pere's father-in-law Manfredi.

Chapter 24

A Lion and a Wildcat

In the summer of 1286, King Edward of England travelled to Oloron in the far southwest of France, part of his own domains in his capacity as duke of Aquitaine, with his wife Leonor of Castile. They left their children – five daughters and a two-year-old son and heir, Edward of Caernarfon – in England, and in Oloron welcomed twenty-year-old Alfonso III of Aragón, their daughter Eleanor's fiancé, and his large retinue. This meeting of two kings occasioned large celebrations and jousts, and the usual lavish and competitive gift-giving of medieval royals; Alfonso gave Edward a lion and a wildcat, though unfortunately the lion killed a horse belonging to a local resident, and Edward had to pay compensation. An agreement was reached fairly quickly and Alfonso agreed to liberate Charles of Salerno, who did, however, have to agree to three of his and Marie of Hungary's nine sons being handed over to the Aragónese instead.[1]

In stark contrast to his father Pere III, who fathered seven known illegitimate children, and his younger brother Jaume II, who married four times and fathered ten legitimate children and several illegitimate ones, Alfonso III of Aragón, according to the chronicler Ramon Muntaner, died a virgin and never even touched a woman. Muntaner states that Alfonso only wished to sleep with his wife and therefore never concerned himself with any other woman. Though Alfonso had been betrothed to Eleanor of England since they were both children in 1273, the marriage never took place. Alfonso died on 18 June 1291 at the age of only twenty-five, while he was in Barcelona arranging his and Eleanor's wedding. Muntaner says that the king had a rash on his upper thigh which became infected, and that the consequent fever plagued Alfonso so violently for ten days that any other man would have died long before.[2] Alfonso was succeeded in Aragón by his much-married brother Jaume II (b.1267), already king of Sicily by right of their mother Costanza (who outlived her eldest son and died in 1302). Sicily passed to Alfonso and Jaume's next eldest brother, Frederic, who ruled the island until his death in 1337, while Jaume II ruled as king of Aragón until 1327.

The kingdom of Sicily, which since 1130 had consisted of the island of Sicily and the Italian mainland below Rome, was now divided into two. The island of Sicily remained the kingdom of Sicily and was ruled by Costanza and Pere III's descendants, while the mainland territory became the kingdom of Naples and was ruled by Charles of Anjou's descendants. On the death of Anjou's son Charles of Salerno in 1309, Naples passed to Salerno's third son, Robert 'the Wise' – his eldest son Charles Martel, titular king of Hungary, had died in 1295, and his second son Louis became bishop of Toulouse and was canonised as a saint in 1317 – and then to Robert's granddaughter Giovanna I (b. *c.*1326) in 1343. As queen regnant of the kingdom of Naples, Giovanna's life was a dramatic one; she married four times and was accused of murdering her first husband and second cousin, András of Hungary, Charles Martel's grandson, in 1345. Her second husband Louis of Taranto was even more closely related to her, her third was Jaume IV, titular king of Majorca, and her fourth was a German duke, Otto of Brunswick. Giovanna's turbulent life came to a suitably turbulent end when she was assassinated in 1382 on the orders of another cousin, Charles of Durazzo.

After a period of a few decades without a Holy Roman Emperor following the death of Friedrich II in 1250, Henry, count of Luxembourg, briefly reigned as emperor, and was crowned in Rome in June 1312. He died the following year, and the next imperial coronation took place in Rome in early 1328 when Ludwig of Bavaria and his wife Margarete of Hainault were crowned. Emperor Ludwig (1282–1347) is perhaps best known for his long and bitter dispute with Pope John XXII (r.1316–34), whom he accused of heresy. In return, John belittled Ludwig by calling him simply 'the Bavarian', excommunicated him, and declared him deposed as emperor. One of Ludwig's staunchest allies against John XXII was the English Franciscan friar William Ockham (*c.*1287–1347), after whom Ockham's or Occam's Razor is named.

The greatest and most famous Holy Roman Emperor of the fourteenth century was Karl or Charles IV, né Wenzel or Wenceslas and renamed in honour of his godfather, Charles IV of France (d.1328). Karl, already king of Bohemia and the founder of the Charles University in Prague, the oldest university in central Europe, was crowned as Emperor in 1355 and died in 1378. Karl's son Zikmund (b.1368), who lost the battle of Nicopolis to the Ottoman Sultan Bayezid in 1396, also became Holy Roman Emperor, though not until 1433, four years before his death. The Holy Roman Empire, like the Byzantine or Eastern Roman Empire, endured for a thousand years and was finally dissolved in the early 1800s, during the Napoleonic Wars.

Part V

France

Dramatis Personae

John de Brienne, b. *c.*1175/78; king of Jerusalem by marriage; Latin Emperor of Constantinople from 1228

Berenguela of León, b. *c.*1204/05, third wife of John de Brienne; sister of Fernando III, king of Castile and León; niece of Blanche of Castile, queen consort of France

Louis VIII, b.1187, king of France 1223 to 1226; son of Philip II Augustus (r.1180–1223) and his first wife Isabelle of Hainault (1170–90); nephew of Baudouin and Hendrik of Flanders, the first two Latin Emperors of Constantinople

Ingeborg of Denmark, b.1174, dowager queen consort of France; widow of Philip II Augustus and stepmother of Louis VIII; called Isambour in France

Blanche (née Blanca) **of Castile,** b.1188, queen consort of France; marries Louis in 1200; daughter of Alfonso VIII, king of Castile, and granddaughter of Henry II, king of England

Louis IX, b.1214, king of France 1226 to 1270; eldest son of Louis VIII and Blanche of Castile; marries **Marguerite of Provence** (b.1221), eldest daughter of Ramon-Berenger, count of Provence, in 1234

Robert of Artois, b.1216, and **Alphonse of Poitiers,** b.1220; sons of Louis VIII and Blanche of Castile; brothers of Louis IX

Charles of Anjou, b.1227; posthumous son of Louis VIII and youngest brother of Louis IX; count of Anjou, Maine and Provence; king of Sicily, titular king of Albania and Jerusalem

Beatrice of Provence, b. *c*. late 1220s; fourth and youngest daughter of Ramon-Berenger, count of Provence, and his sole heir; marries Charles of Anjou in 1246

Charles of Salerno, b.1254; eldest son and heir of Charles of Anjou and Beatrice of Provence; king of Naples, count of Anjou and Provence; marries Marie of Hungary

Henry III, b.1207, king of England 1216 to 1272; eldest child of King John and Isabelle of Angoulême; betrothed to Jeanne, countess of Ponthieu and later queen of Castile-León, in 1235, but marries **Alienor of Provence** (b. *c*.1222), sister of Marguerite and Beatrice, in 1236

Marie de Brienne, b.1225, eldest child of John de Brienne and Berenguela of León; Latin Empress of Constantinople by marriage to Baudouin de Courtenay (b.1217)

Alphonse de Brienne, b. *c*.1228; second child and eldest son of Emperor John de Brienne and Berenguela of León; chamberlain of France; marries Marie de Lusignan, countess of Eu

John de Brienne the younger, b. *c*.1230/32, son of Emperor John de Brienne and Berenguela of León; butler of France; marries Jeanne de Châteaudun, countess of Montfort, and secondly Marie de Coucy, dowager queen of Scotland; stepfather of Alexander III, king of Scotland (b.1241)

Louis de Brienne, b. *c*.1230/32; son of Emperor John de Brienne and Berenguela of León; marries Agnès de Beaumont, viscountess of Beaumont-sur-Sarthe; his children Isabelle, Louis and Henry adopt their mother's last name and move to England

Baudouin II de Courtenay, b.1217, Latin Emperor of Constantinople; son of Yolanda of Flanders and Pierre de Courtenay; marries Marie de Brienne; cousin of Louis VIII

Philippe de Courtenay, b.1243, titular Latin Emperor of Constantinople; son and heir of Baudouin de Courtenay and Marie de Brienne; grandson of John de Brienne and Berenguela of León; married to **Beatrice of Sicily**, daughter of Charles of Anjou and Beatrice of Provence

Catherine de Courtenay, b.1274, titular Latin Empress of Constantinople, countess of Valois by marriage; only child of Philippe de Courtenay and Beatrice of Sicily; great-granddaughter of John de Brienne; second wife of Charles, count of Valois

Catherine de Valois, b.1303, titular Latin Empress of Constantinople in her own right; eldest child of Catherine de Courtenay and Charles de Valois, and her mother's heir; niece of Philip IV, king of France, and half-sister of Philip VI, king of France; marries Philip of Taranto in 1313

Philip of Taranto, b. *c.*1278, son of Charles of Salerno, king of Naples, and Marie of Hungary; king of Albania, despot of *Romania*, prince of Achaea and Taranto

Philip III, king of France, b.1245, r.1270–85; eldest surviving son of Louis IX and Marguerite of Provence; marries Isabel of Aragón in 1262 and Marie of Brabant in 1274

Isabel of Aragón, b. *c.*1247, queen consort of France; sister of Pere III, king of Aragón, and Yolande of Aragón, queen consort of Castile-León

Philip IV, king of France, b.1268, r.1285–1314; elder son of Philip III and Isabel of Aragón; marries Juana I of Navarre in 1284

Charles of Valois, count of Valois, b.1270; younger son of Philip III and Isabel; brother of Philip IV; marries Marguerite of Anjou-Naples (1272–99), daughter of Charles of Salerno, and secondly Catherine de Courtenay; father of Philip VI, king of France, by his first marriage; titular Latin Emperor of Constantinople by his second

Juana I, queen regnant of Navarre, queen consort of France, b.1273, r.1274–1305; only child of Enrique I, king of Navarre (d.1274), and Blanche of Artois; granddaughter of Thibaut of Champagne (b.1201), king of Navarre

Blanche of Artois, queen consort of Navarre, countess of Lancaster, b. *c.*1245/48; daughter of Louis VIII's brother Robert, count of Artois (1216–50); marries Enrique I, king of Navarre, and secondly Edmund of Lancaster; mother of Juana I of Navarre and Thomas and Henry of Lancaster

Marguerite of France, queen consort of England, b.1278/79; daughter of Philip III and Marie of Brabant; half-sister of Philip IV; marries Edward I as his second wife in 1299

Edward I, king of England, b.1239, r.1272–1307; elder son of Henry III and Alienor of Provence; cousin of Philip III of France; marries firstly Leonor of Castile (d.1290) and secondly Marguerite of France

Edmund of Lancaster, earl of Lancaster, b.1245; younger son of Henry III and Alienor of Provence; brother of Edward I; marries Blanche of Artois, dowager queen consort of Navarre; stepfather of Juana I of Navarre

Louis X, king of France and Navarre, b.1289, r.1314–16; eldest son of Philip IV of France and Juana I of Navarre; marries Marguerite of Burgundy and secondly Clemence of Hungary

Marguerite of Burgundy, queen consort of Navarre, b. *c.*1289/90; daughter of Robert II, duke of Normandy, and granddaughter of Louis IX of France; marries Louis of Navarre in 1305

Jeanne/Juana II, queen regnant of Navarre, b.1312, r.1328–49; only child of Louis X and Marguerite of Burgundy; mother of Carlos II, king of Navarre, b.1332, r.1349–87

Clemence of Hungary, queen consort of France and Navarre, b.1293; daughter of Charles Martel, titular king of Hungary, and granddaughter of Charles of Salerno, king of Naples; marries Louis X in 1315

John I, king of France and Navarre, b.1316, r.1316; son of Louis X and Clemence

Philip V, king of France and Navarre, count of Poitiers, b. *c.*1291, r.1316–22; younger brother of Louis X; married to Jeanne of Burgundy

Charles IV, king of France and Navarre, count of La Marche, b.1294, r.1322–28; younger brother of Louis X and Philip V; marries firstly Blanche of Burgundy, secondly Marie of Luxembourg, and thirdly Jeanne of Evreux

Jeanne of Burgundy (b.1287/88), queen consort of France and Navarre, wife of Philip V, and her sister **Blanche of Burgundy** (b. *c.*1296), wife of Charles of La Marche; daughters of Othon IV, count of Burgundy, and Mahaut, countess of Artois; Jeanne is their parents' heir

Marie of Luxembourg, b.1304, queen consort of France; daughter of Henry VII of Luxembourg, Holy Roman Emperor; marries Charles IV in 1322

Jeanne of Evreux, b. *c.*1310, queen consort of France; granddaughter of Philip III of France; marries her cousin Charles IV in 1324

Isabella of France, queen consort of England, b. *c.*1295; only surviving daughter of Philip IV of France and Juana I of Navarre; sister of Louis X, Philip V and Charles IV; marries Edward I and Leonor of Castile's son **Edward II** in 1308 and mother of **Edward III**, b.1312

Philip VI, king of France, b.1293, r.1328–50; son of Charles of Valois and his first wife Marguerite of Anjou-Naples; nephew of Philip IV and cousin of Louis X, Philip V and Charles IV; first king of the house of Valois

Chapter 25

A Barefoot Procession

John de Brienne's grandmother-in-law from his first marriage to Marie of Montferrat, the redoubtable Maria Komnene of Byzantium, queen consort of Jerusalem, died in 1217. She outlived both of her husbands, King Amalric and Balian d'Ibelin, by decades, and also outlived a number of her grandchildren including John's wife Queen Marie. John played a prominent role in the Fifth Crusade of 1217 to 1221 and was instrumental in the Christian capture of the Egyptian port of Damietta in 1219, failed to take control of the kingdom of Armenian Cilicia in 1219/20 after the death of his second wife Stephanie, then undertook what his biographer has called 'a tour of the West'.[1] He travelled to his native France and attended King Philip II Augustus's funeral in Paris in July 1223, Philip having finally died after a long reign of forty-three years. (His younger sister Agnès/Anna, widowed from two Byzantine Emperors by her mid-teens, is thought to have died around 1220, leaving a daughter from her third marriage to Theodoros Branas.) According to the Old French Continuation of William of Tyre's chronicle, Philip Augustus left 50,000 marks of silver 'to the hand of King John', i.e., de Brienne, king of Jerusalem.[2] John stayed in his homeland to attend the coronation of Louis VIII in Rheims on 6 August 1223. Louis was King Philip's only surviving child from his first marriage to the long-dead Isabelle of Hainault (d.1190).

In the early autumn of 1223, not long after Louis's coronation, John de Brienne visited England, where Henry III had succeeded his father King John as a boy of just turned nine in October 1216. Henry was crowned in St Peter's Abbey in Gloucester, later Gloucester Cathedral, rather than in Westminster Abbey as was customary, because King John died with a sizeable part of his kingdom including the Westminster area under the control of Louis of France, later to become Louis VIII. Louis had invaded England at the behest of some of John's disgruntled barons, though lost the battle of Lincoln in May 1217 to the young King Henry's regent William Marshal, earl of Pembroke. In August that year, Louis's forces also lost the naval battle of Sandwich, and he withdrew to his homeland not long afterwards and gave up all hopes of claiming the kingdom of England.

John de Brienne met the young King Henry, who turned sixteen shortly after John's visit, at the shrine of St Thomas Becket in Canterbury Cathedral. He also visited London and Westminster, where he celebrated the Nativity of the Virgin Mary on 8 September. John did not linger long in England, however, and was back in France by 25 September.[3] A few decades ago, historian Steven Runciman made the extraordinary, though sadly unevidenced and unexplained, remark that John de Brienne was 'suggested for the throne of England' around this time. John's biographer Guy Perry plausibly suggests that Runciman must have misread a Latin document to come to this conclusion.[4] It is difficult to imagine how this claim could possibly be true, given that King John of England left two sons, Henry III and Richard of Cornwall, whose legitimacy was not in any doubt, and given that de Brienne was only distantly, if at all, related to the English royal family.

After his wedding to Berenguela of León in northern Spain in the spring of 1224, John travelled again to Paris, this time with his new wife in tow. Berenguela, now acknowledged as queen of Jerusalem – though her eleven-year-old stepdaughter Yolande was queen regnant of the diminished Latin Kingdom, at least in name – took part in a grand procession on 2 August 1224. The procession was headed by Berenguela and two other queens: her aunt Blanche of Castile, the present queen-consort of France as the wife of Louis VIII, and Ingeborg of Denmark, widow of Philip II Augustus and stepmother of Louis VIII. The story of King Philip's marriage to Ingeborg, or Isambour as she was commonly known in France, was a tragi-comic farce: he rejected her immediately after their wedding in 1193 and did his utmost to have the marriage annulled, and instead married his lover Agnès of Merania, with whom he had several children. Ingeborg, however, refused to accept the annulment of her marriage, and, thanks to the intervention of her brother the king of Denmark and the Pope, Philip finally relented and took Ingeborg back as his wife following Agnès of Merania's death in 1201. They had no children together, though two of the king's children with Agnès lived into adulthood.

Whether she knew it yet or not, Berenguela of León was already pregnant at the time of the August 1224 procession: in the Italian town of Capua in April 1225, eleven months after her and John's wedding, she gave birth to their daughter, Marie de Brienne.[5] They might have named their daughter in honour of John's first wife, Queen Marie of Jerusalem. He had travelled to Capua, as noted in Part 3 above, to arrange the marriage of his and the late Queen Marie's daughter Queen Yolande to Emperor Friedrich. Evidently Berenguela accompanied him.

All the religious houses of Paris took part in the procession, which followed a route from Notre-Dame to the abbey of Saint Antoine des Champs. The entire procession went barefoot, even the three queens, and its aim was to pray for Louis VIII's success against Henry III of England.[6] On 5 May 1224, Louis had refused to renew a truce with England agreed by his father Philip Augustus in 1220, and invaded Poitou and Gascony. Henry III's mother, the dowager queen of England, Isabelle of Angoulême, and her second husband Hugues de Lusignan, count of La Marche – a great-nephew of Aiméry and Guy de Lusignan, kings of Cyprus and Jerusalem – defected and came to an agreement with Louis. The king of France took over Poitou, and the English, who had ruled that part of France since the marriage of Henry III's grandparents Eleanor of Aquitaine and Henry of Anjou (later Henry II of England) in 1152, lost everything north of the river Garonne. As a defiant gesture in or around August 1225, Henry made his sixteen-year-old brother Richard of Cornwall count of Poitou, but as the English no longer held the territory, the title was purely nominal.[7] John de Brienne did his best to dissuade Louis VIII from attacking Poitou in 1224, but Louis failed to respond to his efforts. John's aim was almost certainly to ensure that France and England remained at peace and united in their willingness to aid and support him in Outremer.[8]

Louis VIII had married Berenguela of León's aunt Blanche of Castile in May 1200 when they were both twelve. Blanche's maternal grandmother Eleanor of Aquitaine, dowager queen of England – and the first wife of Louis's grandfather Louis VII – travelled to Castile to ready her for her new role and to accompany her to France. Louis of France was the only surviving child of Philip II Augustus and his first wife Isabelle of Hainault, three of whose younger siblings later ruled in Constantinople. The queen, not quite twenty years old, died in 1190 after giving birth to twin boys who also died, and afterwards her widower embarked on his rather ludicrous marital career of being wed to both Ingeborg of Denmark and Agnès of Merania. Louis VIII died in his late thirties on 8 November 1226 after a short reign of three years, leaving Queen Blanche pregnant; she gave birth to her youngest son, Charles of Anjou, on 21 March 1227. Their eldest child succeeded as Louis IX, though as he was only twelve, his mother served as his regent and later as his chief adviser. Queen Blanche's career followed a similar pattern to that of her eldest sister Berenguela, queen of Castile and León, and these two remarkable, powerful women were both the mothers of saints: Louis IX was canonised by the Catholic Church in 1297 and Fernando III in 1671. Queen Blanche's youngest daughter Isabelle of France (b.1224) is also recognised as a saint by the Franciscan Order.

John de Brienne and Berenguela of León were also raising a family. Either John or Louis was the youngest of their children; perhaps Louis, as a French chronicler lists the three de Brienne brothers as 'Alphonse, John and Louis' in that order. John de Brienne the younger married his first wife in 1250 or 1251 and their daughter was born *c.*1252, whereas Louis wed in 1253, which would also indicate that John was older. On the other hand, when the three de Brienne brothers witnessed royal charters in their mother's native Spain they always appeared as Alphonse, Louis and John in that order, which would seem to mean that Louis was older than John, or at least that Spanish clerks believed him to be.[9] In their own lifetimes, the three brothers were often called 'of Acre' because of their father's connections to the Holy Land, though they were born many years after their father left Outremer.

As the three de Brienne sons were young children when they lost their parents in 1237, they might not have remembered them well, though they probably knew their maternal grandmother, the redoubtable Queen Berenguela of Castile and León, who did not die until 1246, and their uncle Fernando III. Berenguela's younger sister, the equally formidable Queen Blanche, died in 1252, and the de Briennes certainly knew her well, as the *Chronique de Guillaume de Nangis* records that John de Brienne sent *ses trois fils, Alphonse, Jean et Louis, encore enfants* ('his three sons, Alphonse, John and Louis, still children') to grow up at the court of Blanche's son Louis IX. According to Guillaume de Nangis, Louis IX 'honourably and graciously received' the three de Brienne boys and raised them 'very high', despite his lack of interest in aiding their sister Marie and her husband Baudouin de Courtenay after they lost their empire.[10] In 1234, Louis married Marguerite, eldest of the four daughters of Ramon-Berenger, count of Provence, and Beatrice of Savoy. Almost certainly born in 1221, Marguerite was just thirteen when she wed, and their eldest child was born in 1240 (and their youngest *c.*1260). The next eldest Provençal sister, Alienor, married Henry III of England in 1236, the year after his betrothal to Jeanne of Ponthieu, later the second wife of Berenguela of León's brother Fernando III, fell through. Marguerite and Alienor's third sister, Sancha of Provence, married Henry III's brother Richard of Cornwall in 1243 and the youngest, Beatrice, married Louis IX's youngest brother Charles of Anjou in 1246: four sisters married two sets of brothers, and famously, all four became queens.

Chapter 26

A Mantle and a Surcoat for Meals

In the late 1240s, several years after an army led by his brother Alphonse of Poitiers routed an army led by Henry III of England and Richard of Cornwall at the battle of Taillebourg, ending English hopes of regaining Poitou and other territories lost to the French during Henry's reign and the reign of his and Richard's father King John, Louis IX led a crusade to Egypt. It is known as the Seventh Crusade and was the first of two crusades led by Louis, and its main aim was to recapture the city of Jerusalem and the Holy Land, once again in Muslim hands since 1244, for Christianity. As with the previous few crusades with this same aim, however, it failed. Queen Marguerite accompanied her husband, as did Louis's three brothers, Robert, count of Artois, Alphonse, count of Poitiers, and Charles, count of Anjou, and Charles's wife Beatrice of Provence.

Robert of Artois was killed while attacking the town of Mansurah in early 1250, and the other three French royal brothers were captured not long afterwards but released on payment of a massive fine and a promise that the Egyptian port of Damietta would be surrendered. An extraordinary woman encountered by the French at this time was Shajar al-Durr, whose name translates as 'Tree of Pearls'. She was a former slave and the widow of the sultan of Egypt, al-Salih Ayyub, and was herself proclaimed sultana and ruled in her own name for three months in 1250. Coins minted in her name call her *Malikat al-Muslimin*, 'Queen of the Muslims'.[1]

While King Louis and Queen Marguerite were staying in Cyprus in 1248 on their way to Egypt, they met Louis's kinswoman Marie de Brienne, Latin Empress of Constantinople. Marie arrived safely at Paphos, but the ship bearing all her clothes had been driven to Acre during a violent storm, and she had nothing but 'the mantle she was wearing and a surcoat for meals'. Jean de Joinville, the historian and chronicler, took her to Limassol where she met the king and queen and was received 'with great honour', though without, as noted above, obtaining any financial support for the Latin Empire. In the same year, Marie sent a letter to Louis's mother Blanche of Castile calling herself *empereris de Romanie*, 'empress of *Romania*'. After meeting Louis and Marguerite, Empress Marie travelled to her late father's native France. Here, she arranged a marriage with Jeanne de Châteaudun, dowager countess of Montfort by her first marriage, for her brother '*Monsignour* Jehan d'Acre', i.e., John de Brienne the younger, who was then in his late teens or at the start of his twenties. Jeanne de Châteaudun's first husband John, the count of Montfort, died in Cyprus in September 1249, and they had one child together, Beatrice de Montfort. An inveterate matchmaker who did her utmost to support and help her younger brothers, Empress Marie also arranged a marriage for her brother Alphonse, eldest of the three Brienne brothers, with the heiress Marie de Lusignan, countess of Eu in her own right. They wed in or before 1250, a couple of years before Alphonse made a pilgrimage to the shrine of St Thomas Becket in Canterbury. The remaining Brienne brother, Louis, married yet another heiress, Agnès de Beaumont, viscountess of Beaumont-sur-Sarthe, in 1253.[2] Several of their children used the name of de Beaumont in preference to their father's family name.

Queen Marguerite gave birth to three of her many children during the six years she and Louis IX spent in Egypt and Outremer, including Blanche, later the wife of Fernando de la Cerda of Castile. Louis's powerful mother Blanche of Castile died in November 1252 without seeing her four sons again; the king and his brothers Alphonse of Poitiers and Charles of Anjou finally returned to France in the spring of 1254, leaving the body of their other brother, Robert of Artois, behind in Egypt. In May 1254, shortly after Louis's return to his homeland, Konrad von Hohenstaufen, the titular king of Jerusalem, died, and was succeeded by his two-year-old son Konradin under the regency of Plaisance of Antioch, dowager queen of Cyprus.

Louis IX of France and Henry III of England were married to sisters, and furthermore, were closely related by blood and were only six and a half years apart in age.[3] After the conflict around the time of the battle of Taillebourg in the early to mid-1240s, relations between the two kingdoms during their reigns were as warm as at any time during the Middle Ages. Henry, Queen Alienor and their children visited Louis and Queen Marguerite in Paris in 1254, and Louis exclaimed 'Have we not married two sisters, and our brothers the other two? All that shall be born of them, both sons and daughters, shall be like brothers and sisters'.[4] On the English royal family's departure, Louis gave Henry a gift of an elephant, and Henry ordered the sheriffs of London to build an enclosure within the Tower of London for the animal.[5] Henry,

Alienor and family also spent the festive season of 1259/60 with Louis and Marguerite, and were still in France when Louis the younger, who was the French royal couple's eldest son and heir to the French throne, died in his teens in early 1260 (Louis and Marguerite's second son Philip of France, born in 1245, became next in line to the throne on his brother's death). Henry and Alienor attended the young man's funeral, and Louis and Marguerite were guests at the wedding of the royal English couple's second daughter Beatrice of England and the duke of Brittany's son shortly afterwards.[6]

Philip, the future king of France, married Isabel of Aragón in the early summer of 1262. She was a daughter of Jaume I of Aragón and one of the younger sisters of Yolande, queen of Alfonso X of Castile-León. Philip was seventeen at the time of his wedding and Isabel was about fifteen. Around the same time, Isabel and Yolande's brother Pere, future king of Aragón, married Costanza of Sicily, the only child of the reigning king of Sicily, Manfredi von Hohenstaufen, from his first marriage.[7]

Chapter 27

The Handsomest Man in the World

The rise of the Mamluks under their powerful leader Sultan al-Zahir Baibars, and their capture of numerous Christian-held cities including Antioch in 1268, triggered the second crusade led by Louis IX, usually known as the Eighth Crusade, in the late 1260s. Louis would never see his kingdom again; he died in Tunis on 25 August 1270, on the same day and in the same place as Alphonse de Brienne, count of Eu, eldest son of Emperor John de Brienne and Berenguela of León. The king's son and successor, now Philip III of France, wanted the body returned to Paris, while Louis's brother Charles of Anjou wished to bury him in Sicily. They compromised, and Louis's bones were taken to Paris and his entrails to Sicily.[1]

Nancy Goldstone accurately describes the French royal family's subsequent return to their homeland as a funeral procession.[2] As well as Louis himself, numerous other members of the French royal family passed away during that dreadful year of 1270/71: Louis and Queen Marguerite's twenty-year-old son Jean Tristan, born in Damietta during the French king's previous crusade; their eldest daughter Isabelle and her husband Thibaut II, king of Navarre; Louis's brother Alphonse of Poitiers and Alphonse's wife Jeanne of Toulouse; and Louis's daughter-in-law Isabel of Aragón, briefly queen consort of France as Philip III's wife. Queen Isabel died in early 1271 after falling from her horse in southern Italy; she was pregnant, and her child died with her. She left three sons, Louis (b.1264), Philip (b.1268), later king of France, and Charles de Valois, who, born in March 1270, was then just a few months old. Marguerite of Provence outlived her husband by a quarter of a century and did not die until December 1295, in her seventies, having also outlived her three younger sisters and seven of her ten children. In 1297 during their grandson Philip IV's reign, and thanks in great part to Philip's promotion of his holiness, Louis IX was canonised as a saint of the Catholic Church.

Louis IX's English nephews Lord Edward and Edmund of Lancaster survived the dreadful years of the early 1270s; in November 1272, Edward succeeded his father Henry as king of England, though he and Leonor of Castile lingered for a while in their duchy of Aquitaine, where Leonor gave birth to her son Alfonso of Bayonne in November 1273 and met her brother Alfonso X of Castile-León. Finally, they returned to England for their coronation at Westminster Abbey in August 1274. In the Treaty of Paris between Henry III and Louis IX in 1259, Henry had given up all claims to the French territories lost by his father King John, including Normandy, Poitou and Anjou, and agreed that he and his successors would perform homage for their duchy of Aquitaine every time there was a new king of England or a new king of France. As the new king of England, therefore, Edward owed homage to his cousin Philip III as his overlord for the duchy, and the ceremony took place in Paris in 1273 before Edward and Leonor returned to England.

Philip III was crowned king of France at Rheims in August 1271, a few months after the death of his wife Isabel, and in 1274 married his second wife Marie of Brabant, with whom he had three more children. Queen Marie's preference for her own offspring over her three stepsons Louis, Philip and Charles is understandable, but it is noteworthy that when Louis died at the age of twelve in 1276, leaving his brother Philip as heir to the throne, many people in France believed that Marie had in some way caused or brought about his death. After Philip the younger became king, he seems to have had as little to do with Marie as possible.[3] It was, perhaps, not particularly tactful that when Marie gave birth to her eldest child in 1276, the year of her eldest stepson's death, he was given the name Louis.

King Philip pulled off a real achievement in 1274/75. The greatest European heiress of the era was Juana, born in 1273 and the only surviving child of the king of Navarre, Enrique I, successor of his brother Thibaut II in 1270 and the youngest son of Thibaut I of Champagne (cousin and rival of Alice and Philippa of Champagne and Jerusalem). When King Enrique died in 1274, baby Juana became queen regnant of Navarre and countess of Champagne. Edward I of England had hoped to marry her to his son Henry of Windsor (b.1268), but his plans were thwarted by his cousin the king of France, and young Henry died later in 1274 anyway, leaving his infant brother Alfonso of Bayonne (d. August 1284) as heir to the English throne. Juana's mother and regent was Blanche of Artois, daughter of Louis IX's brother

Robert, count of Artois, who fell at Damietta in Egypt in 1250. Feeling that her infant daughter's position in Navarre was threatened by internal and especially external forces, Blanche fled to Paris and the protection of her cousin Philip III. They sealed the Treaty of Orléans, whereby King Philip became the guardian of Juana and her small realm, and it was arranged that the baby queen would grow up at the French court and would eventually marry one of Philip's sons. Not long afterwards, in late 1275 or early 1276, Blanche of Artois married her second husband, Edward I's brother Edmund of Lancaster, and moved to England; their sons Thomas and Henry of Lancaster, Queen Juana's half-brothers, were born *c.*1277/78 and *c.*1280/81. The wedding of sixteen-year-old Philip of France, heir to the throne after the death of his brother Louis in 1276, and eleven-year-old Juana went ahead in August 1284.

In 1284/85, Philip III went to war against Aragón after the Sicilian Vespers and the defeat and flight of his uncle Charles of Anjou. This war is often known as the Aragónese Crusade, because Pope Martin IV called for a crusade against Pere III of Aragón following his invasion of Sicily, and excommunicated him. Pere's son the future Alfonso III was placed in charge of defending Aragón's border with Navarre, which was ruled, at least nominally given his youth, by Philip III's son and heir by right of his wife Juana. King Philip's younger son Charles de Valois, who was fourteen in 1284, was endowed with the kingdom of Aragón by Martin IV; as Charles was Pere III's nephew via his late mother Isabel of Aragón, he did have some kind of vaguely plausible claim. Charles never, however, managed to exercise any authority over Aragón, and ultimately renounced his empty, and widely ridiculed, title. Cast rather in the mould of his namesake great-uncle Charles of Anjou, however, over the years Valois attempted to gain control of the Latin Empire of Constantinople and the Holy Roman Empire as well as the kingdom of Aragón.

Philip III, one of the least colourful men who form the long procession of French kings down the ages, died of dysentery in Perpignan on 5 October 1285, aged only forty and defeated in his war, or crusade, against Aragón. Although he had expressed a wish for his body to be buried whole at Saint-Denis, as almost all kings of France were through the centuries, his son and successor had his heart removed and given to the church of the Dominican friars in Paris.[4] Philip's enemy and former brother-in-law Pere III outlived him by mere weeks. Philip IV, aged seventeen, succeeded his father and was crowned, as was customary, in Rheims at the beginning of 1286. He was and is known as *Philippe le Bel*, usually translated into English as 'Philip the Fair' in the sense of handsome, not an observation on his colouring or his fondness for justice. One of Philip's enemies, Bernard Saisset, bishop of Pamiers, declared that 'he is neither man nor beast. He is a statue'. Saisset also likened Philip to an owl, 'the handsomest of birds, which is worth absolutely nothing… such is our king of France, who is the handsomest man in the world and who can do nothing except to stare at men.'[5]

As well as the epithet *le Bel*, Philip IV is known to history as *le Roi de Fer*, 'the Iron King'. He is rather better known to an English-speaking audience than most other medieval French monarchs, thanks mostly to Maurice Druon's popular series of novels about him, the later years of his reign, and his family: *Les Rois Maudits*, 'The Accursed Kings'. His and Juana's eldest child, or at least their eldest son, Louis X of France and Navarre, was born in October 1289, though it may be that their eldest daughter Marguerite was older, born sometime after May 1288. Marguerite was betrothed to Fernando IV of Castile-León but died young in 1294; her younger sister Blanche was then betrothed to Fernando instead, but herself died in 1295, and the planned Franco-Castilian marital alliance never took place. Two other sons were born to Philip IV and Juana I *c.*1291 and in June 1294, Philip and Charles, both kings of France and Navarre, then a daughter, Isabella, queen consort of England, probably in the second half of 1295.[6] Their youngest child, Robert, died in 1308 at the age of about eleven.

Chapter 28

Feuding Fishermen

In 1293, a dispute broke out between fishermen from Normandy on one side and fishermen from England and the English-ruled duchy of Aquitaine on the other, and it developed into something very serious when the Englishmen sacked the port of La Rochelle on their way home after seizing a number of French vessels. The conflict spiralled almost to the point of a war between the two maritime communities. Philip IV sent letters to Edward I regarding the matter that not only failed to address him as duke of Aquitaine, but also did not even acknowledge him as king of England, and he peremptorily summoned Edward to Paris, not as a fellow king and his equal but as a vassal. Edward's brother Edmund of Lancaster, stepfather of Philip's wife Juana I of Navarre, travelled to France and attempted to mediate and soothe the French king's ruffled feathers, but Philip's brother Charles de Valois urged him to war instead. Supposedly, according to a chronicler, Valois 'hated the English with inveterate hatred', and both he and Philip wished nothing more than to destroy Edward I's rule, and English rule more generally, in southwest France.[1] Edmund of Lancaster's attempts at diplomacy failed catastrophically, and his brother the king of England – whose relations with their young kinsmen, their cousin Philip III's sons, had also now failed catastrophically – would spend the rest of the 1290s at war with France.

As a means of ending the conflict between France and England, in July 1299 Pope Boniface VIII issued a dispensation for Edward I to marry Philip IV's half-sister Marguerite, daughter of Philip III and Marie of Brabant, and for Edward's heir, fifteen-year-old Edward of Caernarfon, to marry Philip and Queen Juana's only surviving daughter, the young Isabella.[2] Marguerite, aged twenty, married sixty-year-old Edward I in early September 1299, and became pregnant immediately: their first son Thomas, later earl of Norfolk, was born on 1 June 1300, and their second, Edmund, earl of Kent, fourteen months later. In late 1325, Edmund would marry Margaret Wake, a great-granddaughter of the *Porphyrogennetos* John de Brienne the younger. Also in 1299, Philip IV's sister-in-law Marguerite of Anjou-Naples, Charles de Valois's first wife, died in her twenties. In 1301, Valois married his second wife Catherine de Courtenay, granddaughter of Emperor John de Brienne's daughter Marie and Emperor Baudouin de Courtenay, and began calling himself Latin Emperor of Constantinople. Catherine's heir to her titular empire was their eldest daughter, Catherine de Valois.

Queen Juana I died in early April 1305, aged only thirty-two; her heir in Navarre and Champagne was her eldest son, Louis, who was crowned as king of Navarre in Pamplona in the early autumn of 1307 a few days before he turned eighteen. Juana's will, made a week before she died, survives, though her widower failed to execute some of her testamentary wishes.[3] Juana had never reigned alone in her small realm of Navarre, which, given that she and her mother Blanche fled to the French court when Juana was a toddler, she did not know at all and seems never to have visited later in life. Navarre was ruled during her absence by men appointed by Philip III, and later by Juana's husband. Philip IV's sister-in-law Catherine de Courtenay, titular Latin Empress, soon followed Juana to the grave and died in 1307, also in her early thirties, and another death in 1307 was that of sixty-eight-year-old Edward I of England. He was succeeded by his twenty-three-year-old son Edward II, soon to become Philip IV's son-in-law.

In the autumn of 1307, Philip IV moved against the Knights Templar, a wealthy and influential military and religious order. It was the Templars who had paid the ransom of Isaakios Doukas Komnenos, later *Basileus* of Cyprus, after he was captured in Armenia in the 1180s, and the order took part in, among many other engagements, the defence of Tripoli and Acre against the Mamluks in 1289/91. With the aid of Pope Clement V, who was based in Avignon rather than in Rome, Philip IV accused the Templars of committing heresy and sodomy, renouncing Christ, and spitting on the cross. They were arrested, imprisoned, tortured, and killed, and their lands, goods and wealth were seized. The persecution of the Templars spread to other European countries including England, Sicily and Aragón, after Clement V issued the papal bull *Pastoralis praeeminentiae* ordering all Christian kings to arrest the Templars. One notable exception was Scotland, whose recently (March 1306) crowned king, Robert Bruce, was already under sentence of excommunication and was therefore immune to papal threats.

All three of Philip IV and Juana I's sons who lived into adulthood – Louis, king of Navarre, Philip, count of Poitiers, and Charles, count of La

Marche – married women from Burgundy. Confusingly, there was a duchy of Burgundy and a county of Burgundy, and the latter was also often called the *Franche-Comté* or Free County and was separate from the duchy. Marguerite, who married the eldest royal son Louis in 1305, was a daughter of Robert II, duke of Burgundy (d.1306) and a granddaughter of Saint Louis IX of France via her mother Agnès. Jeanne and Blanche, who married Philip of Poitiers in 1307 and Charles of La Marche in 1308 respectively, were sisters, the daughters of Othon IV, count of Burgundy (d.1302) and Mahaut, countess of Artois (d.1329). Mahaut is a major – and decidedly malevolent and murderous – character in Maurice Druon's *Accursed Kings* series. In the novels and in real life, she was involved in a long struggle with her nephew Robert of Artois over possession of the county of Artois, which Mahaut inherited from her father on his death in 1302; her brother Philip, Robert's father, had died in 1298, and she became her father's heir by nearness of blood in preference to her nephew. Jeanne of Burgundy, as the elder of Othon and Mahaut's daughters, inherited the *Franche-Comté* from her father, and ultimately also inherited the county of Artois from her mother. A week after Charles of La Marche married Jeanne's sister Blanche of Burgundy at their mother Mahaut's castle of Hesdin (now in the Pas-de-Calais department of northern France) in early 1308, his sister Isabella married her long-term fiancé Edward II of England in Boulogne.

Louis of Navarre and Marguerite of Burgundy's daughter Jeanne or Juana, their only child, and a future queen regnant of Navarre, was born in January 1312. Marguerite sent her usher, Jeannot de Samoys, to England to inform her sister-in-law Queen Isabella and Edward II, whose eldest child the future Edward III was born a few months later in November 1312.[4] Louis's brother Philip of Poitiers was also raising a family with Jeanne of Burgundy; they had four daughters who survived into adulthood and a son who died as an infant in 1317, while the youngest royal brother Charles of La Marche and Jeanne's sister Blanche had a son and a daughter. All seemed well in the Capetian royal family in the early 1310s, but one of the greatest royal scandals of the French Middle Ages was about to break.

Chapter 29

The Tour de Nesle and Tennis

As a ten-year-old in July 1313, John de Brienne's great-great-granddaughter and heir to the Latin Empire of Constantinople, Catherine de Valois, married Philip of Taranto, then about thirty-five and one of the many children of Charles of Salerno, king of Naples, in Paris. Philip's first wife Thamar Angelina Komnene was the daughter of the despot of Epirus, and in 1309 Philip accused her of adultery; she died imprisoned in 1311. Catherine's cousin Isabella of France, Philip IV's daughter, and her husband Edward II spent a couple of months in France in the spring and summer of 1313, and although they missed the wedding, Edward met Philip of Taranto before he and Isabella returned to England. Philip, the 'prince of Tarente' (i.e., Taranto) asked the English king to intervene with Pope Clement V and the cardinals on behalf of his older brother Robert, king of Naples.[1] Catherine and Philip's wedding took place a few weeks after the – perhaps rather belated, given their ages – joint knighting of Philip IV's three sons and their cousin Philip de Valois, Catherine's half-brother.

The following spring, Philip IV subjected Jacques de Molay, grand master of the Knights Templar, and his deputy Geoffroi de Charny to a horrific death by being burned alive on a scaffold placed on an island in the middle of the River Seine in Paris. In April 1314, just a few weeks later, Pope Clement V (born Bertrand de Got), who had done much to help Philip bring down the Templars, passed away; it would be twenty-eight months before another pope was elected. The short gap between the hideous deaths of Molay and Charny and the death of the pope who had destroyed them, coupled with the end of the Capetian dynasty only fourteen years later, has proved irresistible for many writers, who claim that Jacques de Molay cursed both Pope Clement, and Philip IV and his dynasty, from his pyre.

Shortly after the awful executions of Jacques de Molay and Geoffroi de Charny, Philip IV's daughter Isabella visited him again in Paris, and a major crisis broke out during her stay at the French court. Two of the king's three daughters-in-law were found to have committed adultery with brothers called Philippe and Gautier d'Aulnay or d'Aunay, who came from the minor French nobility and were members of the households of the king's brother Charles de Valois and the king's son Philip of Poitiers. Isabella may have revealed this, or it may be a coincidence that she was with her father at the time when the scandal, known to posterity as the Tour de Nesle Affair after the tower in Paris where the women were supposed to have met their lovers, broke.[2] Marguerite of Burgundy, queen of Navarre, and Blanche of Burgundy, countess of La Marche, were the guilty parties, and Blanche's older sister Jeanne, countess of Burgundy and Poitiers, was held under house arrest for a few months and questioned extensively, though at the end of 1314 she was finally found not guilty and allowed to go free. The fact that she was the sole heiress to the counties of Burgundy and Artois was, one might cynically assume, a good reason for her to be found innocent and released. The unfortunate d'Aulnay brothers were grotesquely executed by being flayed alive and emasculated, and many others who had known of their liaisons with the two women but had not spoken up were also executed. Marguerite and Blanche were imprisoned in Château Gaillard, a massive fortress in Normandy built by Richard Lionheart of England in the 1190s.[3]

In early 1314, Philip IV was in his mid-forties and had three sons aged between nineteen and twenty-four, all of whom were married with children; the future of the Capetian dynasty must have seemed well assured. Yet within fourteen years of the adultery scandal, all four men would be dead without male heirs, finally breaking the direct line of descent that the dynasty had managed since as far back as 987 (though their successors the Valois family shared the same blood). Mere months after the scandal, Philip IV was mortally injured while hunting, and, aware that he was dying, ordered that he be transported from Pont-Sainte-Maxence to Poissy, birthplace a hundred years earlier of the grandfather he and many others revered, Saint Louis IX. Shortly before Philip died, he was taken by litter to Fontainebleau, his own birthplace in 1268, and passed away there at the end of November 1314.[4] He was buried at Saint-Denis with his three sons present at the funeral, though his daughter Isabella, queen of England, did not travel over the Channel to attend it. This is rather puzzling as the two had always been close, so perhaps Isabella simply had no wish to cross the Channel again in winter only a few months after she had last seen her father. Philip's stepmother Marie of Brabant outlived him and died in 1321, having also outlived her three children including Marguerite (d.1318), stepmother of Isabella of France's husband Edward II. Philip's eldest son the king of Navarre now succeeded him as Louis X of France, and was nicknamed *le Hutin*, the Stubborn or Quarrelsome. A chronicler stated that Louis was extravagant and young for his age, and on his deathbed, Philip IV took the opportunity to lecture his eldest son about comporting himself with more maturity, wisdom and restraint, as befitted a king of France.[5]

At the end of April 1315, Louis's wife the imprisoned Marguerite of Burgundy, queen consort of Navarre and technically also of France for the previous five months, died in Château Gaillard. The cause of her death is uncertain. There were, surely inevitably, rumours at the time that she had been murdered – and centuries later, Maurice Druon titled his novel about Marguerite and the Tour de Nesle Affair *La Reine Étranglée*, The Strangled Queen – though it may simply be that the harsh treatment to which she was subjected hastened a natural death. Three months later Louis X married his second wife, Clemence of Hungary. They were jointly crowned king and queen of France in Rheims shortly afterwards, and their marriage had been planned by various relatives including Louis's uncle Charles de Valois and Clemence's uncle Robert 'the Wise', king of Naples, in December 1314, even though Louis was then still married to the imprisoned Marguerite of Burgundy.[6] After Clement V's death in April 1314 only days after the adultery scandal broke, there was no pope until the election of Jacques Duèse as John XXII in August 1316, and therefore no one with the authority to annul Louis and Marguerite's marriage.

Louis X's reign would be a very short one of a mere eighteen months, though it was eventful: he abolished serfdom in France – though serfs would have to pay to be released from their servitude – readmitted France's Jewish population who had been expelled by his father several years earlier, and led a military campaign against the wealthy county of Flanders. The latter part of his reign also coincided with a terrible natural disaster in northern Europe called the Great Famine, when endless heavy rain caused crops to fail catastrophically and up to ten percent of the inhabitants of France, England and other northern countries died of starvation or malnutrition. A particular feature of Philip IV's reign had been his closeness to two councillors, Guillaume de Nogaret and Enguerran de Marigny. Both men rose from fairly humble beginnings to enjoy great influence at court in Philip's reign and, at first, in Louis X's; Marigny became Philip IV's chamberlain in 1305, a remarkable position to reach for a man of comparatively lowly birth, and was a highly skilled financier and diplomat. He made, however, the error of alienating Philip IV's powerful brother Charles de Valois, and at Valois's instigation, he was imprisoned in December 1314 soon after King Philip died. He was hanged on the public gibbet at Montfaucon at the end of April 1315, seemingly on the same day as the death of Marguerite of Burgundy in captivity at Château Gaillard.[7]

In early June 1316, Louis X died suddenly and rather mysteriously in Vincennes at the age of only twenty-six. Chroniclers blamed either an unspecified illness of rapid onset, or stated that the king overheated while playing an early form of tennis called *jeu de paume* of which he was very fond, then took a deadly chill after drinking icy water or cold wine afterwards. Louis's body, dressed in a fur-trimmed, hooded surcoat, an ermine mantle and a silver-gilt crown, was taken from the Bois de Vincennes to the cathedral of Notre Dame, and then to Saint-Denis, where he was interred.[8] The political situation Louis left behind in France was difficult; his widow Clemence of Hungary was pregnant, and he also had a four-year-old daughter Jeanne/Juana from his marriage to Marguerite of Burgundy, whose legitimacy might well have been deemed rather in doubt given her mother's extramarital relationship. Louis's next eldest brother Philip of Poitiers was appointed regent, and Philip and Queen Clemence came to an agreement that if Clemence bore a son, he would, despite the closeness of the familial relationship – they would be first cousins – marry one of Philip and Jeanne of Burgundy's daughters.[9]

Queen Clemence gave birth to Louis X's posthumous son John, or Jean, in Paris during the night of 13/14 November 1316, and the baby became king of France as soon as he drew his first breath. Sadly, the little boy died at a few days old, perhaps as a result of the feverish illness, probably malaria, from which his mother was suffering at the time of his birth. The unfortunate Clemence was also suffering from depression, presumably brought on or at least exacerbated by her sudden bereavement that year, and wept constantly. Her quarrels with her brother-in-law Philip of Poitiers, who withheld the rightful income promised to Clemence by Louis X, cannot have helped.[10] Despite her child's death at about five days old, he was and is considered a true king of France, and the next King John, who acceded in 1350, has always been known as John II.

Philip of Poitiers, known as *le Long* or the Tall, succeeded his tiny nephew as Philip V of France, and was crowned at Rheims in early January 1317. He thus broke a promise made to the duke of Burgundy, Odo (or Eudes) IV, who was the brother of the late Marguerite and the uncle of Jeanne/Juana, that if Louis X and Queen Clemence's infant was female, Philip would serve as regent only until Louis's daughters came of age and would then step aside. Odo's mother Agnès, youngest child of Louis IX and a great-aunt of Philip V, was infuriated at what she saw as Philip's usurpation in place of her four-year-old granddaughter, and to placate her and any other French nobles who might be uneasy at the turn of events, Philip asked the Estates-General to write a text that would justify his right to the throne. The words 'Salic Law' were not used in the text, but in later decades and centuries were used as a form of shorthand when retrospectively barring female accession to the French throne. To make peace with Odo and Agnès, Philip arranged Odo's marriage to his eldest daughter, yet another Jeanne, who in 1330 would inherit her mother's and grandparents' counties of Burgundy and Artois.[11]

Philip V invited his sister Isabella and brother-in-law Edward II to his coronation, and though they failed to attend, he did meet them in late June 1320 when they travelled to Amiens for Edward to pay homage to Philip as his overlord for Aquitaine and Ponthieu. Philip has been called 'a man of considerable intelligence and sensitivity, arguably the wisest and most politically apt of Philip the Fair's sons'.[12] He managed to restore more cordial relations with the county of Flanders, a thorn in the side of his father and elder brother, instituted some important fiscal and government reforms, and created the *Cour de Comptes* or 'Court of Accounts', the supreme French audit institution, which still exists.

Chapter 30

The Last Capetian King

King Philip V, despite his youth – he was almost certainly only thirty – became mortally ill in August 1321 with dysentery and quartan fever, i.e. malaria. In late October he was taken to the Franciscan nunnery at Longchamp, which had been founded by his great-grandfather Louis IX for his sister Isabelle and was the home of Philip's nine-year-old daughter Blanche, a future nun there. He remained at Longchamp until the beginning of 1322, when he died.[1] As Louis X's daughter Jeanne/Juana had been in 1316 when Philip became king, Philip's own four daughters were overlooked as potential successors to the French throne on his death.

The youngest living son of Philip IV succeeded to the throne as Charles IV at the start of January 1322, and became the fourth king of France in the seven years since Philip IV's death in late 1314. He was the first king of France – or rather, of the territory later known as France – to bear the name Charles since Charles the Simple died in the early 900s. For 400 years, the realm had seen an endless parade of kings called Louis and Philip. Charles also succeeded his brothers and his mother Juana I as king of Navarre. His marriage to Blanche of Burgundy, imprisoned for adultery since 1314, was finally annulled in May 1322 after Pope John XXII discovered that Blanche's mother Mahaut, countess of Artois, was Charles's godmother. As the godparent/godchild connection created a relationship considered every bit as binding as that of a blood tie, and as no papal dispensation had been issued before Charles and Blanche wed in 1308, John declared that their marriage had always been invalid. It is hard to explain why nobody had noticed this relationship, or cared about the legal difficulties that it caused, in the previous fourteen years.

Blanche of Burgundy and Charles IV's son Philip and daughter Jeanne both died young in the early 1320s, though if their son had lived a few years longer, one wonders what might have happened when Charles died, and whether the young Philip would have been recognised as king of France. The boy's paternity must surely have been in some doubt, as was the case with Louis X and Marguerite of Burgundy's daughter, and probably even more so given that Jeanne/Juana had been conceived three years before Marguerite's adultery was discovered and it seems extremely unlikely that her extra-marital relationship had lasted anything like that long. There is no certain evidence that Charles IV and Blanche of Burgundy had any children until early 1314, a couple of months before the adultery scandal broke, and it is unclear when Blanche gave birth to the two children and possible that their son Philip, at least, was born while his mother was incarcerated at Château Gaillard. It is also possible that Charles and Blanche had two more children at some point, suggesting that their marital relationship continued after Blanche was imprisoned, though it may be that in fact the children were illegitimate, fathered by Charles with another woman or women. His brother Louis X fathered an illegitimate daughter called Endeline, whose mother (name unknown) was married to someone else, in the short period between Marguerite of Burgundy's death in April 1315 and Louis's wedding to Clemence of Hungary later that year.[2]

In September 1322, Charles IV married his second wife Marie of Luxembourg, daughter of the Holy Roman Emperor Henry of Luxembourg (d.1313); her brother John 'the Blind' was king of Bohemia, and would be killed fighting against Edward III of England at the battle of Crécy in 1346. Their marriage was a short one. In March 1324, while the royal couple were travelling in a coach, the unfortunate Marie fell out of the bottom. She went into premature labour and gave birth to a boy who died immediately, and herself died soon afterwards as well. Desperate for a son and heir, Charles married his third wife Jeanne of Evreux on 5 July in the same year.[3] As she was the daughter of Philip IV's half-brother Louis of Evreux (1276–1319), Philip III and Marie of Brabant's son, she was his first cousin, and almost certainly was only fourteen years old. Jeanne gave birth to their first daughter in the summer of 1325, a year after her wedding, and bore their second in the autumn of 1326, several months after she was rather belatedly crowned queen of France in May 1326.

Also in 1324, Charles went to war against his brother-in-law Edward II of England, a little-known and comparatively short-lived conflict between the two kingdoms known as the War of Saint-Sardos. Edward, unwilling to leave an England seething with unrest, made endless excuses for his failure to travel to France to pay homage and fealty to Charles IV for his duchy of Aquitaine as well as the county of Ponthieu in northern France that he had inherited from his Spanish mother Leonor of Castile and his French grandmother Jeanne of Ponthieu. Charles's brother Philip V had tolerated Edward's prevaricating and allowed almost four years to pass between his accession to the throne in 1316 and Edward's visit to Amiens to perform the ceremony in the summer of 1320, but Charles was a different kind of person, and, exasperated with his English brother-in-law, invaded the duchy of Aquitaine shortly after he married Jeanne of Evreux. His uncle Charles de Valois, who hated the English and had been heavily involved in the previous Anglo-French war in the 1290s, led the invasion. Charles IV also had to contend with renewed hostilities in the county of Flanders, though was on much better terms with the house of Luxembourg and in particular with his second wife Marie's nephew Wenzel, who grew up at Charles IV's court and was renamed Charles in his honour, and married the French king's cousin Blanche de Valois. Wenzel/Charles inherited his father John the Blind's kingdom of Bohemia in 1346, and became Holy Roman Emperor in 1355.

Isabella of France, queen of England, travelled to her homeland in March 1325, empowered to negotiate a peace settlement between her husband and her brother. Despite her close relationship to both men, this proved far from easy; Isabella sent a letter to Edward II a few weeks after her arrival complaining that her brother was being very difficult, and the matter was not settled until the summer of that year.[4] Isabella's experience stands in stark contrast to 1314, when she visited her and Charles's father Philip IV in and around Paris, and at her request he issued a number of documents in Edward II's favour.[5]

Edward sent his and Isabella's son Edward of Windsor to France in his place to pay homage to Charles IV for Aquitaine and Ponthieu in September 1325. With her son in her custody, Isabella felt confident enough to issue an ultimatum to her husband: that he must send Hugh Despenser the Younger, his chamberlain, 'favourite' and probably lover, and a man whom Isabella hated and feared, away from court, or Isabella and her son would not return. Edward II refused and left Isabella with little other option than to remain at her brother's court. Charles made her welcome for a few months until Isabella left France for the county of Hainault on France's northern border, where she arranged her son's future marriage to the count's daughter Philippa in exchange for money to provide ships and pay mercenaries. In the autumn of 1326 she invaded England, and, having killed the detested Hugh Despenser, brought down her husband – whether she had originally intended to or not – who abdicated in favour of their son in January 1327. The partly French Edward III, aged fourteen and the king of France's nephew, thus became king of England.

Charles IV died on 1 February 1328 at the age of thirty-three, and now all of Philip IV's sons had died at a comparatively young age, though Philip's daughter Queen Isabella, stronger and healthier than her brothers, outlived them all by decades and did not die until August 1358. Exactly two months after Charles's death, on 1 April 1328, his widow Jeanne of Evreux gave birth to their third daughter, Blanche. As had been the case with Louis X's posthumous son John I in 1316, if Blanche had been a boy, he would have become king of France from the moment of birth. Because, however, all three of Philip IV's sons left daughters but no living sons, the French throne passed to their cousin Philip de Valois, son of Philip IV's brother Charles de Valois (d. December 1325). Edward III of England also had a strong claim to become king of France, as he was, other than his younger brother John of Eltham (b.1316), the only living grandson of Philip IV. The French magnates, however, understandably preferred a Frenchman to succeed to the throne of France rather than the king of England, half-French though he might have been, and claimed that not only was it the case that a woman could not inherit the throne, she could not transmit a claim to her descendants either. Edward III officially claimed to be the rightful king of France in 1337 and thus began what we now know as the Hundred Years War, which did not end until 116 years later in 1453. Despite the interminable length of the conflict he created, and despite winning several notable victories over French armies, Edward never sat on the coveted throne of France, though he did reign as king of England for half a century. On his death in 1377, he was succeeded by his ten-year-old grandson Richard II, his eldest son the prince of Wales having died in 1376.

On 9 April 1328, just days after Philip VI became king of France, Marguerite de Brienne passed away. She was the dowager princess of Antioch and countess of Tripoli, the eldest daughter of the *Porphyrogennetos* Louis de Brienne and Agnès de Beaumont, and a granddaughter of Emperor John de Brienne. She was buried at Maubuisson Abbey near Paris, a house founded by Blanche of Castile (d.1252), queen consort of France and a kinswoman of the Brienne/Beaumonts, and the place where the disgraced Blanche of Burgundy had died two years earlier. An inscription on the countess's tomb stated 'Here lies Marguerite, daughter of my lord Louis son of the king of

Jerusalem, viscount of Beaumont, wife of my lord Bohemond, prince of Antioch and count of Tripoli, who passed away in the year of grace 1328, on Saturday 9 April'. Three of Marguerite's siblings outlived her: her sister Isabelle, Lady Vescy, and brothers Louis, bishop of Durham, and Henry, Lord Beaumont, all of whom used their mother's name and lived in England.[6]

As Philip VI de Valois was not the son of the late Juana I, queen regnant of Navarre, the Navarrese throne passed in 1328 to her granddaughter Jeanne/Juana II as the only living child of Juana I's eldest son Louis X of France and Navarre. Juana II's son Carlos II was born in 1332 and succeeded her in the kingdom of Navarre on her death in 1349, and is known to posterity as Carlos the Bad thanks to his constant flip-flopping between England and France during the early decades of the Hundred Years War. Carlos himself had an excellent claim to the French throne as the grandson of Philip IV's eldest son, but the ruler of a small and comparatively insignificant realm such as Navarre could not compete with the kings of France and England, both of them much larger and more powerful kingdoms. The Valois dynasty ruled France for more than two and a half centuries until the death of Henri III in 1589.

Philip VI of France was succeeded in 1350 by his son John II, who was captured by Edward III's eldest son Edward of Woodstock, prince of Wales, at the battle of Poitiers in 1356 and spent the remaining years of his life as a captive in England. The early years of the Hundred Years War were a family affair: Edward III's wife and Edward of Woodstock's mother was Philip VI's niece Philippa of Hainault, whose mother Jeanne de Valois was Philip's sister and was also an older half-sister of Catherine de Valois, Latin Empress of Constantinople. Catherine herself died in Naples in October 1346, a few weeks after her half-brother Philip lost the battle of Crécy to Edward III. Her eldest son Robert, king of Albania and prince of Taranto and Achaea, inherited her claim to *Romania*, the Latin Empire.

Part VI

Scotland

Dramatis Personae

William the Lion, b. *c.* early 1140s, king of Scotland 1165 to 1214; grandson of David I (d.1153); second son of Henry of Scotland (d.1152), earl of Northumbria and Huntingdon; younger brother and successor of Malcolm IV

Ermengarde de Beaumont, b. *c.*1170, queen consort of Scotland; marries William the Lion in 1186; daughter of Richard, viscount of Beaumont-au-Maine; aunt or great-aunt of Agnès de Beaumont, who marries the *Porphyrogennetos* Louis de Brienne (b. *c.*1230/32) in 1253

Alexander II, b.1198, king of Scotland 1214 to 1249; only son of William and Ermengarde; marries firstly Joan of England (b.1210), eldest daughter of King John and sister of Henry III, in 1221, and secondly Marie de Coucy in 1239

Marie de Coucy, b. *c.*1218, queen consort of Scotland, second wife of Alexander II and mother of Alexander III; daughter of Enguerrand, lord of Coucy; marries secondly the *Porphyrogennetos* John de Brienne the younger (b. *c.*1230/32) in 1257

Alexander III, b.1241, king of Scotland 1249 to 1286; only child of Alexander II and Marie de Coucy; marries Margaret of England in 1251 and secondly Yoleta de Dreux in 1285

Margaret of England, b.1240, queen consort of Scotland; eldest daughter of Henry III, king of England, and Alienor of Provence; sister of Edward I, king of England

Maighread of Scotland, b.1261, queen consort of Norway, daughter of Alexander III and Margaret of England; marries **Eirik Magnusson** (b.1268), king of Norway, in 1281

Alexander (b.1264) and **David** (b.1273) **of Scotland**; the younger children of Alexander III and Margaret of England

Margrete of Norway, b.1283, called 'the Maid of Norway'; titular queen regnant of Scotland 1286 to 1290; daughter of Maighread of Scotland and Eirik Magnusson; granddaughter and heir of Alexander III; great-granddaughter of Henry III; betrothed to Edward of Caernarfon in 1289

Yoleta de Dreux, b.1263, queen consort of Scotland by marriage to Alexander III; countess of Montfort in her own right; daughter of Robert, count of Dreux, and Beatrice, countess of Montfort; granddaughter of Jeanne de Châteaudun

John de Brienne the younger, b. *c*.1230/32, son of John de Brienne, Latin Emperor of Constantinople, and Berenguela of León; marries firstly Jeanne de Châteaudun in *c*.1251 and secondly Marie de Coucy, dowager queen of Scotland, in 1257; stepfather of Alexander III of Scotland and step-grandfather of Alexander's second wife Yoleta de Dreux

Jeanne de Châteaudun, b. *c*.1227, marries firstly John de Montfort, count of Montfort (d.1249) and secondly John de Brienne; mother of Beatrice, countess of Montfort, and Blanche de Brienne; maternal grandmother of Yoleta de Dreux, queen consort of Scotland

Blanche de Brienne, b. *c*.1252, only child of John de Brienne and Jeanne de Châteaudun, and her father's heir; stepsister of Alexander III of Scotland, and aunt of Yoleta de Dreux; grandmother of Roger Mortimer, earl of March (d.1330) and Margaret Wake, countess of Kent (d.1349), via her daughters Marguerite and Jeanne de Fiennes

David of Scotland, earl of Huntingdon (d.1219); younger brother of Malcolm IV (d.1165) and William the Lion (d.1214), kings of Scotland; uncle of Alexander II; father of Margaret and Isobel of Huntingdon

John I Balliol, lord of Galloway, king of Scotland, b. late 1240s; son of Devorguilla of Galloway and John Balliol (d.1268); maternal grandson of Margaret of Huntingdon; great-great-great-grandson of David I, king of Scotland (d.1153); father of **Edward Balliol** (b. early 1280s), claimant to the Scottish throne

Robert Bruce, lord of Annandale, b. *c.*1215; son of Isobel of Huntingdon; great-great-grandson of David I, king of Scotland; competitor to the Scottish throne 1290–92; marries Isabel de Clare, daughter of the earl of Gloucester

Robert Bruce, earl of Carrick, b.1243; son and heir of Robert and Isabel; marries Marjorie, countess of Carrick in her own right

Robert I Bruce, earl of Carrick, king of Scotland, b.1274; eldest son of Robert (b.1243) and Marjorie; marries firstly Isabella of Mar, daughter of the earl of Mar, and secondly Elizabeth de Burgh, daughter of the earl of Ulster; father of **David II Bruce** (b.1324), king of Scotland, by his second marriage; grandfather of **Robert II Stewart** (b.1316), king of Scotland, by his first

Henry III, king of England, b.1207; married to Alienor of Provence (b. *c.*1222); father-in-law of Alexander III

Edward I, king of England, b.1239; son of Henry and Alienor; brother-in-law of Alexander III; marries firstly Leonor of Castile and secondly Marguerite of France

Edward II, king of England, aka Edward of Caernarfon, b.1284, fourth but only surviving son of Edward I and Leonor; betrothed to Margrete of Norway in 1289; later marries Isabella of France

Chapter 31

The Red Fox Cub

In July 1174, the king of Scotland invaded the northeast of England, but was captured by English soldiers during the battle of Alnwick and was imprisoned for a few months in England and Normandy. He was William 'the Lion', younger brother and successor of Malcolm IV 'the Maiden' (d.1165). William had invaded England to lay claim to his earldom of Northumbria, which he had inherited from his brother, father and grandmother, but had been forced to give up to Henry II, king of England. In the Treaty of Falaise in December 1174, a few months after his capture, William was forced to concede that he held the realm of Scotland from the king of England and not directly from God, though Henry II's son Richard I Lionheart nullified the treaty in 1189 and absolved King William of his fealty and allegiance in exchange for 10,000 marks at a time when he was raising as much money as he could to pay for the Third Crusade.[1] The precedent was, however, to bedevil the future kings of Scotland, as numerous kings of England down the centuries claimed to be the rightful overlords of Scotland.

As part of the two kings' agreement in 1174, Henry II granted himself the right to choose William the Lion's bride, and selected a teenaged French noblewoman, Ermengarde de Beaumont (who was either the aunt or great-aunt of Agnès de Beaumont, who married the *Porphyrogennetos* Louis de Brienne a few decades later). The couple married at the English royal palace of Woodstock in Oxfordshire on 5 September 1186. Ermengarde's family, the viscounts of Beaumont-sur-Sarthe, are believed to have been descended from Constance, probably one of the many illegitimate children of Henry I, king of England (r.1100–35), the youngest son of William the Conqueror (r.1066–87). If this is indeed the case, then Ermengarde was a relative of Henry II, who was Henry I's grandson. She was, however, of rather low rank to be married to a king. Ermengarde bore William three daughters and one son, Alexander, who was born in August 1198; he succeeded his father as Alexander II of Scotland as a sixteen-year-old in December 1214. Ermengarde and William the Lion's daughters all lived in England, where they married Anglo-Norman noblemen and became countesses of Kent, Norfolk and Pembroke, though none of the three had children who lived past their teens. The eldest royal daughter, Margaret of Scotland, married Hubert de Burgh, earl of Kent, and her daughter Meggotta (or Magota) secretly married the heir to the earldom of Gloucester, Richard de Clare, in the mid-1230s when they were both in their early teens. Meggotta, however, died not long afterwards in 1237; had she had descendants, they would have had an excellent claim to the Scottish throne a few decades later when Alexander II's line ran out.[2]

In August 1216, Alexander II rode all the way from Scotland down to Dover to swear homage for the lands he had inherited in England to Louis, the future Louis VIII of France, who had invaded King John's realm some months earlier. John, however, died that October, Louis retreated to France a few months later, and ultimately, at York Minster in June 1221, Alexander married John's daughter Joan of England. Joan was not quite eleven years old at the time of her wedding to the Scottish king, and was the eldest daughter of John and his queen Isabelle of Angoulême, and the younger sister of Henry III. William the Lion had granted the rights to his son's marriage to King John a decade earlier.[3] Joan had originally been betrothed to Hugues X de Lusignan, count of La Marche, but her widowed mother Queen Isabelle decided to marry him instead, having been betrothed to his father before she married John in 1200. Alexander II, as heir to the Scottish throne, had been knighted by King John in person at Clerkenwell in March 1212 when he was thirteen and a half, and the English king called him a 'red fox cub' on account of his youth and bright red hair.[4] Alexander and his retinue travelled through Thirsk on their way south to York in June 1221, and on hearing that the thirteen-year-old Henry III had not yet arrived in the city, Alexander announced his intention to stay at Easingwold between Thirsk and York until the young king entered the city. He did not wish to be seen to wait for the other king as though he were Henry's vassal.[5] A little over two years after the royal wedding in York, another king travelled to England and met the young Henry III: John de Brienne, king of Jerusalem.

Alexander II and Joan of England's marriage produced no children and was apparently unhappy, and Queen Ermengarde lived until twelve years after their wedding with the result that Joan's influence on Scottish politics was negligible, a fact not aided by her extreme youth. While on a visit to her native England in 1237, two years after her sister married Emperor Friedrich

II von Hohenstaufen, Joan decided to remain there rather than returning to her husband's realm, and her brother Henry granted her some manors to live on. She died at the royal Essex manor of Havering-atte-Bower in March 1238 at only twenty-seven years old, supposedly in the arms of her brothers Henry and Richard of Cornwall, and was buried at Tarrant Abbey in Dorset. King Henry paid for a marble tomb and effigy for her and provided rich silk cloths to lie on her coffin.[6] Joan's sister Isabella, Holy Roman Empress and queen of Sicily, outlived her by less than four years and also died at age twenty-seven, and their affectionate brother Henry fed hundreds of poor people on the anniversaries of their deaths every year (calling Isabella 'empress of Almain', i.e. Germany).[7] Joan's rather brief life is reminiscent of another English Joan, queen of Scotland: her brother Henry's great-granddaughter Joan of the Tower. As a seven-year-old in 1328, this Joan married the four-year-old David Bruce, who succeeded his father as David II of Scotland a year later. Their marriage was also unhappy and childless and the couple were estranged for the last few years of Joan's life, and she died in her native England.

In May 1239, the year after Joan of England's death, Alexander II married the French noblewoman Marie de Coucy, daughter of Enguerrand, lord of Coucy, and their son and only surviving child Alexander was born in Roxburgh in early September 1241. The month after Alexander II and Marie's wedding, in June 1239, Lord Edward, sometimes known as Edward of Westminster after his birthplace, was born. He was the eldest child of Henry III and Alienor of Provence. Their second child Margaret was born in September 1240, a year before the birth of Alexander II and Queen Marie's son Alexander of Scotland, her future husband.

Chapter 32

The Young King of Scotland

Alexander II, called 'the renowned king of Scots' and 'a most gentle prince towards his people' by a chronicler, died in July 1249, two months before his son and successor Alexander III turned eight. Young Alexander was crowned as Alexander III by the bishop of St Andrews at Scone Abbey on 13 July, a week after his father's death.[1] During his long minority, two rival factions battled for power and for the right to govern the kingdom. One was led by Walter Comyn, who came from the most powerful noble family in thirteenth-century Scotland, and the other by Alan Durward, who had married the young king's half-sister Marjorie, illegitimate daughter of Alexander II. Alexander II's widow Marie de Coucy was not appointed as one of the regents for their son, and set off for a long visit to France, passing through England, in September 1250. Her visit to her homeland had much to do with the difficulties caused to her natal family by the death of her brother Raoul, lord of Coucy, who was killed at the battle of Fariskur in Egypt in April 1250 during Louis IX's crusade, a few weeks after the death of Louis's brother Robert of Artois at Damietta also in Egypt. Louis himself and his other two brothers, Alphonse of Poitiers and Charles of Anjou, were taken captive at Fariskur. Before she departed for her native France, Queen Marie and her young son attended the translation of the relics of Queen Margaret of Scotland, recently canonised by Pope Innocent IV, in Dunfermline on 19 June 1250. Margaret (d.1093) was a member of the English royal family displaced by the Norman Conquest, and married Malcolm Canmore, king of Scotland, in 1070. She was an ancestor of Alexander II and III via her son David I, king of Scotland (d.1153).[2]

At Christmas 1251, a royal wedding took place in York Minster, the same location where Alexander II had married Joan of England thirty years earlier. The bridegroom was Alexander III, then aged ten, and the bride was eleven-year-old Margaret of England, eldest daughter of Joan's brother Henry III and his queen Alienor of Provence. King Henry provided vast quantities of food for the guests: 68,500 loaves of bread, 60,000 herring, 10,000 haddock,

25,000 gallons of wine, 7,000 chickens and 170 boars, among much else. He promised to pay Alexander 5,000 silver marks as his daughter's dowry, and for himself and Queen Alienor bought robes, tunics, supertunics and cloaks of samite (expensive silk) lined with ermine and miniver (expensive furs). He also ordered three more robes of violet samite for himself with three leopards embroidered on the front and another three on the back.[3] Margaret's elder brother Lord Edward, the twelve-year-old heir to their father's throne, attended, as did her younger sister Beatrice, who was to marry into the duchy of Brittany in 1260, and her younger brother Edmund, later earl of Lancaster and Leicester and the ancestor of the Lancastrian branch of the English royal family. Henry III's brother Richard of Cornwall and his second wife Sancha of Provence, sister of the queens of France and England and the future queen of Sicily, and herself the future queen of Germany, were also there, as were Henry and Richard's only living sister Eleanor and her French husband Simon de Montfort, earl of Leicester. On the Scottish side, the wedding was attended by Alexander III's mother the dowager queen Marie de Coucy, who had returned to Scotland from an extended visit to France earlier in 1251, and his aunt Margaret of Scotland, dowager countess of Kent.[4] Alexander's wedding present from his parents-in-law was a new bed, while his new wife Margaret's gifts from Henry and Alienor were two saddles with 'ornate and becoming' reins, a gold cup and a gold chalice, and a 'rich and precious' bed.[5]

Henry III knighted his son-in-law on Christmas Day, using a sword, belt of knighthood and silver-gilt spurs procured by his son Edward, and the wedding took place the following day.[6] If Henry had expected the young Scottish king to be biddable, however, he was sorely mistaken. Though he was only ten years old, Alexander refused to swear homage to Henry as his overlord for the kingdom of Scotland, though he did so for the lands that he had inherited in England. After the wedding, the royal couple, young though they were, set out for Edinburgh, where they had guardians who took care of them. They did not live together as husband and wife for a few more years and conceived their first child in 1260 when they were both at the end of their teens, although they seem to have consummated their marriage in August 1255 when they were not quite fourteen and fifteen respectively.[7]

Alexander III had married into a very close family. Henry and his Provençal queen Alienor were loving parents who created remarkably strong bonds with all their children, and Alexander and Margaret were to spend much time with them over the years – though Alexander might not always have taken this as a positive, as his marriage into the English royal family gave the king of England an excuse to interfere in Scottish affairs. Queen Alienor, perhaps rather unexpectedly, became pregnant again in 1253, a good few years after the birth of her previous child, Edmund, in January 1245. Henry III asked Alexander and his regents if Margaret might return to England for a while for Alienor's 'solace and recreation' until her purification forty or so days after giving birth.[8] The queen of England gave birth to a daughter on the feast day of St Katherine, 25 November 1253, and named her after the saint, though sadly the little girl died at age three and a half. Henry and Alienor's teenage nephew Heinrich von Hohenstaufen, the late Empress Isabella's son, died in the same year.

According to the English chronicler Matthew Paris, a monk of St Albans, reports came to the ears of King Henry and Queen Alienor that their daughter and Scottish son-in-law were being kept apart by their guardians and that Margaret was ill and unhappy, almost a prisoner, and not allowed to have her own household or choose her own attendants. Henry and Alienor rode north in August 1255 to set things right, having first sent the earls of Gloucester and Albemarle, the provost of Beverley in Yorkshire and the steward of Henry's household to see to the 'reformation and amelioration of the condition of the king [Alexander] and M. his queen'. Henry himself declared in late August that he was 'about to approach the Scottish borders' to see Alexander and Margaret, 'according to the great desire of his heart' and 'bound by the link of paternal affection'. He further declared that he had no intention of harming Scottish liberties or doing anything prejudicial to Alexander III or his kingdom. The royal English couple stayed at Wark in Northumberland and the royal Scottish couple at Roxburgh, a few miles over the border.[9]

Alienor of Provence was ill at the time, or at least she claimed to be as an excuse for her eldest daughter to remain in England with her for a while after Alexander returned north. It might not have been wholly untrue, however, as decades later, Alienor told her son Edward that the climate of the north of England made her ill, and begged him not to take his young son there but to let him stay in the more temperate climate of the south.[10] During her stay in England with her parents in the autumn of 1255, Queen Margaret of Scotland probably had the chance to meet her Spanish sister-in-law Leonor of Castile, who married Edward in Burgos in November

1254 and arrived in England to great fanfare in October 1255. Leonor was accompanied to England by two of her seven older half-brothers: Don Sancho, future archbishop of Toledo, and Don Enrique, long a thorn in his brother Alfonso X's side, who would be captured a few years later at the battle of Tagliacozzo fighting for Konradin von Hohenstaufen against Charles of Anjou. Alexander III and Margaret visited England again in the summer of 1256, when Alexander would also have had the opportunity to meet Leonor, and spent the feast of the Assumption (15 August) at the royal palace of Woodstock.[11]

Chapter 33

Queen Marie and John de Brienne the Younger

Sometime before 6 June 1257, perhaps in September 1256 when she was given permission to travel through England on her way between Scotland and France, Alexander III's mother Marie de Coucy married her second husband. He was the *Porphyrogennetos* John de Brienne the younger, second or third son of John de Brienne, Latin Emperor of Constantinople and king of Jerusalem, and Berenguela of León. The younger John was called 'John of Acre, son of the king of Jerusalem' in Henry III's letters about him at this time (Emperor John de Brienne had been dead for twenty years by the time his son married the dowager queen of Scotland). John the younger's kinsman Louis IX made him butler of France around the time of his marriage to Marie de Coucy, while his older brother Alphonse, count of Eu, was appointed grand chamberlain of the kingdom. The Brienne brothers were reckoned among King Louis's most influential counsellors, and also spent much time in Spain in the 1250s with another of their royal kinsmen, Alfonso X of Castile-León.[1] As the city of Constantinople did not fall to Mikhael Palaiologos until 1261, John de Brienne's sister Marie and her husband Baudouin de Courtenay were still the reigning Latin Emperor and Empress of Constantinople at the time of his wedding to the king of Scotland's mother.

John de Brienne was about twelve or fourteen years younger than Marie de Coucy, and in 1257 was approximately twenty-five or twenty-seven to her approximately thirty-nine. It perhaps did not escape his attention that his father had also been married to a Queen Marie long before he was born; given that he was so often called John of Acre in his own lifetime, he must have been well aware of his father's career in the Latin Kingdom of Jerusalem and his marriage to Jerusalem's young queen regnant. John's first wife Jeanne de Châteaudun had died in 1254, leaving two daughters: Beatrice de Montfort from her first marriage and Blanche de Brienne, born around 1252, from her second. Beatrice was heir to her late father the count of Montfort (d.1249), and Blanche was heir to her father John. John apparently lived in Scotland for a while with Queen Marie, as in November 1258 he was named with Marie, the bishop of St Andrews, the earls of Menteith, Buchan and Mar and four other Scottish noblemen as the people who 'have assumed the government of Scotland'. Earlier in 1258 he had, as the 'son of King John of Acre, Emperor of Constantinople, and Empress Doña Berenguela', witnessed two Castilian court documents, and was named as count of Montfort, a title he continued to hold after Jeanne de Châteaudun's death. His two brothers were also there; Alphonse was called the *Conde Do*, i.e. the count of Eu, and Louis the *Conde de Belmont* or count of Beaumont.[2]

John was, therefore, closely involved with the governance of three European realms in the 1250s: Scotland, France, and Castile-León; a real achievement for a man who did not even turn thirty until the early 1260s. Something must have gone badly wrong in John de Brienne and Marie de Coucy's personal relationship, however. Marie and John had returned to France by the mid-1260s when her son Alexander III was well into his twenties and the father of two children, and a chronicler says that Marie, 'wife of John of Acre' (*uxor Johannis de Aconia*), 'fled from her husband' and 'came to Scotland from parts overseas' around this time.[3] The reason for Marie's flight from her homeland and her husband to the kingdom ruled by her son was not given, though the wording implies that something unpleasant had happened.

In the autumn of 1260, John de Brienne's stepson Alexander III and Queen Margaret visited her parents in England again. Margaret was expecting their first child, though might not have informed her husband how advanced her pregnancy was because she was determined to stay in her homeland with her mother Alienor until she gave birth. On 16 October 1260, Alexander III 'granted that his spouse should remain with her mother in England until her lying-in'. He was, however, concerned that a child who might be the next king of Scotland would be born in England, and that the infant might be used as a hostage or a means of leverage against him in some way. King Henry therefore promised his son-in-law that his daughter and her child would return to Scotland forty days after the birth (i.e. after Margaret's purification, which took place around forty days after childbirth). If Margaret died, Henry swore an oath that her child would be sent to Scotland, and if Alexander III died in the meantime – unlikely as he was only nineteen, but all eventualities had to be covered – Henry promised that the child would be given into the custody of any three or four from a group of four Scottish bishops, five earls and three barons named by Alexander. These oaths were also taken by Henry's brother Richard of Cornwall and son Edward, and a number of important England earls, barons and bishops.[4] In the end, the royal Scottish child was a girl, born at Windsor Castle at the end of February 1261. She was named Margaret after her mother, though is called Maighread in the Gaelic form here to avoid confusion.

In January 1264 Queen Margaret gave birth to a son, named Alexander after his father and heir to the Scottish throne from the moment of his birth, and a few years later in 1273 a second son, David. Her two older children Maighread and Alexander the younger kept in touch with their uncle Edward of England and sent him affectionate letters, while in June 1284 King Alexander III himself sent his brother-in-law a gift of four gerfalcons. Relations between Scotland and its larger southern neighbour were, at least at the highest level, more cordial in the thirteenth century than is often supposed, and the notion perpetuated by the Hollywood film *Braveheart* that the English occupied Scotland for most or all of the century is absolute nonsense.[5]

Alexander III and Margaret were in England in the autumn of 1269 to witness the ceremony of St Edward the Confessor's (d.1066) bones being moved into a shrine dedicated to him in Westminster Abbey, and also saw the consecration of the shrine and its chapel.[6] It took place on 13 October, St Edward's feast day, and the saint was a popular one in the English royal family; Margaret's brother Edward was named in his honour. A few months later, Edward and his younger brother Edmund of Lancaster set off on a crusade led by their uncle Louis IX of France, which was triggered by Sultan al-Zahir Baibars and the Mamluks' capture of important Frankish cities such as Antioch, Tyre and Beirut. Numerous English and Scottish noblemen also went. David Strathbogie, earl of Atholl, died in Tunis on 6 October 1270, less than three weeks before King Louis and Alphonse de Brienne, count of Eu, the older brother of Alexander III's stepfather, also died in Tunis. Adam, earl of Carrick, survived the Crusaders' attack on Tunis but died in Acre the following year, and his widow Marjorie later married another Scottish nobleman; her eldest son Robert Bruce, born in 1274, was to become king of Scotland in the early 1300s.[7]

The visit to Westminster in October 1269 was the last time that Queen Margaret would see her father. Henry III died on 16 November 1272 after a reign of fifty-six years, the fourth longest in English history after Elizabeth II, Victoria and George III. He was buried in the new chapel of St Edward the Confessor in Westminster Abbey. Edward succeeded him as king of England though was still in Outremer with his wife Leonor and his brother Edmund, and did not return to his kingdom until August 1274. His and Leonor's coronation took place that month, and King Alexander and Queen Margaret travelled all the way south to Westminster with a large retinue of Scottish nobility to attend.[8] Margaret was pregnant with her third child David at the time her father died, and surely to her great sorrow was therefore unable to travel south for his funeral.

Chapter 34

The Lord Had Shaken His Sword Against Him

The kings of Scotland owned lands in England, and Alexander now owed homage to Edward as his new overlord for them (as Edward himself owed homage to the kings of France for the duchy of Aquitaine he inherited from his father and great-grandmother Eleanor of Aquitaine). Alexander managed, however, to postpone the ceremony until October 1278, and at the same time attended the wedding of his (then late) wife's cousin Eleanor de Montfort to Llywelyn ap Gruffudd, prince of Wales. He also took the opportunity to visit the shrine of St Thomas Becket in Canterbury, as his stepfather's older brother Alphonse and their father Emperor John de Brienne had also done.[1] Alexander made a point of specifying during the ceremony of October 1278, as he had done as a ten-year-old at his wedding in December 1251, that he was performing homage to Edward only for the lands he held in England and not for his kingdom of Scotland. His grandfather William the Lion's feudal subjection to Edward I's great-grandfather Henry II gave subsequent English kings what they believed was a right to interfere in Scottish affairs and to act as overlord of the kingdom, and as the historian G.W.S. Barrow has pointed out, the thirteenth-century kings of England 'did not always behave as though they recognized the political independence of Scotland'.[2]

Margaret of England, queen of Scotland, died in February 1275, aged thirty-four, and whether coincidentally or not, her sister Beatrice, daughter-in-law of the duke of Brittany, died a month later at the age of thirty-two. The Lanercost chronicler in the far northwest of England wrote that Queen Margaret was 'a woman of great beauty, chastity, and humility'. He was, for some reason, far less impressed with Alexander III, talking frequently of his 'sins' and 'wrongdoing', and declared that 'the Lord had shaken His sword against him'. The chronicle portrays Alexander as a lecher who would visit 'matrons and nuns, virgins and widows, by day or by night as the fancy seized him' after he lost his wife in 1275.[3] There is no other evidence of this, and the king, unlike his father Alexander II and his grandfather William the Lion, is not known to have fathered any illegitimate children. It does not seem very likely that he ran his way through half the women in his kingdom, though as he did not marry again until a decade after Margaret's death, however, it would hardly seem surprising if he had some other relationships in the meantime. Lanercost's other remarks about Alexander also seem inaccurate as well as unfair.

In 1281, Alexander and Margaret's eldest child Maighread of Scotland married the young king of Norway, Eirik Magnusson.[4] Born sometime in 1268, he was seven years her junior and only at the start of his teens, and had succeeded his father Magnus Haakonsson on the throne in May 1280. Shortly before his death, King Magnus had written to Edward of England asking him to take his sons Eirik and Haakon under his protection. Maighread sailed to Bergen in August 1281, married Eirik, and was crowned queen of Norway at the end of that month.[5] Despite her husband's youth, Maighread became pregnant in the summer of 1282 and gave birth to a daughter, yet another Margaret, named Margrete here in the Norwegian form, in or not long before early April 1283.

Disaster struck the Scottish royal family in the early 1280s. King Alexander and the late Queen Margaret's youngest child David died at the age of eight in June 1281, their daughter the queen of Norway died in April 1283 after giving birth to her Norwegian daughter Margrete, and their elder son and heir Alexander the younger died just past his twentieth birthday in early 1284, married to a daughter of the count of Flanders, but childless. Called a 'gallant youth' by a chronicler, the young Alexander was buried at Dunfermline Abbey as his brother David already had been, both of them 'amid the boundless grief of the whole people, the tears and groans of all the clergy, and the endless sobs of the king and the magnates'.[6] Within a painfully short time frame, all three royal Scottish children were dead, and Alexander III's only heir was his infant granddaughter Margrete in Norway.

Alexander sent a letter in Latin to 'his most beloved brother' King Edward on 20 April 1284, five days before Queen Leonor gave birth to her youngest child, also Edward – who would be betrothed to Margrete of Norway a few years later – in Caernarfon, North Wales. (Edward I had recently conducted a successful campaign against Llywelyn ap Gruffudd, prince of Wales, who was killed in an ambush on 11 December 1282, the same day that the Byzantine

Emperor Mikhael VIII Palaiologos died.) Alexander thanked Edward for his sympathy over the 'grievous and unbearable trials and tribulations which we have suffered, and do suffer, from the death of our dear son, your beloved nephew', and reminded him that 'the daughter of your niece, of our beloved, the late queen of Norway' was now Alexander's heir apparent (*apparens heres nostra*). If a young girl were to sit on the Scottish throne, she would, as Alexander III's biographer has remarked, require the goodwill of Edward of England, and Alexander himself was only too aware of this. He was therefore at pains to point out the 'indissoluble bond' between himself and Edward, which 'between men who are faithful and constant, should never be broken'.[7]

Alexander had his granddaughter Margrete of Norway recognised as his heir on 5 February 1284 during a parliament held in Scone, only a week after his son's death and when the little girl was not even a year old.[8] Margrete was, however, hardly ideal as the future ruler of Scotland, being both female and foreign. The king, therefore, decided to remarry in the hope of fathering a son and heir; a male child from his second marriage would take precedence over his granddaughter. In the nine years between Margaret of England's death in 1275 and the death of their elder son in 1284, Alexander had not taken another wife, but now the issue was pressing, and as his father had, he chose a French noblewoman as his second wife. She was Yoleta or Yolande de Dreux, born in 1263 as the daughter of Robert, count of Dreux. Her mother was Beatrice de Montfort, only child of Jeanne de Châteaudun and her first husband the count of Montfort, and Yoleta was, therefore, the step-granddaughter of the *Porphyrogennetos* John de Brienne the younger – who, confusingly, was also Alexander III's stepfather. The Lanercost chronicler, a harsh critic of Alexander for reasons which are not entirely clear, sniped at Yoleta as well, claiming that she had intended to become a nun, but 'altered her mind with the levity of a woman's heart and through ambition for a kingdom'.[9]

Chapter 35

The Great Cause

Yoleta de Dreux and Alexander III wed at Jedburgh Abbey in the late autumn of 1285, but their marriage was doomed to be a short one. Mere months later, on 19 March 1286, Alexander made the fateful decision to ride from Edinburgh to Kinghorn in Fife to visit Yoleta during a terrible storm. After crossing the River Forth by ferry, the king became separated from his attendants in the dark, wind and rain, and fell from his horse. The following morning, the king of Scotland was found dead at the bottom of an embankment. Alexander outlived Charles of Anjou, king of Sicily, Pere III, king of Aragón, and Philip III, king of France, by only a few months; the period from January 1285 to March 1286 saw the deaths of no fewer than four western European kings (and Alfonso X of Castile-León had died in April 1284). Alexander's stepfather the *Porphyrogennetos* John de Brienne the younger survived him by a decade. Born in September 1241, Alexander III was still only forty-four when he died, and his unexpected death was a tragedy for Scotland that was to usher in a long period of uncertainty and conflict with England. Chronicler John Fordun lamented 'How worthy of tears, and how hurtful, his death was to the kingdom of Scotland, is plainly shown forth by the evils of after times'.[1]

For a while in 1286 there remained the hopeful possibility that Queen Yoleta might be carrying her late husband's child, and according to the Lanercost chronicle, 'she, resorting to feminine craft, was pretending to be pregnant'. Supposedly, the queen carried on the pretence for so long that she even claimed to have given birth and 'contrived to have the son of a play-actor' smuggled into her residence at Stirling Castle. Given the chronicler's intense dislike of Alexander and Yoleta, however, it seems highly unlikely that this story bears any resemblance to reality, though it may be that Yoleta was indeed pregnant at the time of Alexander's accident and miscarried. G.W.S. Barrow correctly states that the Lanercost chronicle is 'deeply imbued with a pathological misogyny' and that its tale of Yoleta's fake pregnancy cannot be trusted.[2] Had the dowager queen borne a son, he would have become king of Scotland from the moment of birth, but as it was, Alexander's only heir was his toddler granddaughter Margrete, known to history as 'the Maid of Norway'. Around late April 1286, at a parliament held at Scone, the Scottish magnates swore to preserve the realm for the little girl, just three years old.[3] Yoleta departed from Scotland, having been its queen for less than half a year, and some years later married her second husband Arthur II, duke of Brittany. Duke Arthur had children from his first marriage, including his son and heir John III, born in 1286, and had another family with Yoleta in the 1290s; this was to lead to the War of the Breton Succession when Yoleta's stepson Duke John III died childless in 1341.[4]

In the summer of 1286, a few months after his Scottish brother-in-law's death, Edward I and Queen Leonor departed from England, firstly to swear homage to eighteen-year-old Philip IV for Edward's French lands, and secondly to negotiate between France and Aragón over Charles of Salerno (see Part 4 above). His cousin Edmund, earl of Cornwall, son of Richard of Cornwall and Sancha of Provence, acted as regent. On his return in 1289, Edward arranged the marriage of his only living son and heir Edward of Caernarfon, born in April 1284 and then aged five, to his (Edward I's) six-year-old great-niece the Maid of Norway. The following year, the young girl set off from her homeland to the kingdom she had never seen.

Sadly, Margrete died in Orkney on or about 26 September 1290 at just seven years old, during her journey. Her body was returned to Bergen to be buried alongside her mother.[5] Had she lived long enough to marry Edward of Caernarfon, the future king of England, British history would look very different, and the couple would also have had a strong claim to the Norwegian throne on the death of Margrete's father King Eirik in 1299. News of her death was slow to travel; on 7 October 1290, the bishop of St Andrews informed Edward I in a letter that he had heard rumours of her death and that the realm of Scotland was troubled as a result, but that he could not yet confirm them.[6] Margrete's fiancé Edward of Caernarfon was betrothed to two other girls in the 1290s before his final engagement to Philip IV of France's daughter Isabella, his future queen, at the end of the century.

Alexander III's descendants were now all dead, and adjudicators were appointed to determine who had the best claim to become Scotland's next king. Except for his illegitimate half-sister Marjorie, Alexander III had no siblings. Of his father Alexander II's three sisters, only one had a child, Meggotta de Burgh, and she had died childless all the way back in 1237. The adjudicators thus had to go back through several generations of the Scottish royal family, and the whole matter became rather complex. Alexander II's father William the Lion had an older brother, Malcolm IV 'the Maiden', king of Scotland, who died childless, and a younger brother, David of Scotland, earl of Huntingdon, who died in 1219.[7] David had one son who lived into adulthood, John the Scot, earl of Huntingdon and Chester, who died without issue in 1237, and three daughters who had children. In the early 1290s, the men with the strongest claim to the Scottish throne were the descendants of these daughters, and it came down to a straight battle between two men: John Balliol, lord of Galloway (b. late 1240s), maternal grandson of David of Scotland's eldest daughter, Margaret; and the elderly Robert Bruce, lord of Annandale (b. *c.*1215/20), son of David's second daughter, Isobel. Balliol claimed by primogeniture as the descendant and heir of the eldest daughter, and Bruce by nearness of blood, as he was David of Scotland's grandson, not a great-grandson as Balliol was, and therefore a generation closer. Furthermore, as the son of Alexander II's cousin Isobel, it is possible that Bruce had been considered heir presumptive to the Scottish throne between the death of John the Scot, earl of Huntingdon and Chester, in 1237 and the birth of Alexander II's son and heir Alexander III in 1241.[8]

The man with the third-best claim was the English baron John Hastings (b.1262), grandson of David of Scotland's youngest daughter Ada, while Floris V, count of Holland (b.1254), also had a plausible claim: his great-great-grandmother was David of Scotland's sister. Most of the other claimants to the throne were descended through an illegitimate line. The English baron William Vescy (b.1245), for example, brother-in-law of the *Porphyrogennetos* Louis de Brienne's daughter Isabelle de Beaumont, was the grandson of one of William the Lion's illegitimate daughters; another English baron, William Ros, was the great-grandson of another of William the Lion's illegitimate daughters; and the Scottish baron Nicholas Soulis was the grandson of Marjorie, illegitimate daughter of Alexander II and older half-sister of Alexander III. King Eirik Magnusson of Norway also put in a claim, not by right of descent but as the father of the late Margrete, the Maid.

The Guardians of Scotland asked Edward I, ruler of their powerful neighbour, to help judge the matter, though the death in November 1290 of Leonor, the Spanish queen of England and aunt of the reigning king of Castile-León, Sancho IV, delayed proceedings. Finally, in November 1292, Edward and the other adjudicators chose John Balliol as the grandson of

David of Scotland's eldest daughter Margaret in preference to Robert Bruce, even though primogeniture had never previously applied in Scotland or England to female heirs; in the absence of a male heir, they were entitled to equal portions of an inheritance. On the other hand, as recently as April 1290, Edward I had issued a document declaring that if he and his only living son Edward of Caernarfon died without male heirs, the kingdom of England would belong to his eldest daughter Eleanor (b.1269), then betrothed to Alfonso III of Aragón. Clearly, there was an idea that a kingdom was not divisible in the same way that a magnate's inheritance might be, and belonged by right to the eldest daughter if there were no son.[9] The Balliol decision was almost certainly the correct and most supported one, even if the Bruce family did not see it that way.

John Balliol was duly crowned king of Scotland at the end of November 1292. His mother Devorguilla of Galloway (d.1290) was the wealthy daughter and heir of Alan, lord of Galloway and his royal wife Margaret of Scotland and Huntingdon, and his father John Balliol the elder (d.1268) was a partly English, partly French nobleman who founded one of the first colleges at Oxford University in *c.*1263, still called Balliol College. King John Balliol was the youngest of his parents' four sons, but his three older brothers all died in the 1270s. In 1281, he married the English noblewoman Isabel de Warenne, daughter of the earl of Surrey, and their son, born *c.*1283, was called Edward. As this name was all but unknown in Scotland at the time and was rare even in England, it seems likely that Edward I of England, Isabel de Warenne's cousin, was the boy's godfather.

Chapter 36

Toom Tabard

In 1294, Edward I went to war against his kinsman Philip IV of France, and the cordial relations between England and France that had been fostered since the 1240s ended abruptly. It began with a quarrel between English sailors and sailors from Normandy that resulted in the English sailors attacking La Rochelle, and after Philip IV sent Edward rather peremptory and rude letters ordering him to appear in Paris to explain himself, Edward sent his brother Edmund of Lancaster to Paris instead to try to resolve the matter. This seemed an excellent idea, as Edmund's wife Blanche of Artois was King Philip's mother-in-law, and at first Edmund thought that he had sorted it all out, but to his horror Philip confiscated all of King Edward's French territories permanently, and thus England and France found themselves at war.[1]

John Balliol, king of Scotland, allied with Philip IV against Edward I, and Edward thus invaded Scotland in the spring of 1296. At the battle of Stirling Bridge in September 1297, William Wallace and Andrew Moray defeated the English army led by John de Warenne, earl of Surrey, who happened to be John Balliol's father-in-law. Contrary to the film *Braveheart*, the pretext of which is that England had occupied Scotland for about a century by this point, fewer than eighteen months passed between Edward I's invasion of the kingdom and the emergence of William Wallace as an important military leader in Scotland. One of the opening scenes of the film shows Edward I having a group of Scottish nobles massacred in 1280, a year when Edward's brother-in-law Alexander III was very much alive and had his kingdom well under control.

In the same year as Edward of England's invasion of Scotland and capture of its king, the late Alexander III's stepfather John de Brienne died (John's wife, the dowager queen Marie de Coucy, had died in 1284 or 1285, a year or two before her son the king). John de Brienne had no children in Scotland, but at the time of his death in 1296 was great-grandfather to two English children who would have a large impact on fourteenth-century history: Roger

Mortimer of Wigmore, born in 1287, who played a vital role in the downfall of Edward II in 1326/27; and Margaret Wake, born in the mid-1290s, who in late 1325 married her second husband, Edward II's half-brother Edmund, earl of Kent, and was the mother of Joan of Kent, princess of Wales, and the grandmother of Richard II, king of England. In Paris in October 1294, calling himself 'Jehan, son of King Jehan of Jerusalem, butler of France', John had paid for masses to be said at the church of St Paul in Paris for the souls of 'our father, King Jehan of Jerusalem and Emperor of Constantinople, and Lady Berangiere [Berenguela], his wife, our mother', as well as for his own soul after he died. He did not mention either of his late wives, Jeanne de Châteaudun or Marie de Coucy, any of his siblings, his daughter Blanche or his grandchildren and great-grandchildren.[2]

John Balliol spent several months in flight around his kingdom, trying to evade Edward I, though eventually he was captured and forced to submit to the English king in July 1296, then forced to abdicate his throne. Balliol subsequently spent a while under house arrest in England and in captivity at the Tower of London, though he was allowed to go to the Continent in 1299. He was derisively known as *Toom Tabard* or 'Empty Jacket': his surcoat carried a blazon of the royal arms of Scotland, which was torn off and thrown to the floor to humiliate him and to make clear that he was now king of nothing and nobody.[3] He died in exile in 1314; his son Edward was also held in the Tower of London until 1299, then released into the custody of his English grandfather John de Warenne, earl of Surrey (d.1304). Decades later, in the early 1330s, Edward Balliol claimed the throne of Scotland with the aid of Edward I's grandson Edward III of England, though unsuccessfully. Another of Balliol's allies was Henry de Beaumont, son of the *Porphyrogennetos* Louis de Brienne.

John Comyn (b. *c.* mid-1270s), lord of Badenoch and known as 'the Red Comyn', was a nephew of John Balliol and one of the Guardians of Scotland. Badenoch was stabbed to death by his rival Robert Bruce, earl of Carrick, in a Dumfries church in February 1306, and with his most powerful enemy out of the way, Bruce moved to have himself crowned king of Scotland the following month. Badenoch's three children moved to England, their mother Joan de Valence's homeland; his only son Sir John Comyn married Margaret Wake, great-granddaughter of the *Porphyrogennetos* John de Brienne the younger.[4] Isobel MacDuff, countess of Buchan, exercised the hereditary right of her natal family the MacDuffs by crowning Robert Bruce as king at

Scone Abbey. A furious Edward I exacted harsh revenge on Bruce's family and supporters. Three of his four younger brothers were executed, as were several of his brothers-in-law including the earl of Atholl, while his wife Elizabeth de Burgh, Marjorie, his daughter from his first marriage, two of his sisters, and his underage nephew Donald of Mar were imprisoned in England. Robert's sister Mary Bruce was imprisoned in Roxburgh Castle and placed in the custody of Louis de Brienne's son Henry de Beaumont and his wife Alice Comyn, the niece and co-heir of Isobel MacDuff's husband the earl of Buchan (who, unlike Isobel herself, was an enemy of Robert Bruce).[5] After Bruce defeated Edward II's forces at the battle of Bannockburn in 1314, Edward was forced to release all the Scottish prisoners in England, though Isobel MacDuff appears to have been dead by then.

Robert Bruce, one of the great Scottish heroes of history, spent years consolidating his position as king, gaining allies, and capturing the English-held castles in his kingdom then destroying them so they could not be retaken. His defeat of Edward II and his huge army at the battle of Bannockburn in June 1314 is probably Scotland's most famous military victory ever, and the Declaration of Arbroath in 1320, sent to Pope John XXII by the Scottish barons and the community of the realm, stated passionately that 'As long as but a hundred of us remain alive, never will we under any conditions be brought under English rule'.[6] In 1327 after Edward II's deposition, Edward's wife Isabella of France, ruling England in the name of their underage son Edward III, sealed a peace settlement with Robert and recognised him as king of Scotland.

Robert died in his mid-fifties in 1329 and was succeeded by his young son David II Bruce (b.March 1324), who had married the partly English, partly French Joan of the Tower (b.July 1321), youngest child of Edward II and Queen Isabella, the previous year. David and Joan had no children and David had none with his second wife Margaret Drummond either, so on his death in 1371, he was succeeded by his nephew Robert II. Robert was the son of Robert I Bruce's daughter Marjorie and her husband Walter the Steward, and was, as Marjorie was three decades her half-brother David's senior, eight years older than his uncle. He was the first king of the house of Stewart, later Stuart, which was to rule Scotland and then England for centuries.

Part VII
England

Dramatis personae

Louis de Brienne, b. *c.*1230/32, *Porphyrogennetos*; son of John de Brienne, Latin Emperor of Constantinople, and Berenguela of León; half-brother of Yolande de Brienne, queen of Jerusalem; father of Isabelle, Louis and Henry de Beaumont, and John, Marguerite, Marie and Jeanne de Brienne; ancestor of the English Beaumonts

Agnès de Beaumont, marries Louis de Brienne in 1253, and mother of his children; daughter or granddaughter and heir of Raoul VIII, viscount of Beaumont-sur-Sarthe; niece or great-niece of William the Lion and Ermengarde de Beaumont, king and queen of Scotland, and cousin of Alexander II, king of Scotland (r.1214–49)

Isabelle de Beaumont, Lady Vescy, b. *c.*1260s; second daughter of Louis de Brienne and Agnès de Beaumont, and uses her mother's name; moves to England *c.*1279/80 when she marries **John Vescy,** b.1244

Louis de Beaumont, b. *c.*1271, son of Louis de Brienne and Agnès de Beaumont, and brother of Isabelle, Lady Vescy; joins the Church and moves to England in or shortly after the mid-1280s; elected bishop of Durham in 1317

Henry de Beaumont, titular earl of Buchan, b. *c.* late 1270s or early 1280s; son of Louis de Brienne and Agnès de Beaumont, and brother of Lady Vescy and Louis, bishop of Durham; moves to England as a child in or before 1290; marries Alice Comyn in 1310, and ancestor of the English Beaumonts

Alice Comyn, b.1296/97, niece and co-heir of John Comyn, earl of Buchan (d.1308); marries Henry de Beaumont in 1310

Isabella de Beaumont, b. *c.*1315/20, duchess of Lancaster, countess of Derby, Leicester and Lincoln; second daughter of Henry and Alice; marries Henry of Grosmont in 1330; mother of Blanche of Lancaster, duchess of Lancaster (b.1342)

John de Beaumont, b.1317/18, son and heir of Henry and Alice, and Isabella's brother; marries Eleanor of Lancaster in 1330; ancestor of the English Beaumonts

Marguerite de Brienne, sister of Isabelle, Louis and Henry de Beaumont; eldest daughter of Louis de Brienne and Agnès de Beaumont; marries **Bohemond VII of Antioch**, count of Tripoli and titular prince of Antioch, b. *c.*1260, grandson of Zabel, queen regnant of Armenian Cilicia, in 1278

Henry of Lancaster, earl of Lancaster and Leicester, b. *c.*1280/81; grandson of Henry III and nephew of Edward I; younger half-brother of Juana I, queen regnant of Navarre, and great-grandson of Louis VIII of France; marries Maud Chaworth in 1297; father-in-law of Isabella de Beaumont and her brother John de Beaumont

Henry of Grosmont, b. *c.*1310/12, son and heir of Henry of Lancaster; first duke of Lancaster, earl of Leicester, Derby and Lincoln; marries Isabella de Beaumont in 1330

Edward I, b.1239, king of England 1272 to 1307; son of Henry III, grandson of King John and great-nephew of Richard Lionheart; marries firstly **Leonor of Castile**, b.1241, niece of Berenguela of León, Latin Empress of Constantinople, and secondly **Marguerite of France**, b.1278/79, daughter of Philip III and granddaughter of Louis IX

Edward II, b.1284, king of England 1307 to 1327; son of Edward I and Leonor; nephew of Alfonso X *el Sabio*, king of Castile-León; second cousin of the Brienne/Beaumont siblings; marries Isabella of France in 1308

Isabella of France, b. *c.*1295, queen consort of England; daughter of Philip IV, king of France, and Juana I, queen regnant of Navarre; niece of Henry of Lancaster (b. *c.*1280/81)

Edward III, b.1312, king of England 1327 to 1377, son of Edward II and Isabella; marries Philippa of Hainault in 1328

Philippa of Hainault, b. *c*.1314, queen consort of England; daughter of Willem, count of Hainault and Holland; granddaughter of Charles, count of Valois (b.1270) and great-niece of Philip IV of France; niece of Philip VI

John of Gaunt, b.1340, second duke of Lancaster, earl of Richmond, Lincoln, Leicester and Derby; third eldest surviving son of Edward III and Queen Philippa

Blanche of Lancaster, b.1342, younger daughter and ultimately the sole heir of Henry of Grosmont and Isabella de Beaumont; great-granddaughter of the *Porphyrogennetos* Louis de Brienne; marries John of Gaunt in 1359; mother of Henry IV, king of England, and Philippa of Lancaster, queen consort of Portugal

Henry de Beaumont, b. *c*. late 1339; only child of John de Beaumont and Eleanor of Lancaster, and the Beaumont heir; marries Margaret, daughter of John de Vere (b.1312), earl of Oxford; ancestor of the later English Beaumonts

Chapter 37

The Brienne/Beaumonts Move to England

A grand royal wedding took place in Reading Abbey on 19 May 1359, attended by the king and queen of England, Edward III and Philippa of Hainault, and the king and queen of Scotland, David II Bruce and Edward III's sister Joan of the Tower. The groom was John of Gaunt, aged nineteen, the fourth (but third eldest surviving) son of King Edward and Queen Philippa, and the bride was Blanche of Lancaster, aged seventeen, younger daughter and co-heir of Henry of Grosmont, the partly royal first duke of Lancaster and earl of Leicester, Derby and Lincoln. John and Blanche received valuable gifts from the royal guests, and afterwards John, his father and his brothers took part in a jousting tournament at Smithfield in London.[1] Eight years after they married, John and Blanche became the parents of a baby boy named Henry, a future king of England, and their eldest child, born in March 1360 and named after her grandmother and godmother Queen Philippa, would marry João I, king of Portugal.

Another of those present at the royal wedding was Isabella de Beaumont, who was the mother of the bride, the first English duchess in history, and the great-granddaughter of John de Brienne, Latin Emperor of Constantinople and king of Jerusalem. Isabella's father Henry de Beaumont (d.1340) was one of the seven or eight children of the *Porphyrogennetos* Louis de Brienne, youngest or second youngest child of Emperor John and Berenguela of León. Louis married the French heiress Agnès de Beaumont, viscountess of Beaumont-sur-Sarthe and lady of Loué, La Flèche, L'Aigle, Fresnay, Sainte-Suzanne and du Lude, on 12 February 1253 when he was about twenty-one.[2] Agnès's exact parentage is uncertain, though she was either a daughter of Raoul de Beaumont (d.1237), and if so, must have born late in his life decades after his other children, or a daughter of one of his sons. Three of Agnès and Louis's children adopted their mother's last name and moved to England: Isabelle, probably their second daughter, and their sons Louis and Henry. The other siblings remained in France and used their father's name.

The Brienne/Beaumont siblings were born over a period of many years and at widely spaced intervals. Marguerite de Brienne, countess of Tripoli, was old enough to marry Bohemond VII of Antioch-Tripoli in 1278; Isabelle de Beaumont, the second daughter, married in 1279 or 1280; Louis de Beaumont was probably born in 1271; and Henry de Beaumont was born around the late 1270s or early 1280s, twenty-five or thirty years after his parents' wedding. Some of the siblings probably spent part of their childhoods in Spain, and might have been born there rather than in France: the *Porphyrogennetos* Louis de Brienne witnessed documents issued by his cousin Alfonso X of Castile and León in November 1264, March 1265, December 1266, July 1268, November 1271, and April and December 1272. His brother John, count of Montfort and stepfather of the reigning king of Scotland, Alexander III, witnessed all the same documents.[3] Neither Louis nor John de Brienne witnessed any royal Castilian documents after December 1272, and presumably returned to their native France.

In 1279 or 1280, Leonor of Castile, queen of Edward I of England and the niece of Berenguela of León, Latin Empress of Constantinople, arranged her kinswoman Isabelle de Beaumont's marriage to John, Lord Vescy. Born on 18 July 1244, a baron of Northumberland, a grandson of the earl of Derby, and a close friend of King Edward and Queen Leonor, Vescy was much Isabelle's senior and in his mid-thirties at the time of their wedding. He was the widower of the Italian noblewoman Agnese di Saluzzo, who had died *c.*1265, and evidently was in no great rush to marry again even though he and Agnese had no children. John died in Montpellier on 10 February 1289; he and Isabelle had no children either, and John's heir was his brother William (b.1245). Isabelle did not marry again in the remaining four and a half decades of her life. John de Vescy's heart was buried at the Blackfriars' church in London with the heart of King Edward and Queen Leonor's third son Alfonso of Bayonne (1273–84), godson and nephew of Alfonso X of Castile-León. Leonor's own heart was also buried there after her death in late 1290.[4] Isabelle, Lady Vescy, spent the remainder of her long life in England rather than returning to her native France, and in 1305 was appointed custodian of Bamburgh Castle on the northeast coast of England.[5] For a woman to be appointed to such a position was unprecedented and speaks volumes about Edward I's trust and liking for his late wife's cousin.

Isabelle's younger brother Louis de Beaumont, at the beginning of a long and successful career in the Church, followed her to England. Louis was said to be twenty years old in 1291 and therefore was born *c*.1271, perhaps in Castile, where their father Louis de Brienne spent part of that year.[6] Louis de Beaumont was made a canon of York in 1285 so might have been in England then, though these positions did not always require residency, and he was probably only fourteen years old then. By 1291 he was treasurer of Salisbury Cathedral; by 1308 he was also canon of Le Mans in his native France; and in 1317 he would be elected to a bishopric in the north of England.[7] The Lanercost chronicler, also resident in the north of England, stated that Louis was 'a Frenchman of noble birth, but lame in both feet, nevertheless liberal and agreeable'. The royal clerk and chronicler Adam Murimuth also wrote that Louis was lame in both feet (*claudus utroque pede* in the Latin original) and added the rather xenophobic comment 'as are many Frenchmen'.[8] Most unfortunately for a man in his position, Louis de Beaumont struggled endlessly to read or understand Latin. On one occasion he stumbled over the word *Metropoliticae*, and finally said, in his native French, *Seit pour dite* or 'Take it as said'. He then came to *In Aenigmate*, and exclaimed 'By Saint Louis, he who wrote this word was not courteous'.[9] One wonders if Louis managed to master any English during the forty-plus years that he lived in England, even if Latin was beyond him.

At an uncertain date in or before April 1290, Henry de Beaumont, Isabelle and Louis's brother and probably the youngest child of the *Porphyrogennetos* Louis de Brienne and Agnès de Beaumont, moved to England as well. He was perhaps not even born when his sister Isabelle married John de Vescy, and was still very young in 1290 when Edward I's wardrobe accounts referred to him as a 'child' and a 'boy'. King Edward gave Henry money for his expenses in April/May 1290 as he was ill, and he had to be left behind in Winchester when the royal court left there. Henry received just under 40 shillings for his food, bread, wine and hay and oats for his horses. He was still unwell a few months later in mid-November 1290, and was staying in Laxton, Nottinghamshire with a carer named Arnold Comound.[10] The royal court was also in Laxton at the time, and Queen Leonor died in nearby Harby on 28 November. Presumably the Beaumont siblings attended their kinswoman's funeral in Westminster Abbey on 17 December. Of the fourteen or more children Leonor had borne, only six outlived her: her daughters Eleanor, Joan, Margaret, Mary and Elizabeth, and her youngest child, only surviving son and heir Edward of Caernarfon, six years old in 1290 and not much younger than Henry de Beaumont. Queen Leonor's mother-in-law Alienor of Provence, the dowager queen and widow of Henry III, outlived her and died in June 1291; Alienor's older sister Marguerite, widow of Louis IX of France, lived even longer and did not die until late 1295. When Marguerite died, her grandson Philip IV was at war with her nephew Edward I.

It was perhaps Isabelle, Lady Vescy, who decided that it would be a good idea for her little brother Henry to move to England in 1290, though their parents Louis de Brienne and Agnès de Beaumont were still alive and must have consented. The decision for young Henry to make a home in England would result in many generations of the Beaumont family in that country, and Henry de Beaumont was the great-grandfather of King Henry IV and an English-born queen of Portugal, Philippa of Lancaster.

The Brienne/Beaumont family had numerous connections to Scotland, and it was there that Henry de Beaumont would spend much of his career from the 1290s to the 1330s. Henry was present on 14 March 1296 when a number of Scottish nobles submitted to Edward I, four months before John Balliol's forced abdication. A knight named Sir John Cambus did not perform homage to the English king on this occasion, because, according to a note in the margin of the document recording this event, he was 'challenged by Sir H. de Beaumont'. Henry was, therefore, already a knight by March 1296, and he joined Edward I's household as a knight in or before 1297.[11] He was possibly still a teenager, or perhaps in his early twenties at most.

Probably in 1297, though the date is uncertain, Isabelle de Vescy and Henry de Beaumont's father Louis de Brienne the *Porphyrogennetos* died at the age of about sixty-five, leaving his widow Agnès de Beaumont, who died in the early 1300s. Given that Louis was born as the son of a reigning Emperor and had the most illustrious family connections imaginable, it is rather sad that we do not know the date of his death. He was the last survivor of Emperor John de Brienne's children, his brother John having died the year previously in 1296, his siblings Alphonse and Empress Marie in the 1270s, and his older half-sister Queen Yolande of Jerusalem as far back as 1228.

Chapter 38

In the New King's Favour

Edward I died at the age of sixty-eight on 7 July 1307 and was succeeded by his eldest living son Edward of Caernarfon, prince of Wales, duke of Aquitaine, earl of Chester and count of Ponthieu (he also left two young sons from his second marriage to Philip IV of France's half-sister Marguerite). Edward, as the maternal grandson of Fernando III, king of Castile and León, was the second cousin of the Brienne/Beaumont siblings and seems to have been very fond of them. In September 1307, Edward gave Henry de Beaumont three manors in Lincolnshire: Folkingham, Edenham and Barton.[1] Henry received a licence to crenellate Folkingham in April 1312, and rebuilt a castle there which had originally been built in the twelfth century.[2] Sadly, Folkingham Castle was already a ruin in the sixteenth century, and nothing remains of it now except earthworks. It stood on a rectangular island surrounded by a moat, with a larger moat outside which enclosed a large area.[3] Edward II confirmed his father's appointment of Isabelle, Lady Vescy, as constable of Bamburgh Castle in Northumberland in November 1307, and she had probably been in his company on 30 October when he ordered an inquisition into an attack on her servants in Yorkshire.[4] Edward II married Isabella of France, only surviving daughter of Philip IV and the late Juana I of Navarre, in January 1308, and Lady Vescy and her brother Henry travelled together to their homeland with Edward to attend his wedding. Lady Vescy became one of the young queen's chief attendants, alongside Edward's eldest niece Eleanor, Lady Despenser.[5]

Edward alienated many of his earls and barons in 1308 with his excessive favouritism towards Piers Gaveston, a nobleman of Gascony who was his close friend and probably his lover, and in June that year was forced to send Gaveston out of England, though he returned a year later. Within a few months of his accession, the young king had already brought his realm to the brink of civil war. Henry de Beaumont was one of the few barons who remained staunchly loyal to Edward during the crisis year of 1308, and was rewarded by being jointly appointed, with the earl of Angus and Sir William

Ros, 'to guard this side of the Scottish sea, between Berwick[-on-Tweed] and the water of Forth'.[6] Henry was appointed constable of Roxburgh Castle in Scotland on 23 February 1310, and its constable for life on 21 March. He went to reside there with sixty armed men.[7] Roxburgh overlooked the Tweed and Teviot rivers and stood close to Scotland's border with England, and was often in English hands. During Edward I's ferocious campaign against Robert Bruce and his relatives and followers in 1306/07, the king had captured and imprisoned several of Bruce's female relatives and supporters. One of them was Bruce's sister Mary, held captive in a wooden or iron cage on the walls of Roxburgh Castle and thus, horribly, visible to public view and exposed to the elements. Edward II ordered Henry on 30 March 1310 to release Mary Bruce, who was to be exchanged for Walter Comyn, an ally of the English king held prisoner by Mary's brother King Robert.[8] The other Scottish prisoners in England, who included Robert and Mary's sister Christina, Robert's daughter Marjorie (ancestor of the Stewart/Stuart dynasty), his second wife Elizabeth de Burgh, his nephew the underage earl of Mar, and Isobel MacDuff, countess of Buchan, had to wait for a few more years before they were able to gain their freedom.

On 16 March 1310, Edward II granted Henry the lordship of the Isle of Man, an island of 220 square miles off the north-west coast of England, and on 1 May 1311 gave it to him for life.[9] On 11 May 1310, Henry was in Woodstock near Oxford when he witnessed the king's great seal being handed to Edward, and judging by the number of times he appears in the chancery rolls asking the king to grant favours to others, he spent much of 1310 at court. Edward gave Henry the Lincolnshire manor of Heckington on 14 December.[10] The church dedicated to St Andrew which still stands in the village was built in Henry de Beaumont's lifetime by Richard de Potesgrave, who worked as a chaplain for Edward II and his son Edward III, and was a man Henry must have known well. Edward II spent all of the period from the autumn of 1310 to the autumn of 1311 in the far north of England and in Scotland, attempting without success to defeat Robert Bruce. It was, despite the grants of the Isle of Man and Heckington, not a good year for Henry either: a ship he owned was robbed at sea by a group of German merchants in or before July 1310.[11]

Henry de Beaumont's favour with his kinsman Edward II enabled him to make an excellent marriage to the Scottish heiress Alice Comyn. One of Robert Bruce's chief enemies was John Comyn, earl of Buchan (b. *c.*1260), who died in England in 1308 after a defeat to Bruce at the battle of Inverurie that year. Buchan had no children, but he had a younger brother, Alexander, sheriff of Aberdeen, who died in 1308 or earlier. From his marriage to the English noblewoman Joan Latimer, Alexander Comyn had two daughters, Alice and Margaret. They were the heirs of their father, their uncle the earl of Buchan, and Master William Comyn, a clerk, their father's other brother.[12] Nothing is known of Alice and Margaret's early life. Alice must have moved to England from Scotland in 1308, if not before, the year of her uncle the earl's defeat at the hands of Robert Bruce, and she would spend the rest of her life there.

Alice Comyn was married to Henry de Beaumont by 14 July 1310, though she and Margaret were still minors at the time. Alice had come of age by 22 January 1311; Margaret was still underage on 14 December 1312.[13] As Alice was female and already married, 'of full age' meant fourteen years old (men came of age at twenty-one and unmarried women at sixteen), which means that she was born after 14 July 1296 and before 22 January 1297. Her sister Margaret was born sometime after 14 December 1298, and returned to their native Scotland and to the allegiance of Robert Bruce at some point; she married firstly the earl of Ross's brother and secondly Sir William Lindsay. Alice was considerably younger than Henry de Beaumont, at least a dozen years younger and perhaps twenty or so, and would have been old enough to bear children from *c.*1312/13. Henry called himself earl of Buchan by right of his wife, though it was a nominal title as he and Alice never held the lands that had belonged to her uncle John, and the inheritance was not worth a great deal anyway: after defeating John Comyn, earl of Buchan, at Inverurie in 1308, Robert Bruce sacked and destroyed the Buchan lands. This is known as the *Herschip* or 'Harrying' of Buchan. The Beaumont/Comyn couple, partly Scottish, partly English, partly French and partly Spanish, were to spend almost all their lives in England.

John de Beaumont, the first son of Alice and Henry and the Beaumont/Comyn heir, was born either *c.* 25 December 1317, or *c.* 30 November 1318. Henry and Alice also had a younger son, Thomas de Beaumont (born *c.* 30 November 1324), and five daughters.[14] Their eldest, Katherine, became titular countess of Atholl by marriage – her husband's Scottish family, the Strathbogies, also moved permanently to England – and their younger daughters Joan, Elizabeth and Agnes became Lady Fitzwarin, Lady Audley and Lady Lucy. Their second daughter Isabella, born around 1315/20, made a brilliant marriage to the partly royal duke of Lancaster and was the mother-in-law of Edward III's son John of Gaunt and the grandmother of King Henry IV. Elizabeth, Lady Audley, one of the younger Beaumont daughters, lived a very long life, and did not die until October 1400. As she had no children, her heir was her brother John's great-grandson; she not only outlived her brother by almost sixty years, but also his son and grandson.[15]

Chapter 39

Not a Good Englishman

A number of bishops, earls and barons, unhappy with Edward II's rule, formed themselves into a group called the Lords Ordainer in 1310, and appointed themselves to reform the king's household and government. In the autumn of 1311, they presented their reforms to Edward, and to his horror they limited his powers severely. The Ordainers' demand that caused him the most personal grief, however, was the exile of Piers Gaveston from England and all of Edward's other territories including Gaveston's native Gascony, for the third time. The Lords Ordainer also ordered Henry de Beaumont's removal from court, in the belief that his influence over the king was malign and self-interested. Edward temporarily took all of Henry's lands into his own hands on 24 October 1311, and Henry's sister Isabelle de Vescy was also ordered to leave court.[1] The Beaumont siblings were two of the four people named in the Ordinances as bad influences on the king, the other two being Piers Gaveston and an influential Italian banker named Amerigo dei Frescobaldi.[2] The Ordainers also demanded that the Isle of Man, which Henry held for life, be given instead to 'some good Englishman' (this demand was made in French, *askun bon homme Engleys*).[3] This was a dig at him that was both xenophobic and hypocritical; Henry, though born in France and with no English ancestry, had lived in England since he was a child, and some of the Ordainers themselves were partly French or partly Italian.

Henry de Beaumont was high in the king's favour between 1311 and 1313. In February 1312, Edward II made him keeper of Somerton Castle in Lincolnshire, which belonged to the king personally, and Henry also replaced his sister Lady Vescy as constable of the great fortification of Bamburgh on the Northumberland coast and was keeper of the town of Maidstone in Kent.[4] Henry spent almost all of 1312, the second major crisis year of the reign, with Edward, and on 26 June the king ordered the keeper of his stud-farm in Burstwick to send Henry a 'bay colt'.[5] Henry was therefore on hand to witness the king's grief when news came to him in York on

26 June 1312 that Piers Gaveston had been killed in Warwickshire a week earlier. For a few weeks, England teetered again on the brink of civil war after the earls who had killed Gaveston brought their armies near London, though Edward's father-in-law Philip IV of France and Pope Clement V (r.1305–14) sent envoys, and they and the most moderate of the English earls, Gloucester, Pembroke and Richmond, negotiated between the two sides and managed to avert a war. On 7 August 1312, Henry and the royal cousin Aymer de Valence, earl of Pembroke, were at Dover waiting to cross to France as Edward II's envoys. Henry went overseas again on the king's affairs in May 1313.[6]

Chapter 40

A Defence Like a Stone Wall

Queen Isabella visited her father Philip IV's court in Paris in the spring of 1314, and both Henry de Beaumont and Isabelle de Vescy went with her.[1] Not long after their return to England, war clouds began to gather. In 1313, Robert Bruce's brother Edward Bruce had begun a siege of Stirling Castle, the most important fortification in Scotland and the only one still held by English forces. Edward II duly marched north to relieve the siege, taking with him the largest army ever assembled in England, and on 23 and 24 June 1314 his forces met Robert Bruce's near Stirling. The English side, who massively outnumbered the Scottish army and were hopelessly over-confident, could not imagine how they could possibly lose the battle, but Robert had home advantage, knew the terrain well, and was a brilliant general. The battle of Bannockburn has gone down in history as one of England's most humiliating military defeats ever.

Henry de Beaumont fought with Edward II at Bannockburn, and was active on the first day, when he and the northern lord Robert Clifford (b.1274) attempted, unsuccessfully, to strike a definitive blow against Bruce's schiltrons. Schiltrons were formations of a few hundred men in concentric rings, standing or kneeling by pikes of 14 to 18 feet long and with a sharpened steel point, facing outwards and positioned at the height of a horse's neck or chest. They were extremely effective against cavalry charges, and Beaumont and Clifford failed to make any headway against them and sustained heavy losses. On the second day of the battle, Edward II's twenty-three-year-old nephew Gilbert de Clare, earl of Gloucester, was killed during another attack on the Scottish schiltrons. The young earl had forgotten to put on a surcoat identifying himself as a great nobleman, and the Scottish soldiers had no idea who he was. If they had, they would instead have captured him for ransom, as happened to the English king's brother-in-law Humphrey de Bohun, earl of Hereford. Robert, Lord Clifford was probably also killed during this period of the battle, and was the second highest ranking Englishman who fell at Bannockburn.

At a parliament held in York in the autumn of 1314, Edward II's cousin and enemy the earl of Lancaster, in league with his ally the earl of Warwick, drastically reduced the king's household income. Edward, knowing what was coming, deliberately arrived very late to the parliament, and empowered the bishop of Exeter, the earl of Pembroke and Henry de Beaumont to convene it in his absence.[2] Politically weakened by his military defeat in Scotland, Edward was in no position to refuse anything to his baronial enemies. The mid-1310s was a comparatively quiet time in Edward II's turbulent reign, though a natural disaster, a widespread famine caused by endless rain and the subsequent catastrophic failure of several harvests, held England and northern Europe in its dread grip from 1315 to 1317. Henry de Beaumont continued his active political and military career, and he and Edmund Fitzalan, earl of Arundel, were appointed to 'safeguard the Scottish march' in 1315 and 1316. Henry was with Edward II in Beverley, Yorkshire on 12 September 1316, and spent that Christmas with him in York.[3]

On 9 October 1316, the bishop of Durham, Richard Kellawe, died, and much politicking ensued at the royal court as the king, the queen and others promoted their preferred candidates for election as the new bishop. Edward II put forward his clerk Thomas Carleton; his powerful cousin the earl of Lancaster promoted John Kynardsey; his brother-in-law the earl of Hereford promoted John Walwayn; and Queen Isabella preferred Louis de Beaumont. Edward changed his mind and also began promoting Louis, supposedly at his wife's instigation, and on 9 February 1317 Pope John XXII duly appointed Louis de Beaumont as bishop. The monks of Durham claimed that Queen Isabella persuaded Edward II to promote Louis to the bishopric to demonstrate that he loved her, and stated disapprovingly that he was *incantatus per reginam* or 'enchanted by the queen'.[4] On the other hand, Edward II himself stated a few years later that he promoted Louis's candidacy to the bishopric because Henry de Beaumont persuaded him that Louis would be a 'defence like a stone wall' against the Scots in the north of England.[5] Evidently Henry's statement was well-known, as the Lanercost chronicler, an excellent source for events in Scotland and northern England in the early fourteenth century, wrote that Louis was appointed because of the 'deceitful suggestion that… he himself would hold the March of England [i.e. the English-Scottish borderlands] against the Scots'.[6]

The royal couple's promotion of Louis to John XXII worked wonders, and the Pope officially appointed him as bishop of Durham on 9 February

1317 and sent two cardinals, Luca Fieschi and Gaucelin Duèse, to England to conduct the consecration. While travelling between Darlington and Durham in the company of the cardinals on 1 September 1317, Henry and Louis were attacked, robbed and taken prisoner by Sir Gilbert Middleton. This attack may have been the work of the earl of Lancaster, annoyed at the failure of his own candidate to gain the bishopric of Durham, though an indignant Pope John XXII blamed the Scots. Gilbert Middleton was captured and subjected to an appalling death by hanging, drawing and quartering in early 1318.[7]

Edward II's inability to defeat Robert Bruce or gain control of Scotland gradually eroded his close relationship with his kinsman Henry de Beaumont. Bruce seized the vital port of Berwick-on-Tweed in 1318, and Edward's attempt to recapture it in 1319 ended in failure. In 1323, the king came to terms with Robert Bruce and sealed a peace treaty for thirteen years. Henry was furious, as this meant he had no chance of gaining his and Alice Comyn's lands inherited from her uncle the earl of Buchan. During a session of the royal council held at Bishopthorpe near York, Henry made his feelings vehemently known to his kinsman. When Edward asked his council's advice about the truce, Henry, 'with an excessive motion and irreverent mind,' refused to offer counsel, and continued to refuse. Edward lost his temper and ordered him out of the room, whereupon Henry retorted that 'it would please him more to be absent than to be present.' Five days later, Edward ordered his arrest for this 'contempt and disobedience'.[8] The same year, Edward II sent a viciously sarcastic letter to Louis de Beaumont, stating that although Henry had promised that his brother would be a 'defence like a stone wall' against the Scots if he was bishop of Durham, Louis had failed entirely in this endeavour (a rather hypocritical point to make, given that Edward himself failed utterly to protect the north of his own kingdom from Scottish raids).[9]

In the late 1310s, Edward had begun a relationship with his nephew-in-law and chamberlain, the English nobleman Hugh Despenser the Younger. The nature of the two men's relationship is not completely certain, but Edward came to love, trust and depend on Despenser. In the early 1320s, they provoked a rebellion which resulted in the execution of twenty or so noblemen and knights and in the exile or imprisonment of others. Edward II also went to war against his brother-in-law Charles IV of France, youngest of Queen Isabella's three brothers, in 1324. Queen Isabella travelled to her homeland in March 1325 to negotiate a peace settlement between her husband and her brother. Six months later, Edward decided that his best option was to send his son and heir Edward of Windsor, who turned thirteen in November 1325, to pay the necessary homage for the duchy of Aquitaine (Gascony) and the county of Ponthieu to Charles IV on his behalf. Henry de Beaumont, finally forgiven for his behaviour in 1323, was sufficiently in favour with the king in September 1325 to travel abroad with Edward's son, and witnessed the young duke of Aquitaine performing homage to Charles IV on 24 September 1325.

With her son in her custody at the French court, Isabella felt safe enough to issue her husband an ultimatum: he must send Hugh Despenser the Younger, a man Isabella loathed and feared, away from him so that she could return to England and resume their marriage. Edward, dependent on Despenser in some way, refused, and left Isabella with little option but to remain in France and to plot the downfall of Despenser another way. Unlike other supporters of the queen, Henry de Beaumont did not remain in France with her, but returned to England. This would prove to be a bad mistake: two chronicles say that he was imprisoned at Kenilworth Castle in February 1326 'because he would not swear to the king and to Sir Hugh Despenser the son, to be of their part to live and die.' That this story was correct is confirmed by the judgement on Hugh Despenser the Younger at his trial a few months later, and Henry was certainly in prison at Warwick Castle (not, in fact, at nearby Kenilworth) by early August 1326.[10]

In the summer of 1326, Queen Isabella moved to the county of Hainault on France's northern border, and agreed to the marriage of her son Edward of Windsor to the count of Hainault's third daughter Philippa in exchange for money to pay for ships and mercenaries. The invasion force landed in Suffolk on 24 September 1326, and two months later the detested royal favourite Hugh Despenser the Younger was executed. Two months after that, Edward II was forced to abdicate his throne to his son Edward III. Henry de Beaumont and his sister Isabelle de Vescy were at Queen Isabella's side during the revolution of 1326/27, the first time in English history that a king had been forced to abdicate his throne.

Fourteen-year-old Edward III was hastily crowned king of England in Westminster Abbey on 1 February 1327, mere days after his father's forced abdication. Henry de Beaumont was specifically named as one of the important men of the realm who attended the coronation, and was in the company of the young king, the dowager queen Isabella, her ally Roger Mortimer and her uncle the earl of Lancaster, in Westminster on 28 January.[11] Alice Comyn, the 'lady of Beaumount', was with Edward III or his mother Isabella on 17 February 1327, when a royal favour was granted at her request.[12] Henry was granted the Leicestershire manor of Loughborough which had belonged to the executed Hugh Despenser the Elder, Despenser the Younger's father. Beaumanor, later an important place for the Beaumont family, was one of its 'hamlets and members'. On 30 April, Henry was 'about to set out for Scotland' as one of the ambassadors being sent to Robert Bruce, and when negotiations failed, a military campaign against Bruce was fought in the summer of 1327 which almost resulted in the young king's capture by Scottish forces.[13]

In September 1327, news of the death of the former king Edward II at Berkeley Castle in Gloucestershire was taken to his son. Edward II's death was at first presented as natural, though as he was only forty-three and had always been a powerfully strong, fit and healthy man, plenty of people must have wondered. His funeral took place in St Peter's Abbey in Gloucester, later Gloucester Cathedral, on 20 December 1327 in the presence of his son, his widow Isabella, and most of the English nobility, including presumably Henry de Beaumont. Rumours soon spread, however, that Edward was not dead at all.

Chapter 41

The Catch of the Century

Edward III married Philippa of Hainault in York in January 1328 a few weeks after his father's funeral, and Philippa's maternal uncle Philip de Valois succeeded his cousin Charles IV, Edward III's uncle, as King Philip VI of France on 1 April 1328. Eight days later on 9 April, also in France, Henry de Beaumont's sister Marguerite de Brienne, dowager countess of Tripoli and princess of Antioch, passed away more than forty years after losing her husband Bohemond VII.

In 1328, the English and Scottish governments signed the treaty of Edinburgh and came to a perpetual peace settlement. This angered a group of barons who were resident in England but believed they had the right to lands in Scotland and were known as the Disinherited, including Henry de Beaumont and his kinsman Thomas, Lord Wake (b.1298).[1] They would now never be able to claim their Scottish lands, the earldom of Buchan in Henry's case. Contemporary chroniclers held Roger Mortimer responsible for the unpopular wedding of Edward III's sister Joan of the Tower (b.1321) and Robert Bruce's son David (b.1324), and for the equally unpopular peace treaty.[2]

As if to rub salt into the wound, Roger Mortimer created the grandiose earldom of March, i.e. earl of all the English-Welsh borderlands, for himself in October 1328. Henry de Beaumont was furious, and in late 1328 and early 1329 took part in a rebellion against Isabella and Mortimer which was led by Henry, earl of Lancaster and Leicester, the dowager queen's uncle, who had been ousted from his rightful position as the young Edward III's guardian and the head of the regency council. Ultimately the rebellion failed, and Henry de Beaumont and several other men were ordered to be arrested on 18 January 1329.[3] Henry fled from England and went to his native France. In 1332, Edward III repaid £500 which the Italian banking society the Bardi had lent Henry there during his exile. Several of his fellow exiles, Thomas Roscelyn, Thomas Wyther and William Trussell, joined him in France; Henry, earl of Lancaster paid Roscelyn's expenses, and perhaps the others' as well.[4]

In 1329/30, Edward II's half-brother Edmund of Woodstock, earl of Kent (b.1301), became convinced that the former king was alive, even though he had attended Edward's funeral in December 1327, and made plans to free him from captivity. Many dozens of noblemen, knights, merchants and others, including the archbishop of York and the bishop and mayor of London, joined him. Kent was arrested in mid-March 1330, and in his confession named some of his most important supporters; one of them, surprisingly enough, was Henry de Beaumont. Another was Richard of Pontefract, confessor of Henry's sister Lady Vescy, who carried messages to the archbishop of York, William Melton, regarding Edward II's release.[5] Whether Henry truly believed that his kinsman was still alive is uncertain, and perhaps he saw Kent's plot more as an opportunity to bring down Isabella and Roger Mortimer. Other adherents of Kent apparently did genuinely believe that the former king was alive years after his funeral, including Archbishop Melton, who sent a letter to his friend and kinsman the mayor of London asking him to procure clothes, boots, money and other items for 'our liege lord Edward of Caernarfon [who] is alive and in good bodily health, and in a safe place'. Henry met the earl of Kent in Paris, where they discussed Edward's survival and what to do about it.[6]

In the summer of 1330, Henry and his allies planned an invasion of England intended to bring down Queen Isabella and Roger Mortimer. This caused panic, and in mid-July 1330, the pair ordered all the sheriffs of England to array knights, squires and others who bore arms; they should prepare themselves 'to set out against certain contrariants and rebels who lately withdrew secretly from the realm and who have assembled a multitude of armed men in parts beyond the sea'. Evidently this was not considered sufficient, and the pair ordered London and more than thirty other towns up and down the country in late July and early August 1330 to array knights and men-at-arms against 'certain rebels who lately withdrew from the country by stealth [and] are said to intend to return and do what mischief they can'. Louis de Beaumont, bishop of Durham, was ordered on 10 August to array knights, squires and others to be ready 'to set out against the said rebels if they invade the realm'. As Beaumont's brother was one of the men plotting the invasion, presumably Mortimer and Isabella must have suspected that the bishop would aid the invasion force and that the rebels might land in his bishopric.[7] In the end, the planned invasion never happened, perhaps because the rebels did not want to appear as though they were attacking the young king, with whom they had no quarrel. Edward III stayed at Folkingham and Heckington, two Lincolnshire manors which belonged to Henry de Beaumont, from 16 to 21 August 1330.[8] Heckington was in the hands of Henry's sister Lady Vescy, who was never arrested for any role she might have played in the plot to restore the supposedly dead Edward II to the throne.

Sometime before he fled from England, Henry de Beaumont arranged marriages for two of his and Alice Comyn's children: their second daughter and their first son. Isabella de Beaumont, probably somewhere between ten and fifteen years old, married Henry of Grosmont, only son and heir of Henry of Lancaster, earl of Lancaster and Leicester, before 24 June 1330. Isabella's brother John de Beaumont married Grosmont's sister Eleanor, fifth of Henry of Lancaster's six daughters, some months later.[9] Henry, earl of Lancaster, was the heir of his older brother Thomas, executed by their cousin Edward II in 1322, and via his father Edmund (d.1296) was a grandson of Henry III and nephew of Edward I. Via his mother Blanche of Artois, Earl Henry was also a great-nephew of Louis IX of France, and perhaps because of his French background, found the idea of two of his children marrying into the Brienne/Beaumont family appealing. His father Edmund had known Henry de Beaumont's uncle John de Brienne the younger (d.1296) in the 1280s when Brienne acted as regent of the county of Champagne (then held by Edmund of Lancaster and Blanche of Artois), so there was a long association between the families. It is possible that the Lancaster-Beaumont marriages had been planned as early as February 1327, when Henry de Beaumont and Isabelle de Vescy acknowledged a staggeringly large debt of £14,000 to Henry of Lancaster, and he acknowledged that he owed them £3,000.[10] Henry, earl of Lancaster, was the richest nobleman in England with an annual gross income of around £11,000.

For the Beaumonts, Lancaster's son and heir Henry of Grosmont (b. *c.*1310/12) was the catch of the century. Not only born into extraordinary wealth, he was related to both the English and French royal families, was sole heir to his father's earldoms of Lancaster and Leicester, and was also sole heir to the earldom of Lincoln, which belonged to his aunt-in-law Alice de Lacy (1281–1348). As well as the three earldoms, Grosmont inherited the estates of his late mother Maud Chaworth (d.1322), who brought the Welsh lordships of Carmarthen and Kidwelly and lands in five English counties to the Lancasters. Under normal circumstances, one of the most eligible bachelors in Europe would probably not have married the second daughter of a mere baron who was not her father's heir or even co-heir, but the times were anything but normal. Henry of Lancaster was currently out of favour after his failed rebellion, and languishing on his estates. He and Henry de Beaumont's goals coincided in 1329/30: they both wished a speedy end to the regime of the dowager queen and Roger Mortimer.

The marriage arranged in 1330 resulted in the births of two daughters, Maud in 1340 and Blanche in 1342, and after Maud of Lancaster died without children in 1362, Isabella de Beaumont's younger daughter Blanche carried the entire enormous Lancastrian inheritance to her royal husband John of Gaunt and their son, the future Henry IV. Edward III gave his kinsman Henry of Grosmont the earldom of Derby in 1337, and in 1351, a few years after Henry had inherited his father's earldoms of Lancaster and Leicester, Edward III made him the first duke of Lancaster. He was only the second English duke in history after the king's son and heir Edward of Woodstock, who had been made duke of Cornwall in 1337, and as Edward did not marry until 1361, Isabella de Beaumont was the first English duchess in history.

Fortunately for Henry de Beaumont and his family, and for Queen Isabella and Roger Mortimer's numerous other enemies, they did not have long to wait for the pair's downfall. Edward III was also sick of their misrule and the way they had bankrupted his kingdom, and in Nottingham Castle on 19 October 1330, four months after the birth of his and Queen Philippa's first son Edward of Woodstock, Edward arrested Roger Mortimer and had him hanged on 29 November. The king took over the governance of his own kingdom, and forced his mother the dowager queen into retirement. That November and December, Edward III invited all those who had fled from England to come back, including Henry de Beaumont, declared them guiltless of any crime, and restored them to their lands and goods.[11] Henry returned to England and to his wife and children after an absence of almost two years. During his enforced exile, his friend Henry, earl of Lancaster, who developed remarkably close bonds with his own children and their spouses, had taken the Beaumont/Comyn children under his protection. The two young Beaumont/Lancaster couples were too young to consummate their marriages – John and Isabella de Beaumont and Eleanor of Lancaster were all around twelve or so in 1330 – but lived in the same household under the benign eye of the royal earl of Lancaster.

Chapter 42

Cohabiting Continually

In 1296, the king of Scotland, John Balliol, had been forced to flee abroad after Edward I of England invaded his kingdom. John died in exile in 1314, but his son Edward Balliol lived to a ripe old age and did not die until 1364. In the early 1330s, Edward Balliol claimed the Scottish throne with the aid and support of Edward III. The young English king repudiated the peace settlement his mother had made with Scotland in 1328, even though the young David II – who succeeded his father Robert Bruce at the age of five in 1329 – was his brother-in-law. As the titular earl of Buchan, Henry de Beaumont enthusiastically supported the Balliols' claims as well, in the hope that he and Alice would be able to take possession of the lands of her inheritance; but it was not to be.

Louis de Beaumont, bishop of Durham, died in September 1333. He left a very short will in Latin, which, given his endless struggles with that language, was surely translated by a clerk from Louis's French.[1] Louis was probably in his early sixties at the time of his death, and was succeeded as bishop of Durham by Richard de Bury (d.1345), former tutor of Edward III and a famous scholar and collector of books. Louis's siblings Isabelle de Vescy and Henry de Beaumont worked together in Newcastle-upon-Tyne on 16 June 1334, regarding a grant previously made to Bridlington Priory on the Yorkshire coast; their servant John Cadinot had 'wilfully torn the document', and they therefore renewed the damaged charter and affixed their seals to it. The siblings' closeness is apparent from the description of Cadinot as 'their' servant.[2] Isabelle evidently was in good enough health to travel to Newcastle, but died later that year, sometime before 1 November 1334; she was perhaps in her late sixties or thereabouts. The four Lincolnshire manors which Henry had given his sister to hold during her lifetime reverted to him.[3] He was now the only living child of Louis de Brienne the *Porphyrogennetos*.

John de Beaumont and his wife Eleanor of Lancaster spent much time with Edward III and Queen Philippa in the duchy of Brabant in the late 1330s; Edward claimed the throne of France in 1337 as the only living grandson of Philip IV (d.1314), and from 1338 to 1340 travelled outside England seeking allies on the Continent. The king's own testimony reveals firstly that he and the queen were deeply fond of John and Eleanor and very much enjoyed spending time with them, and secondly that John and Eleanor were deeply fond of each other and had a happy, mutually satisfactory marriage. The couple 'were cohabiting continually in Brabant in his company in marital intercourse', Edward III declared in 1340. Eleanor became pregnant around March or April 1339, and gave birth to her and John's only child, named Henry after both his grandfathers, not long before the middle of January 1340.[4] Henry de Beaumont was born in the duchy of Brabant; Eleanor and John had intended to return to England for the birth, but the king and queen persuaded them to stay with them as their company was so desirable. As the law held that landowners in England, Wales, Ireland and Gascony had to be born within those territories – the ones ruled by the kings of England – young Henry's birthplace was bound to cause him issues when he came of age. In December 1340, Edward III promised 'to provide for the security of the offspring in its succession to its parents in England' and declared that Henry should succeed John as his 'legitimate heir within the realm of England, notwithstanding that his birth was not in the realm'.[5]

In October 1338, Henry de Beaumont the grandfather stayed at Tutbury Castle in Staffordshire with his old friend Henry, earl of Lancaster.[6] Beaumont, who was now around sixty, did not have much longer to live, and died in his Leicestershire town of Loughborough, or 'Luthburg(h)' as contemporaries spelt it, on 10 March 1340. Two chroniclers, Lanercost and Anonimalle, state that *mounsire Henri de Bewemond* was buried in the 'Abbey of Valle Dei', i.e. Vaudey Abbey in Lincolnshire, on 13 March 1340.[7] On or around 4 April 1340, shortly after Henry died, another of his grandchildren was born: Maud of Lancaster, future duchess of Bavaria and countess of Leicester, Holland and Hainault, daughter of Isabella de Beaumont and Henry of Grosmont. She and her sister Blanche (b. *c*.25 March 1342) were the Lancaster heirs, though Blanche became sole heir to lands in more than thirty counties on Maud's death in 1362.[8]

John de Beaumont did not long outlive his father: he died two years later in the spring of 1342, though the exact date is uncertain. The chronicler Adam Murimuth says that he was killed in a jousting tournament on 14 April that year.[9] There is, however, an entry on the Patent Roll dated 10 May 1342 giving John royal permission to grant three of his own manors

(Folkingham, Barton-upon-Humber and Heckington) to himself and his wife Eleanor of Lancaster jointly.[10] Either this permission was only recorded by royal clerks a few weeks after John died, or the date of his death given by Adam Murimuth is wrong. John was certainly dead by 25 May 1342, when an entry on the Close Roll talks of '...Eleanor de Bello Monte [Beaumont], executrix of the will of John de Bello Monte, for the obsequies of John'. On 26 June, a writ was issued to take John's lands into the king's hands and to hold his inquisition post mortem (IPM), and Eleanor was called 'late his wife' on 10 August.11 John's inquisition post mortem was held in August/September 1342, though unfortunately it does not specify the date of his death. The jurors of all the counties knew that his son Henry was his heir, and they all said that Henry was two or two and a half years old. The list of castles and manors was considerably shorter than in his father's IPM of 1340, as much of the family's inheritance was still in the hands of John's mother Alice Comyn, who outlived him by a few years.[12]

Edward III granted the marriage rights of John's young son and heir Henry de Beaumont to his mother Eleanor of Lancaster and his stepfather, Eleanor's second husband the earl of Arundel, on 23 October 1345.[13] Via Eleanor and Arundel's marriage, Henry was an older half-brother of the countesses of Hereford and Kent, an archbishop of Canterbury (Thomas Arundel, d.1414), and another earl of Arundel who was beheaded outside the Tower of London in 1397. At an uncertain date in or before 1360, Eleanor and Arundel arranged Henry's marriage to Margaret de Vere, one of the daughters of the earl of Oxford. Margaret's father Earl John was born in March 1312, and her brother Thomas de Vere, their father's eldest son and heir, around Christmas 1336.[14] It is likely that she was close to her husband's age. Margaret and Henry's son and heir John de Beaumont was born in March 1361, and was ten months older than his cousin Robert de Vere, earl of Oxford, later the notorious 'favourite' of King Richard II.[16] Henry died in June 1369, not yet thirty.

John de Beaumont and his wife Katherine Everingham had four sons and four daughters, of whom the eldest son was Henry de Beaumont – the family alternated the names John and Henry in each generation – born at the family seat of Folkingham Castle, Lincolnshire, on 16 August 1381 when John was twenty. John became the third Beaumont heir in a row to die at a young age when he passed away on 9 September 1396, the day after he made his will, several years before the dramatic end of Richard II's reign in September 1399.[17] Richard II, a great-great-great-grandson of Emperor John de Brienne, was deposed and later killed by Emperor John's great-great-grandson Henry IV, grandson of Isabella de Beaumont. Isabella's younger sister Elizabeth de Beaumont, Lady Audley, one of the five daughters of Henry de Beaumont (d.1340) and Alice Comyn, was still alive to witness the accession of her great-nephew to the English throne.

Appendix

List of Kings/Queens and Emperors/ Empresses

The dates given are reigns.

Kings and queens of Jerusalem

Baldwin I 1100–18
Baldwin II 1118–31
Melisende with Fulk of Anjou 1131–43
Melisende with Baldwin III 1143–61
Baldwin III alone 1161–63
Amalric 1163–74
Baldwin IV 1174–85
Baldwin V 1185–86
Sibilla with Guy de Lusignan 1186–90
Isabella 1190–1205; with Corrado of Montferrat 1190–92, Henri of Champagne 1192–97, and Aiméry de Lusignan 1198–1205
Marie 1205–12; with John de Brienne 1210–12
Yolande 1212–28; with Friedrich II von Hohenstaufen 1225–28
Konrad 1228–54 (titular)
Konradin 1254–68 (titular)
Hugh of Antioch-Lusignan 1268–84
John de Lusignan 1284–85
Henry de Lusignan 1285–91

Byzantine Emperors

Alexios I Komnenos 1081–1118
Ioannes II Komnenos 1118–43
Manuel I Komnenos 1143–80
Alexios II Komnenos under the regency of Maria of Antioch 1180–82
Alexios II Komnenos jointly with Andronikos I Komnenos 1182–83
Andronikos I Komnenos 1183–85
Isaakios II Angelos 1185–95

Alexios III Angelos 1195–1203
Isaakios II Angelos (again) jointly with Alexios IV Angelos 1203–04
Nikolaos Kannavos 1204
Alexios V Doukas 1204
Constantine Laskaris 1204 (?)
Mikhael VIII Palaiologos 1261–82

Latin Emperors and Empresses of Constantinople
Baudouin I of Flanders 1204–05
Hendrik of Flanders 1205–16
Yolanda of Flanders 1216–19 with Pierre de Courtenay 1216–17
Robert de Courtenay 1219–28
Baudouin II de Courtenay jointly with John de Brienne 1228–37
Baudouin II de Courtenay alone 1237–61; 1261–73 titular
Philippe de Courtenay 1273–83 (titular)
Catherine de Courtenay 1283–1307 (titular) with Charles de Valois 1301–07
Catherine de Valois 1307–46 (titular) with Philip of Taranto 1313–31

Holy Roman Emperors
Friedrich I Barbarossa 1155–90
Heinrich VI von Hohenstaufen 1191–97
Otto IV von Welf 1209–18
Friedrich II von Hohenstaufen 1220–50
Henry VII of Luxembourg 1312–13

Kings of Cyprus
Aiméry de Lusignan 1194–1205
Hugh I de Lusignan 1205–18
Henry I de Lusignan 1218–53
Hugh II de Lusignan 1253–67
Hugh III of Antioch-Lusignan 1267–84
John de Lusignan 1284–85
Henry de Lusignan 1285–1324

Kings and queens of Armenian Cilicia
Levon I 1198–1219
Zabel 1219–52; with Philip of Antioch 1222–25 and Hethum of Baberon 1226–70
Levon II 1270–89

Kings and queens of Sicily
Guglielmo II de Hauteville 1166–89
Tancredi of Lecce 1189–94 with Ruggero III 1192–93
Costanza I de Hauteville 1194–98 with Heinrich VI von Hohenstaufen 1194–97
Friedrich II von Hohenstaufen 1198–1250
Konrad von Hohenstaufen 1250–54
Konradin von Hohenstaufen 1254–58
Manfredi von Hohenstaufen 1258–66
Charles of Anjou 1266–82
Costanza II with Pere III of Aragón 1282–85
Jaume of Aragón 1285–95
Frederic of Aragón 1295–1337

Kings of Castile and León
Alfonso VIII of Castile 1158–1214
Alfonso IX of León 1188–1230
Enrique I of Castile 1214–17
Fernando III of Castile 1217–52 and León 1230–52
Alfonso X of Castile and León 1252–84
Sancho IV of Castile and León 1284–95
Fernando IV 1295–1312
Alfonso XI 1312–50
Pedro I 1350–69
Enrique II of Trastámara 1369–79
Juan I 1379–90
Enrique III 1390–1406
Juan II 1406–54

Kings of Aragón
Jaume I 1213–76
Pere III 1276–85
Alfonso III 1285–91
Jaume II 1291–1327
Alfonso IV 1327–36
Pere IV 1336–87

Kings of Portugal
Diniz 1279–1325

Afonso IV 1325–57
Pedro I 1357–67
Fernando I 1367–83
[Interregnum 1383–85]
João I 1385–1433

Kings and queens of Navarre
Thibaut I 1234–53
Thibaut II 1253–70
Enrique I 1270–74
Juana I 1274–1305 with Philip IV of France 1284–1305
Louis X of France 1305–16
Philip V of France 1316–22
Charles IV of France 1322–28
Juana II 1328–49 with Philip of Evreux 1328–43
Carlos II 1349–87

Kings of France
Louis VII 1137–80
Philip II Augustus 1180–1223
Louis VIII 1223–26
Louis IX 1226–70
Philip III 1270–85
Philip IV 1285–1314
Louis X 1314–16
John I 1316
Philip V 1316–22
Charles IV 1322–28
Philip VI 1328–50
John II 1350–64

Kings and queens of Scotland
William the Lion 1165–1214
Alexander II 1214–49
Alexander III 1249–86
Margrete of Norway 1286–90 (titular)
[Interregnum 1290–92]
John Balliol 1292–96

[Interregnum 1296–1306]
Robert I Bruce 1306–29
David II Bruce 1329–71
Robert II Stewart 1371–90

Kings of England
Henry II 1154–89
Richard I Lionheart 1189–99
John 1199–1216
Henry III 1216–72
Edward I 1272–1307
Edward II 1307–27
Edward III 1327–77
Richard II 1377–99
Henry IV 1399–1413

Notes

Abbreviations

CCR: Calendar of Close Rolls
CChR: Calendar of Charter Rolls
CDS: Calendar of Documents Relating to Scotland
CFR: Calendar of Fine Rolls
CPR: Calendar of Patent Rolls
Deeds Done: A History of Deeds Done Beyond the Sea, by William, Archbishop of Tyre, vol. 2
O City: O City of Byzantium: Annals of Niketas Choniatēs
TNA: The National Archives (London)

Glossary

1. Peter H. Wilson, *The Holy Roman Empire: A Thousand Years of Europe's History* (2016), 1, 19.

Part I: Outremer

Chapter 1: Vivacity of Disposition

1. *A History of Deeds Done Beyond the Sea, by William, Archbishop of Tyre*, vol. 2, translated and annotated by Emily Atwater Babcock and A.C. Krey (1943), 1, 5.
2. Jaroslav Folda, *Crusader Art in the Holy Land, From the Third Crusade to the Fall of Acre* (2005), 74–5, 105 (the 'genteel poverty' quotation is on p.74); Steven Runciman, *History of the Crusades*, vol. 3 (1987), 133; Sarah Lambert, 'Queen or Consort: Rulership and Politics in the Latin East, 1118–1228', *Queens and Queenship in Medieval Europe*, ed. Anne J. Duggan (1995), 167. Jacques de Vitry is cited in Roger Crowley, *Accursed Tower: The Crusaders' Last Battle for the Holy Land* (2019), 8–9.
3. Peter Frankopan, *The Silk Roads: A New History of the World* (2015), 136; Malcolm Lambert, *Crusade and Jihad: Origins, History and Aftermath* (2016), 95–6.
4. Sharan Newman, *Defending the City of God: A Medieval Queen, The First Crusades, and the Quest for Peace in Jerusalem* (2014), 13, 21; Katherine Pangonis, *Queens of Jerusalem: The Women Who Dared to Rule* (2021), 32–4.
5. *History of Deeds Done*, vol. 2, 47.
6. Bernard Hamilton, 'Women in the Crusader States: The Queens of Jerusalem (1100–1190)', *Studies in Church History Subsidia*, 1 (1978), 152; Alan V. Murray, 'Women in the Royal Succession of the Latin Kingdom of Jerusalem (1099–1291)', *Mächtige Frauen? Königinnen und Fürstinnen im europäischen Mittelalter*, ed. Claudia Zey (2015), 142; Jonathan Phillips, *Holy Warriors: A Modern History of the Crusades* (2009), 72–4.
7. *Deeds Done*, vol. 2, 139–40.

8. *Deeds Done*, vol. 2, 274–5; Hamilton, 'Women in the Crusader States', 157; Phillips, *Holy Warriors*, 106–7.
9. Melisende herself founded the convent. *Deeds Done*, vol. 2, 399; Bernard Hamilton, *The Leper King and his Heirs: Baldwin IV and the Crusader Kingdom of Jerusalem* (2005), 24; Bernard Hamilton, 'Women in the Crusader States', 164; https://sourcebooks.fordham.edu/source/tyre-cde.asp#baldwin1, accessed 5 December 2022.
10. *Deeds Done*, vol. 2, 397–8.
11. *Deeds Done*, vol. 2, 344; https://www.defenderofjerusalem.com/maria-comnena-1.html, accessed 25 November 2022; Murray, 'Women in the Crusader States', 144, 161, 163. Ioannes Doukas Komnenos was the son of Andronikos Komnenos, elder brother of Emperor Manuel, who died in 1142 the year before their father Emperor Ioannes II; Theodora Komnene, Baldwin III's queen, was the daughter of Isaakios, another older brother of Manuel.
12. *O City of Byzantium: Annals of Niketas Choniatēs*, ed. Harry J. Magoulias (1984), 8.
13. Natalia Pushkareva, *Women in Russian History from the Tenth to the Twentieth Century* (1997), 16. Dobrodjeja was a granddaughter of Gytha of Wessex, daughter of Harold Godwinson (d. 1066), last king of Anglo-Saxon England. Gytha married Vladimir Monomakh, grand prince of Kievan Rus.
14. *Deeds Done*, vol. 2, 450; *Joinville and Villehardouin: Chronicles of the Crusades*, trans. M.R.B. Shaw (1963), 92; Clari, *Conquest*, 101–3. 'Greek filth' is cited in Natasha R. Hodgson, *Women, Crusading and the Holy Land in Historical Narrative* (2007), 189.

Chapter 2: The Leper King

1. *Deeds Done*, vol. 2, 399.
2. Helena P. Schrader, *The Holy Land in the Era of the Crusades: Kingdoms at the Crossroads of Civilizations, 1100–1300* (2022), 45; Hamilton, *Leper King*, 41–2; Peter W. Edbury and John Gordon Rowe, *William of Tyre: Historian of the Latin East* (1991), 83.
3. Hamilton, *Leper King*, 25.
4. *Deeds Done*, vol. 2, 296–7, 398, 492; Hamilton, *Leper King*, 43; Edbury and Rowe, *William of Tyre*, 70–71.
5. Baldwin V had been crowned as his uncle's co-king in 1183: *Deeds Done*, vol. 2, 501–2.
6. Étienne's sister Adèle was married to Louis VII of France (r. 1137–80) and was the mother of Louis's heir Philip, b. 1165, and his brothers were married to Louis VII's two daughters from his first marriage to Eleanor of Aquitaine.
7. *Deeds Done*, vol. 2, 508.
8. Pangonis, *Queens of Jerusalem*, 275.
9. Runciman, *History of the Crusades*, vol. 2, 460.
10. *The Crusade of Friedrich Barbarossa: The History of the Expedition of the Emperor Friedrich and Related Texts*, ed. G.A. Loud (2010), 114–16.

Chapter 3: Queen Isabella and Queen Marie

1. *Deeds Done*, vol. 2, 499–501; Jonathan Phillips, *The Life and Legend of the Sultan Saladin* (2019), 156.
2. Hamilton, *Leper King*, 161; Hamilton, 'Women in the Crusader States', 168–9. Raynald de Châtillon was the father-in-law of the reigning king of Hungary, Béla III; see Part 3.
3. Hamilton, 'Women in the Crusader States', 172–3.
4. *O City of Byzantium*, 114, 210; M.M. Gilchrist, 'Conrad de Monferrat in English-language Fiction and Popular Histories', *Bollettino del Marchesato*, 6 (2005), 6–12.
5. *History of the Crusades*, vol. 3, 66.

6. *Deeds Done*, vol. 2, 137, 296–300, 416.
7. *O City*, 210; Runciman, *History of the Crusades*, vol. 3, 19–20, 30–31; Hodgson, *Women, Crusading*, 146.
8. Jonathan Phillips, *The Fourth Crusade and the Sack of Constantinople* (2004), 84–5.
9. *Crusade of Friedrich Barbarossa*, ed. Loud, 121–2.
10. Murray, 'Women in the Royal Succession', 153–5; Schrader, *Holy Land*, 77; Runciman, vol. 3, 82, believes Isabella gave birth before Corrado's death.
11. Lambert, 'Queen or Consort', 162–3; Schrader, *Holy Land*, 77.
12. Runciman, vol. 3, 93; Robert Lee Wolff, Harry M. Hazard and Kenneth M. Setton, *A History of the Crusades, Volume Two: The Later Crusades, 1189–1311* (1969), 529.
13. Runciman, *Crusades*, vol. 3, 104.
14. Runciman, *History of the Crusades*, vol. 3, 134–5; Murray, 'Women in the Latin Kingdom', 156; Folda, *Crusader Art in the Holy Land*, 105.
15. Guy Perry, *The Briennes: The Rise and Fall of a Chempenois Dynasty*, 48; Murray, 'Women in the Royal Succession', 155. Via her mother Eudokia Komnene, Marie of Montpellier was, like the queens of Jerusalem Theodora Komnene and Maria Komnene, a close relative of Emperor Manuel I Komnenos.
16. Runciman, vol. 3, 133; Lambert, 'Queen or Consort', 167.
17. Dana Celest Asmoui Ismail, 'A History of the Counts of Brienne (950–1210)', PhD thesis, Royal Holloway, Univ. of London (2013), 180, estimates John's year of birth as *c.* 1178; Perry, *John of Brienne*, 17, thinks mid-1170s. A Byzantine historian, Acropolites, who saw John in 1231 said much later that John was about eighty then, but Acropolites was himself only fourteen at the time, and his statement was given far too much weight by some later writers. In the same way, William of Tyre thought that Fulk of Anjou, whom William saw when he was ten, was 'more than sixty' when he became king of Jerusalem in 1131, at least twenty years older than he in fact was. James Michael Buckley, 'The Problematic Octogenarianism of John of Brienne', *Speculum*, 32 (1957), 315–22; *Deeds Done*, vol. 2, 47.
18. Bernard Hamilton, 'Queen Alice of Cyprus', *The Crusader World*, ed. Adrian J. Boas (2016), 227.
19. Schrader, *Holy Land*, 87, and see Guy Perry, 'Isabella II or Yolanda? The Name of the Queen of Jerusalem and the Spouse of the Emperor Friedrich II', *Medieval Prosopography*, 30 (2015), 78–9, stating that thirteenth-century narrative sources named her as Isabella, as did her father and husband. I call her Yolande here to avoid possible confusion with her grandmother.
20. Hamilton, 'Queen Alice of Cyprus', 227.
21. David-Linus-Emanuel Neagu, 'The War of the Antiochene Succession: Lewon I's Game of Diplomacy', *Revue des Études Sud-Est Européenes*, 57 (2019), 226.
22. Thibaut's mother Blanca of Navarre was the younger sister of Berengaria of Navarre, who married Richard Lionheart of England in 1191. If Berengaria and Richard had had a son, he would – as well as succeeding his father as king of England – have had a stronger claim to the kingdom of Navarre than Thibaut of Champagne, as Berengaria was the older sister.

Chapter 4: Lords of the Mountains

1. Neagu, 'Antiochene Succession', 222.
2. Jochen Burgtorf, 'The Antiochene War of Succession', *The Crusader World*, ed. Adrian J. Boas (2015), 197.

3. Jacob G. Ghazarian, *The Armenian Kingdom in Cilicia During the Crusades: The Integration of Cilician Armenians with the Latins (1080–1393)* (2000), 123; T.S.R. Boase, 'The History of the Kingdom', in ed. Boase, *The Cilician Kingdom of Armenia* (1978), 18; *History of the Crusades*, vol. 2, ed. Wolff, Hazard and Setton, 534; Vahan M. Kurkjian, *The Armenian Kingdom of Cilicia* (1919), 8–9; *The Crusade of Friedrich Barbarossa*, 114.
4. John Armenia, *Armenian Cilicia XII-XIV Century: Dawn, Splendor and Twilight of a Christian Kingdom in the Near East During the Crusades* (2010), 77–8; Boase, 'History of the Kingdom', 21.
5. http://attalus.org/armenian/kg6.htm, accessed 26 November 2022.
6. *Joinville and Villehardouin: Chronicles of the Crusades*, 206–7.
7. Runciman, *History of the Crusades*, vol. 3, 134, 164–5.
8. Runciman, vol. 3, 171; Boase, 'History of the Kingdom', 22–3. Raymond-Roupen was married to Helvis or Heloise of Cyprus, daughter of Aiméry de Lusignan and his first wife Eschiva d'Ibelin. She was a full sister of Hugh I de Lusignan, king of Cyprus, and a half-sister of Zabel of Armenia's mother Sibilla of Cyprus and Jerusalem.
9. John Armenia, *Cilician Armenia XII-XIV Century*, 78–9; Boase, 'History of the Kingdom', 23. Philip's stepmother, the much younger second wife of Bohemond IV of Antioch, was Zabel's aunt Melisende of Cyprus and Jerusalem.
10. http://attalus.org/armenian/kg7.htm, accessed 26 July 2022; Armenia, *Cilician Armenia*, 79.
11. Wolff, Hazard and Setton, *Crusades*, 586–8.
12. Nigel Saul, Richard II (1997), 12; Richard Barber, *Edward, Prince of Wales and Aquitaine: A Biography of the Black Prince* (1978; reprinted 1996), 193.
13. https://digital.janeaddams.ramapo.edu/items/show/20308, accessed 13 November 2022; *Foedera 1373–97*, 480.
14. The National Archives PROB 11/1/53.

Chapter 5: Shot Up Like Lethal Hemlock

1. Runciman, vol. 3, 134–5; Hamilton, 'Queen Alice of Cyprus', 226.
2. *O City of Byzantium: Annals of Niketas Choniatēs*, 160–62 (also for the 'passionately desired' quote); Schrader, *Holy Land*, 78. Isaakios Komnenos the *Sebastokrator* and brother of Emperor Manuel was the father of Theodora Komnene, who married Baldwin III, king of Jerusalem, in 1158, and had a relationship with Andronikos Komnenos; see part 3.
3. *Crusade of Friedrich Barbarossa*, 121; *O City*, 161–2, 229, 254.
4. *O City*, 229, 254–55; *Crusade of Friedrich Barbarossa*, 121. The count of Toulouse who married the Damsel of Cyprus was Raymond VI (1156–1222), who married no fewer than six times; the Damsel was his fifth wife.
5. *O City*, 229–30.
6. Schrader, *Holy Land*, 146.
7. https://ims.leeds.ac.uk/wp-content/uploads/sites/29/2019/10/Estoire-dEracles.pdf; accessed 6 September 2022.
8. Aiméry and Eschiva's younger daughter was Helvis or Heloise, who married Raymond-Roupen of Antioch.
9. Peter W. Edbury, *The Kingdom of Cyprus and the Crusades, 1191–1374* (1993), 44–5.
10. Edbury, *Kingdom of Cyprus*, 43–4; Hamilton, 'Queen Alice of Cyprus', 225–6.
11. Bernard, 'Queen Alice of Cyprus', 229; Edbury, *Kingdom of Cyprus*, 49–51.
12. Plaisance was a granddaughter of Bohemond IV, prince of Antioch, from his first marriage to Plaisance of Jebail; her father Bohemond V had been married firstly, and rather briefly, to Alice of Champagne, queen of Cyprus, Plaisance's mother-in-law. Her

brother Bohemond VI of Antioch married Queen Zabel of Armenia's daughter Sibilla, and their son married John de Brienne's granddaughter Marguerite de Brienne.

13. Walter Rhodes, 'Edmund, Earl of Lancaster', *English Historical Review*, 10 (1895), 27; *Issues of the Exchequer*, ed. Friedrich Devon (1837), 35.

Chapter 6: The Last Crusades

1. Schrader, *The Holy Land in the Era of the Crusades*, 113–14. Hugh of Antioch-Lusignan was the son of Alice's daughter Isabelle de Lusignan; was the cousin of Hugh II, king of Cyprus; and himself became king of Cyprus in 1267 after Hugh II died without children.
2. Hugh was Maria's nephew; she was Bohemond IV's daughter from his second marriage, and Hugh was Bohemond IV's grandson from his first marriage.
3. The National Archives E 101/333/15: *Un cultell dount le Roi Edward estoit naufray en la terre seinte en Acres*.

Part II: Spain

Chapter 7: The Kings of León

1. *Estoire d'Eracles: the Old French Continuation of William of Tyre*, extracts translated by G.A. Loud, available online at https://ims.leeds.ac.uk/wp-content/uploads/sites/29/2019/10/Estoire-dEracles.pdf; Guy Perry, *John of Brienne*, 126–28; H. Salvador Martínez, *Alfonso X, the Learned: A Biography* (2010), 32.
2. H. Salvador Martínez, *Berenguela the Great and Her Times (1180–1246)* (2021), 35–7.
3. Fernando III of Castile and León, canonised in 1671; Louis IX of France, canonised in 1297; and Louis's youngest sister Isabelle of France (1224–70), venerated as a saint by the Franciscan order.
4. Martínez, *Alfonso X, the Learned*, 33–35; Alfonso made a point of specifying that his grandmother Eleanor was 'the daughter of the king of England'.
5. Martínez, *Alfonso X, the Learned*, 38–9; Simon Doubleday, *The Wise King: A Christian Prince, Muslim Spain, and the Birth of the Renaissance* (2015), 3. Beatriz's sisters made impressive marriages across Europe: they were the Holy Roman Empress, the queen of Bohemia, and the duchess of Brabant in modern-day Belgium.
6. Martínez, *Alfonso X*, 35.
7. Martínez, *Alfonso X*, 25. Alfonso VIII of Castile and Alfonso IX of León were both grandsons of Alfonso VII, king of both Castile and León (1105–57). Berenguela of Castile had previously been betrothed to Konrad of Swabia, d. 1196, one of Emperor Friedrich Barbarossa's sons and the uncle of her future daughter-in-law Beatriz of Swabia.
8. Martínez, *Alfonso X*, 27; Bartlett, *Blood Royal*, 45–7.
9. Perry, *John of Brienne*, 130; Janna Bianchini, *The Queen's Hand: Power and Authority in the Reign of Berenguela of Castile* (2012), 186–87, 190; Martínez, *Alfonso X*, 32.
10. Perry, *John of Brienne*, 131; Perry, 'A King of Jerusalem in England: The Visit of John of Brienne in 1223', *History*, 100 (2015), 635.
11. Bianchini, The Queen's Hand, 202–5; Martínez, *Alfonso X*, 32–3. Teresa of Portugal, queen consort of León, was beatified in 1705, as were her sisters Sancha and Mafalda.

Chapter 8: The Learned King

1. Georgius Heinricus Pertz, ed., *Ryccardi de Sancti Germano Notarii Chronica* (1864), 55. I owe this reference to the Medieval Lands Project on the Foundation for Medieval Genealogy site, https://fmg.ac/.

2. Martínez, *Alfonso X*, 97.
3. *Memorial Histórico Español: Colección de Documentos, Opúsculos y Antigüedades que Publica la Real Academia de la Historia*, vol. 1 (1851), nos. 37, 40, 44, 53, 60, 63, 66, etc; Perry, *John of Brienne*, 165.
4. *Foedera, Conventiones, Litterae, et Cujuscunque Acta Publica 1066–1272*, 282; Robert Lee Wolff, 'Mortgage and Redemption of an Emperor's Son: Castile and the Latin Empire of Constantinople', *Speculum*, 29 (1954), 57–8.
5. *Memorial Histórico Español*, nos. 27, 32, 35, 37. A few months after Edward and Leonor's wedding, her niece Berenguela (b. 1253) was betrothed to Louis IX of France's eldest son Louis (b. 1244), but he died in early 1260.
6. Leonor inherited her mother's county of Ponthieu on Jeanne's death in 1279, as she was the only one of Jeanne's five Spanish children who outlived her, and the county of Ponthieu was subsequently held by Leonor's English son and grandson, Edward II and Edward III.
7. The National Archives SC 1/12/103 to 113.

Chapter 9: Poisoned Cherries

1. Martínez, *Alfonso X*, 95. Yolande of Aragón's name usually appears in her husband Alfonso X's documents as Yolant or Iolant, and she is sometimes called 'Violante' by modern writers. According to Sandy Bardsley (*Women's Roles in the Middle Ages* (2007), 82–3), Alfonso X was concerned about Yolande's failure to conceive and invited another woman to Castile to marry instead, presumably intending to have his first marriage annulled; but by the time she arrived, Yolande was pregnant.
2. Doubleday, *Wise King*, 127–30; *Memorial Histórico Español*, nos. 109, 124, 128, 130.
3. Doubleday, *Wise King*, 169. Fernando de la Cerda's maternal grandfather Jaume I of Aragón outlived him by a year.
4. Martínez, *Alfonso X*, 96, 407–8; Doubleday, *Wise King*, 200–01; Kinkade, 'Violante of Aragón', 8–9; Georges Daumet, *Mémoire sur les Relations de la France et de la Castille de 1255 à 1320* (1913), 51–2. In 1277, Alfonso X had Don Fadrique, the brother closest to him in age, secretly executed.
5. Richard P. Kinkade, 'Violante of Aragón (1236?-1300?): An Historical Overview', *Exemplaria Hispanica*, 2 (1992–93), 3; Martínez, *Alfonso X*, 96–7. Costanza married Alfonso X's brother Manuel (1234–83), seventh and youngest son of Fernando III and Beatriz of Swabia, supposedly after falling in love with his older brother Enrique.
6. Martínez, *Alfonso X*, 407; Paulette Pepin, 'A Case Study: Contract and its Consequences for the Kingdom of Castile-León', *The Historian*, 75 (2013), 814.
7. Runciman, *Sicilian Vespers*, 204, 209.
8. Doubleday, *Wise King*, 210; Pepin, 'A Case Study', 816.
9. Paulette Lynn Pepin, *María de Molina, Queen and Regent: Life and Rule in Castile-León, 1259–1321* (2016), 23; Jaume Aurell, 'The Self-Coronations of Iberian Kings: A Crooked Line', *Imago Temporis: Medium Aevum*, 8 (2014), 171.
10. Philip III's uncle Charles of Anjou, king of Sicily, also died in 1285, and Alexander III of Scotland died in 1286; see Parts 4 and 6. Philip III and Pere III were brothers-in-law: Philip had been married to Pere's late sister Isabel (d. 1271).
11. Carlos Estepa, 'The Strengthening of Royal Power in Castile Under Alfonso XI', *Building Legitimacy: Political Discourses and Forms of Legitimacy in Medieval Societies*, ed. Isabel Alfonso Antón, Hugh Kennedy and Julio Escalona Monge (2004), 186.

Chapter 10: An Extraordinary Queen

1. César González Mínguez, 'La Minoría de Fernando IV de Castilla (1295–1301)', *História: Revista Da Faculdade De Letras Da Universidade Do Porto*, 15 (2019), 1072.
2. Teofilo F. Ruiz, *Spain's Centuries of Crisis 1300–1474* (2007), 53 ('resourcefulness' quotation); Pepin, *María de Molina, Queen and Regent*, xxiv, 28; Peter Linehan, 'The English Mission of Cardinal Petrus Hispanus, the Chronicle of Walter of Guisborough, and News from Castile at Carlisle (1307)', *English Historical Review*, 117 (2002), 617; Pepin, 'A Case Study', 819. The queen's baptismal name was María Alfonso de Meneses: Pepin, *María de Molina*, 4.
3. Pepin, *María de Molina*, xi, xiv-xv, 11.
4. Ruiz, *Spain's Centuries of Crisis*, 53–4; Estepa, 'Strengthening of Royal Power in Castile under Alfonso XI', 186.
5. Jaume II instead married Blanche of Anjou-Naples, one of the daughters of Charles of Salerno and Marie of Hungary; see Part 4 below. Isabel of Castile married Duke John III of Brittany (1286–1341).
6. King Diniz of Portugal (b. 1261) was a grandson of Alfonso X of Castile-León via Alfonso's illegitimate daughter Beatriz (b. *c.* 1244); Diniz's wife and queen, Isabel of Aragón, was the daughter of Pere III, king of Aragón, and the sister of Alfonso III and Jaume II. She was canonised in 1626. Fernando IV was betrothed in the 1290s to a daughter of Philip IV of France, but she died in infancy.
7. Linehan, 'English Mission of Cardinal Petrus Hispanus', 615–18; Johnstone, *Edward of Carnarvon*, 120.
8. *Vita Edwardi Secundi Monachi Cuiusdam Malmesberiensis*, ed. N. Denholm-Young (1957), 40; *Foedera 1272–1307*, 1007 (*doit especialement amer Edward nostre chier filz qui est du sank Despaigne).*
9. *Manuel García Fernández, 'Alfonso XI y Andalucía. Un Rey en Tierra de Frontera (1312–1350)', Andalucía en la Historia, 38 (2012), 42.*
10. *Foedera 1307–27*, 144; The National Archives SC 1/16/14; *Calendar of Close Rolls 1307–13*, 457; *CCR 1318–23*, 123; *Calendar of Patent Rolls 1317–21*, 262; W.R. Childs, 'England in Europe in the Reign of Edward II', *The Reign of Edward II: New Perspectives*, ed. Gwilym Dodd and Anthony Musson (2006), 105–6.
11. Pepin, *María de Molina*, 11.
12. José Hinojosa Montalvo, *Jaime II y el Esplendor de la Corona de Aragón* (2005), 77–8, 82; H.T. Sturcken, 'The Unconsummated Marriage of Jaime of Aragón and Leonor of Castile (October 1319)', *Journal of Medieval History*, 5 (1979), 185–201.
13. *Pruebas de la Historia de la Casa de Lara*, ed. Luis Salazar y Castro (1694), 32–5.

Chapter 11: Natural and Gracious Good Qualities

1. *CCR 1323–27*, 175–76. 253–54, 344, 350–51, 515–16, 556–57.
2. Maria of Portugal's mother was Beatriz of Castile (b. 1293), youngest child of Sancho IV and María de Molina, and sister of Fernando IV.
3. Clara Estow, *Pedro the Cruel of Castile 1350–1369* (1996), 21–2; Nicholás Agrait, 'The Reconquest During the Reign of Alfonso XI (1312–1350)', *Essays in Honour of Joseph F. O'Callaghan*, ed. Donald J. Kagay and Theresa M. Vann (1998), 154.
4. *Foedera 1344–61*, 46–7, 59, 74, 147.
5. Estow, *Pedro the Cruel*, 36; Manuel *García Fernández, 'Alfonso XI y Andalucía. Un Rey en Tierra de Frontera (1312–1350)', Andalucía en la Historia, 38 (2012), 44.*

6. *Crónicas de los Reyes de Castilla Don Pedro, Don Enrique II, Don Juan I, Don Enrique III por D. Pedro López de Ayala*, ed. Don Eugenio de Llaguno Amirola, vol. 1 (1779), 83, 130–31, 194, 350, 366–7, 558–70.
7. *Crónicas de los Reyes de Castilla ... por D. Pedro López de Ayala*, 563 (*la corona Francesa que fué de Doña Blanca fija del duc de Borbon*).
8. Pedro's will is cited in full in *Crónicas de los Reyes de Castilla ... por D. Pedro López de Ayala*, 558–70; Estow, *Pedro the Cruel of Castile*, 131–2, 139–40, 146–7, 211–12. Estow (p. 211) discusses the possibility that Pedro had Blanche killed, and states that it is impossible to come to a firm conclusion based on the available evidence; some contemporary Castilian chronicles thought he was guilty of poisoning her, others believed she died naturally.

Chapter 12: The Cruel King

1. *Crónicas de los Reyes de Castilla Don Pedro, Don Enrique II, Don Juan I, Don Enrique III por D. Pedro López de Ayala*, ed. Don Eugenio de Llaguno Amirola, vol. 1 (1779), 293.
2. *Crónicas de los Reyes de Castilla ... por D. Pedro López de Ayala*, 561–64. For Pedro's seizure of e*l Bermejo*, meaning 'russet' or 'the red one', see L.P. Harvey, *Islamic Spain, 1250 to 1500* (1990), 213–14.

Part III: Constantinople

Chapter 13: The Sack of Constantinople

1. *O City of Byzantium: Annals of Niketas Choniatēs*, xxv-xxvii; *A History of Deeds Done Beyond the Sea*, vol. 2, 461–62, 465.
2. Phillips, *Holy Warriors*, 181, citing Geoffroi de Villehardouin.
3. *O City*, xvi-xvii.
4. Folda, *Crusader Art in the Holy Land*, 70, 73.
5. *Deeds Done*, vol. 1, 123, 129–30, 146; vol. 2, 129; https://sourcebooks.fordham.edu/basis/AnnaComnena-Alexiad00.asp, accessed 12 March 2023; *O City*, 50–51.

Chapter 14: A Lively Form of Air and Crystal

1. *History of Deeds Done*, vol. 2, 449–50; Runciman, *History of the Crusades*, vol. 2, 422; Paul Magdalino, *The Empire of Manuel I Komnenos, 1143–1180* (1993), 100. Emperor Manuel's mother, born Piroska of Hungary (d. 1134), was also renamed Eirene.
2. *O City of Byzantium*, 210.
3. Michael Jeffreys, 'The Vernacular Εἰσιτήριοι for Agnes of France', *Proceedings of the First Australian Byzantine Studies Conference* (1981), 107 (also for the 'cornerstone' quote). Bertha von Sulzbach's sister Gertrud married Konrad III of Germany, uncle of Barbarossa.
4. *O City*, 78, 97, 130.
5. *Deeds Done*, vol. 2, 450; *O City*, 97.
6. Raymond of Poitiers was the younger brother of Queen Eleanor's father William X, duke of Aquitaine. Maria's brother Bohemond III (d.1201) was the father of Bohemond IV, prince of Antioch, and the grandfather of both Raymond-Roupen of Antioch, claimant to Armenian Cilicia, and Philip of Antioch, first husband of Queen Zabel of Armenian Cilicia.
7. After Constance's death, Raynald became the third husband of Stephanie de Milly, heiress of Oultrejourdain and the mother of Queen Isabella of Jerusalem's first husband Humphrey of Toron (b. *c.*1166).

8. Melisende of Tripoli was the daughter of Queen Melisende of Jerusalem's sister Hodierna, countess of Tripoli; Maria of Antioch was the maternal granddaughter of Queen Melisende and Hodierna's sister Alice, princess of Antioch.
9. *Deeds Done*, vol. 2, 288–91; *O City*, 66, 149; Lynda Garland, *Byzantine Empresses: Women and Power in Byzantium, AD 527–1204* (1999), 201; Hodgson, *Women, Crusading*, 88–91.
10. *O City*, 78; Paul Stephenson, *Byzantium's Balkan Frontier: A Political Study of the Northern Balkans* (2000), 257.
11. After Agnes of Antioch, the mother of all his legitimate children, died, Béla married Marguerite of France, one of the daughters of Louis VII.
12. *O City*, 96; Magdalino, *Empire of Manuel I*, 100, 243; Jeffreys, 'Vernacular Εἰσιτήριοι', 107. Agnès was the only full sister of Philip Augustus, though they had four older half-sisters from their father's first two marriages, including Marie, mother of Queen Isabella of Jerusalem's third husband Henri of Champagne, and Marguerite, second wife of Béla III of Hungary.
13. *Deeds Done*, vol. 2, 452, 461.

Chapter 15: He Who Stank of the Dark Ages

1. Confusingly, her adviser and perhaps lover bore the same name as her son, Alexios Komnenos, and was the brother of Ioannes Doukas Komnenos (d. 1176) and uncle of Maria Komnene (b. 1154/55), mother of Queen Isabella of Jerusalem.
2. *O City*, 51, 127, 231.
3. *O City*, 8; https://sourcebooks.fordham.edu/basis/AnnaComnena-Alexiad00.asp. Anna died in 1153, around the same time that her great-niece Maria the *Porphyrogennete* was born.
4. *O City*, 81, 130–31; *Deeds Done*, vol. 2, 462–63. Andronikos's father was the *Sebastokrator* and *Porphyrogennetos* Isaakios Komnenos (b. 1093), younger brother of Emperor Ioannes II and the *Porphyrogennete* Anna Komnene.
5. *O City*, 137, 140, 149, 152.
6. *O City*, 144–45.
7. Phillips, *Holy Warriors*, 119.
8. *O City*, 78.
9. *Deeds Done*, vol. 2, 416–17; Hodgson, *Women, Crusading*, 218–19; Hamilton, 'Women in the Crusader States', 161–62; A.A. Vasiliev, 'The Foundation of the Empire of Trebizond (1204–1222), *Speculum*, 11 (1936), 5.
10. *O City*, 78–9, 153.
11. Isaakios's father was Andronikos Angelos, who was, like Andronikos Komnenos and Emperor Manuel, a grandson of Emperor Alexios I. Andronikos Angelos so angered his cousin Manuel in 1179 by his 'ignominious flight' from a Turkish army that the emperor threatened to have him paraded through the streets of Constantinople wearing women's clothes: *O City*, 110–11.
12. *O City*, 190–94, 197–98.
13. *The Conquest of Constantinople: Robert of Clari*, trans. Edgar Holmes McNeal (1936), 79.
14. *O City*, 231–32, 253–54.
15. *O City*, 250–53.
16. *O City*, 294.
17. http://attalus.org/armenian/kg6.htm, accessed 26 November 2022; John Hutchins Rosser, *Historical Dictionary of Byzantium* (2012), 35.

18. *O City*, 294–95, 301–02; *Chronicles of the Crusades: Contemporary Narratives of the Crusade of Richard Coeur de Lion by Richard of Devizes and Geoffrey de Vinsauf, and of the Crusade of Saint Louis by Lord John de Joinville*, ed. Margaret R.B. Shaw (1903), 44–5, 50.
19. *O City*, 295.
20. *O City*, 309, 334; *Conquest of Constantinople: Robert of Clari*, 124. Alexios III Angelos and Euphrosynē Doukaina Kamatera both died of natural causes in 1211.
21. *O City*, 307–09, 405; Phillips, *Fourth Crusade*, 256.

Chapter 16: The Incendiary Angel of Evil

1. *O City*, xiv, 304.
2. *Joinville and Villehardouin: Chronicles of the Crusades*, 94–6; Thomas F. Madden, 'The Latin Empire of Constantinople's Fractured Foundation: The Rift between Boniface of Montferrat and Baldwin of Flanders', *The Fourth Crusade: Event, Aftermath, and Perceptions*, ed. Madden (2017), 45.
3. Phillips, *Fourth Crusade*, xi-xii, 287–88; *Joinville and Villehardouin*, 110–11. Henri and Marie's brother Thibaut had intended to participate in the Fourth Crusade, but died in May 1201; his son Thibaut the younger, count of Champagne and king of Navarre, was born six days later.
4. *Joinville and Villehardouin*, 97. Bonifacio was Emperor Isaakios Angelos's first choice to marry his sister Theodora Angelina in 1187, but he was already married to his first wife: *O City of Byzantium*, 210.
5. John V.A. Fine, *The Late Medieval Balkans: A Critical Survey from the Late Twelfth Century to the Ottoman Conquest* (1994), 63.
6. Fine, *Late Medieval Balkans*, 62–3; *Joinville and Villehardouin*, 92; Bartlett, *Blood Royal*, 17.
7. *Joinville and Villehardouin*, 74, 82, 92, 101.
8. Some decades later, Erzésbet the Cuman, daughter of the Cumans' chieftain, married Béla III's great-grandson István V of Hungary.
9. *O City*, 353; Fine, *Medieval Balkans*, 81–2. Hendrik of Flanders married Bonifacio of Montferrat's daughter Agnese in 1207, and secondly *Tsar* Kaloyan/Ioannitsa's daughter Marija in 1213.
10. Robert Lee Wolff, 'Baldwin of Flanders and Hainaut, First Latin Emperor of Constantinople: His Life, Death, and Resurrection, 1172–1225', *Speculum*, 27 (1952), 294–98.

Chapter 17: The Latin Emperors

1. Michael Angold, 'The Latin Empire of Constantinople, 1204–1261: Marriage Strategies', *Identities and Allegiances in the Eastern Mediterranean after 1204*, ed. Judith Herrin and Guillaume Saint-Guillain (2011), 54.
2. Folda, *Crusader Art*, 158; Perry, *John of Brienne*, 151, 164.
3. Fine, Late Medieval Balkans, 124; Perry, *John of Brienne*, 156, 162; Peter Lock, *The Franks in the Aegean, 1204–1500*, 63; and see also https://ims.leeds.ac.uk/wp-content/uploads/sites/29/2019/02/Latin-Empire.pdf for the Treaty of Perugia, accessed 21 February 2023.
4. This number of John's children includes his little son from his second marriage to Stephanie of Armenia, who died in 1220 aged about four and was probably also called John de Brienne.
5. There are numerous examples in *Memorial Histórico Español: Colección de Documentos*.
6. Folda, *Crusader Art*, 158; *History of the Crusades*, vol. 2, ed. Hazard, Setton and Wolff, 670.
7. Perry, *John of Brienne*, 157–61; Tyerman, *God's War*, 555–57; Phillips, *Fourth Crusade*, 304–05.

8. Perry, *The Briennes*, 71–3.
9. Nikoloas G. Chrissis, 'A Diversion that Never Was: Thibaut IV of Champagne, Richard of Cornwall and Pope Gregory IX's Crusading Plans for Constantinople, 1235–1239', *Crusades*, 9 (2010), 123–45. Gautier de Brienne married Marie of Cyprus, eldest child of Alice of Champagne and Jerusalem and Hugh I de Lusignan, king of Cyprus.
10. Perry, *John of Brienne*, 164; Perry, *The Briennes*, 73.
11. Cited in Perry, *John of Brienne*, 193.
12. Phillips, *Fourth Crusade*, 307; Jonathan Harris, *Byzantium and the Crusades* (2003), 170–71; Wolff, 'Mortgage and Redemption of an Emperor's Son', 73 ('great name' quotation).
13. Hodgson, *Women, Crusading*, 123–24.

Chapter 18: Nicaea, Trebizond and Epirus

1. Perry, *John of Brienne*, 162.
2. Vasiliev, 'Foundation of Trebizond', 5–6, 8ff; Kelsey Jackson Williams, 'A Genealogy of the Grand Komnenoi of Trebizond', *Foundations*, 2 (2006), 173.
3. Kinkade, 'Violante of Aragón (1236?-1300?): An Historical Overview', 4. Violante of Aragón's maternal grandmother was Yolande de Courtenay, queen of Hungary, older sister of Marie de Brienne's husband Baudouin de Courtenay.
4. Ian Mortimer, *The Fears of Henry IV: The Life of England's Self-Made King* (2007), 131.
5. Rosser, *Historical Dictionary of Byzantium*, 308.
6. Mortimer, *Fears of Henry IV*, 230. Manuel II Palaiologos was a great-great-grandson of Zabel, queen regnant of Cilician Armenia, via Zabel's granddaughter Rita of Armenia.
7. Fine, *Medieval Balkans*, 165.

Part IV: Holy Roman Empire

Chapter 19: The Wonder of the World

1. All the details in these two paragraphs are from *Estoire d'Eracles: the Old French Continuation of William of Tyre*, available at https://ims.leeds.ac.uk/wp-content/uploads/sites/29/2019/10/Estoire-dEracles.pdf (accessed 11 April 2023), 2–4. After the coronation of her niece, Alice of Champagne and Jerusalem, dowager queen of Cyprus, married Bohemond V, prince of Antioch; the marriage was annulled in 1227.
2. Runciman, *History of the Crusades*, vol. 3, 176.
3. David Abulafia, *Friedrich II: A Medieval Emperor* (1992), 153.
4. Wilson, *The Holy Roman Empire: A Thousand Years of Europe's History*, 27.
5. Walter Fröhlich, 'The Marriage of Henry VI and Constance of Sicily: Prelude and Consequences', *Anglo-Norman Studies*, 15 (1992), 113; Runciman, *The Sicilian Vespers: A History of the Mediterranean World in the Later Thirteenth Century* (1958), 11.
6. *O City of Byzantium*, 263–64.
7. *O City*, 261, 263–64.

Chapter 20: A Terrifying Marvel

1. Imre was the son of *Despot* Béla III and Agnes of Antioch, and brother of Margit of Hungary, Byzantine Empress and queen of Thessaloniki. Costanza and Imre's son László died as a child in 1205 and was succeeded by Imre and Margit's brother András II.
2. Runciman, *Crusades*, vol. 3, 176; Runciman, *Sicilian Vespers*, 8–9; *The Art of Falconry, Being the De Arte Venandi cum Avibus of Friedrich II of Hohenstaufen*, trans. Casey A. Wood and F. Marjorie Fyfe (1943; reissued 2010), vol. 1, 2 ('eastern sultan' quotation); Phillips, *Holy Warriors*, 219 ('harmonious' quotation).

3. Phillips, *Holy Warriors*, 219–20. Friedrich was the cousin of Alfonso X's mother Beatriz of Swabia, who like him was a grandchild of Barbarossa (which means 'red beard' in Latin, giving some indication of what Barbarossa and perhaps his descendants looked like).
4. Folda, *Crusader Art*, 118.
5. *Estoire d'Eracles: the Old French Continuation of William of Tyre*, 2–3; Perry, 'Isabella II or Yolanda?', 74; Christopher Tyerman, *God's War: A New History of the Crusades*, 741; *History of the Crusades*, vol. 2, ed. Hazard, Setton, Wolff, 442; Phillips, *Holy Warriors*, 229–30; Abulafia, *Friedrich II*, 152.
6. Folda, *Crusader Art*, 150, 213; *History of the Crusades*, vol. 2, ed. Hazard, Setton, Wolff, 670.
7. Folda, *Crusader Art*, 148.
8. Abulafia, *Friedrich II*, 241.
9. Runciman, *Sicilian Vespers*, 26, 42.

Chapter 21: Taking Hold of the Moon

1. Abulafia, *Friedrich II*, 239.
2. *Calendar of Liberate Rolls 1226–40*, 275; *Calendar of Close Rolls 1234–37*, 167; *Calendar of Documents Relating to Scotland 1108–1272*, no. 1227.
3. *Oxford Dictionary of National Biography*.
4. T.W.E. Roche, *The King of Almayne: A Thirteenth-Century Englishman in Europe* (1966), 84; *Oxford Dictionary of National Biography*.
5. Weiler, Henry III and the Staufen Empire, 89.
6. Abulafia, *Friedrich II*, 406; Weiler, *Henry III and the Staufen Empire*, 114; *Constitutiones et Acta Publica Imperatorum et Regum*, vol. 2, 1198–1272, ed. Ludewicus Weiland (1896), no. 274.
7. Weiler, *Henry III and the Staufen Empire*, 115. Elisabeth was a great-granddaughter of Heinrich 'the Lion', duke of Saxony and Bavaria, and Matilda of England, eldest daughter of Henry II.
8. *Foedera 1066–1272*, 302.
9. Rhodes, 'Edmund, Earl of Lancaster', 23–4, 27; *Calendar of Patent Rolls 1247–58*, 343–44, 450, 507–8, 567–68; *Oxford Dictionary of National Biography*.
10. Edmund's first wife was the heiress Aveline Forz, who died aged fifteen in 1274. Blanche's first husband was Enrique I of Navarre (*c.* 1244–74), one of the younger sons of Thibaut of Champagne (1201–53).

Chapter 22: The Putrid Corpse of That Pestilential Man

1. *CPR 1281–92*, 343; *CPR 1317–21*, 341; *CCR 1323–27*, 136; *CPR 1364–67*, 330; *Calendar of Entries in the Papal Registers Relating to Great Britain and Ireland: Papal Letters*, vol. 4, 1362–1404, ed. W.H. Bliss and J.A. Twemlow (1893–1902), 99; *Foedera 1361–77*, 830.
2. Runciman, *Sicilian Vespers*, 71. The third Provence sister, Sancha, was the second of the three wives of Richard of Cornwall, and the mother of his second son and ultimate heir Edmund of Cornwall (1249–1300). Beatrice of Provence had once been courted by Konrad von Hohenstaufen: Runciman, *Sicilian Vespers*, 73.
3. Runciman, *Sicilian Vespers*, 95–6, 99.
4. Runciman, *Vespers*, 115; Jean Dunbabin, *Charles I of Anjou. Power, Kingship and State-Making in Thirteenth-Century Europe* (1998), 4–5, 58. Konradin's heir male to the Latin Kingdom of Jerusalem, Hugh II of Cyprus, had died in late 1267 at the age of fourteen or fifteen.

5. Runciman, *Sicilian Vespers*, 146.
6. Fine, *Medieval Balkans*, 170.

Chapter 23: Death to the French

1. Runciman, *Sicilian Vespers*, 211–12.
2. In 1252 before marrying Costanza, Pere III's marriage to Henry III of England and Alienor of Provence's second daughter Beatrice (b. 1242) had been considered: *Foedera 1066–1272*, 290.
3. Runciman, *Sicilian Vespers*, 215–16.
4. In Castile-León at the same time, Pere III's maternal nephew Sancho, the future Sancho IV, was marrying María de Molina and rebelling against his father Alfonso X.
5. István V's mother Maria Laskarina was the daughter of the first Emperor of Nicaea and a granddaughter of Alexios III Angelos, Byzantine Emperor. István was the first son of his parents and was born after seven sisters, and had a younger sister and brother as well. Three of his sisters have been canonised or beatified.
6. Giorgio Bordin and Laura Polo d'Ambrosio, *Medicine in Art* (2010), 160.
7. Charles, born 1270, had previously been married to Marguerite of Anjou-Naples (1272–99), eldest daughter of Charles of Salerno and Marie of Hungary.
8. *Chronique de Ramon Muntaner, Traduite pour la Première Fois du Catalan*, ed. J.A. Buchon (1827), vol. 1, 438–39; vol. 2, 58–60.

Chapter 24: A Lion and a Wildcat

1. Morris, *A Great and Terrible King*, 209–10.
2. *Chronique de Ramon Muntaner*, ed. Buchon, vol. 2, 58–60.

Part V: France

Chapter 25: A Barefoot Procession

1. Perry, *John of Brienne*, 123–35; Perry, 'King of Jerusalem in England', 627.
2. https://ims.leeds.ac.uk/wp-content/uploads/sites/29/2019/10/Estoire-dEracles.pdf, accessed 25 March 2023.
3. Perry, 'King of Jerusalem in England', 633–35.
4. Runciman, *History of the Crusades*, vol. 3, 177; Perry, 'King of Jerusalem', 636–37; Perry, *John of Brienne*, 132–33.
5. Perry, *John of Brienne*, 126–28; Georgius Heinricus Pertz, ed., *Ryccardi de Sancti Germano Notarii Chronica* (1864), 55.
6. Antoine-Martial Le Fèvre, *Calendrier Historique et Chronologique de l'Église de Paris, Contenant l'Origine des Paroisses, Abbayes, Monastères, Prieurés, Collégiales &c. de Paris* (1847), 285; Julien Philippe de Gaulle and Charles Nodier, *Nouvelle Histoire de Paris et de ses Environs* (1839), vol. 1, 619.
7. David Carpenter, *Henry III: The Rise to Power and Personal Rule, 1207–1258* (2020), 29–30; Björn K.U. Weiler, *Henry III of England and the Staufen Empire, 1216–1272* (2006), 20; N. Denholm-Young, *Richard of Cornwall* (1947), 2, 5, 44.
8. Perry, 'King of Jerusalem in England', 636.
9. *Memorial Histórico Español: Colección de Documentos*, nos. 60, 63, 66; Perry, *The Briennes*, xii, 67.
10. Cited in Perry, *John of Brienne*, 164, and Wolff, 'Mortgage and Redemption of an Emperor's Son', 76 note 77.

Chapter 26: A Mantle and a Surcoat for Meals

1. Josef W. Meri, ed., *Medieval Islamic Civilization: An Encyclopedia, volume 2, L–Z, index* (2006), 730.
2. *Joinville and Villehardouin: Chronicles of the Crusades*, 198–99; Perry, *The Briennes*, xiii, 80, 97. Marie de Brienne's letter to Queen Blanche is in Paul André Roger, *La Noblesse de France aux Croisades* (1845), 121–22. Jeanne de Châteaudun's first husband John de Montfort, count of Montfort, was a nephew of Simon de Montfort (d.1265), earl of Leicester, brother-in-law of Henry III of England. Alphonse and Marie had several children and numerous descendants in France, though Alphonse's direct male line came to an end in November 1350 when his great-great-grandson Raoul de Brienne, count of Eu and Guînes and constable of France, was beheaded in the Hôtel de Nesle in Paris: S.H. Cuttler, *The Law of Treason and Treason Trials in Later Medieval France* (1981), 154. Another of Alphonse's descendants was the partly Spanish, partly French nobleman Carlos de la Cerda, a notorious pirate defeated by Edward III of England at the naval battle of Winchelsea in August 1350.
3. Henry III was a grandson of Henry II of England and Eleanor of Aquitaine; Louis was their great-grandson via his mother Blanche of Castile. Henry was born in October 1207 and Louis in April 1214.
4. Margaret Howell, *Eleanor of Provence: Queenship in Thirteenth-Century England* (1998), 137.
5. *Oxford Dictionary of National Biography*; *Calendar of Liberate Rolls 1251–60*, 197.
6. Howell, *Eleanor of Provence*, 165–66. In 1258, Henry discussed a marriage for Beatrice with one of Alfonso X of Castile's many younger brothers at the same time as planning a match for her into Brittany: *Foedera 1066–1272*, 372, 382.
7. Kinkade, 'Violante of Aragón', 4.

Chapter 27: The Handsomest Man in the World

1. Jim Bradbury, *The Capetians: Kings of France 987*–1328 (2007), 235.
2. Nancy Goldstone, *Four Queens: The Provençal Sisters Who Ruled Europe* (2007), 192.
3. Joseph R. Strayer, *The Reign of Philip the Fair* (1980), 6–7.
4. Elizabeth A.R. Brown, 'Moral Imperatives and Conundrums of Conscience: Reflections on Philip the Fair of France', *Speculum*, 87 (2012), 9.
5. Gita Deneckere and Jeroen Deploige, *Mystifying the Monarch: Studies on Discourse, Power, and History* (2006), 58; Strayer, *The Reign of Philip the Fair*, 3.
6. For Philip and Juana's children and their ages, see Elizabeth A.R. Brown, 'Philip the Fair and His Family: His Sons, Their Marriages, and Their Wives', *Medieval Prosopography*, 32 (2017).

Chapter 28: Feuding Fishermen

1. Morris, *Great and Terrible King*, 264–68.
2. *Calendar of Entries in the Papal Registers Relating to Great Britain and Ireland: Papal Letters*, vol. 1 (1198–1304), 576–77, 579. Edward I and Marguerite of France were first cousins once removed: Edward's aunt Marguerite of Provence, queen of France, was his wife's grandmother.
3. Brown, 'Moral Imperatives and Conundrums of Conscience', 7–9.
4. Elizabeth A.R. Brown, 'The King's Conundrum: Endowing Queens and Loyal Servants, Ensuring Salvation, and Protecting the Patrimony in Fourteenth-Century France', *Medieval Futures: Attitudes to the Future in the Middle Ages*, ed. Ian P. Wei and John Anthony Burrow (2000), 134 note 45.

Chapter 29: The Tour de Nesle and Tennis

1. *Calendar of Chancery Warrants 1244–1326*, 392.
2. Elizabeth A.R. Brown, 'Philip the Fair of France and His Family's Disgrace: The Adultery Scandal Revealed, Recounted, Reimagined, and Redated', *Mediaevistik*, 32 (2019), 78–80, believes that Isabella was heavily involved in the matter, and furthermore, that she subsequently played a vital role in 'breaking news of the scandal (and offering comments on it) to many high-placed and influential individuals' before returning to England.
3. Cuttler, *Law of Treason and Treason Trials in Later Medieval France*, 29–30, 54, 118.
4. Elizabeth A.R. Brown, The Ceremonial of Royal Succession in Capetian France: The Funeral of Philip V', *Speculum*, 55 (1980), 269–70.
5. Elizabeth A.R. Brown, 'Philip the Fair's Sons, Their Statuses, and Their Landed Endowments', *Medieval Prosopography*, 32 (2017), 189.
6. Mariah Proctor-Tiffany, *Medieval Art in Motion: The Inventory and Gift Giving of Queen Clémence de Hongrie* (2019), 16. Clemence was a granddaughter of Charles of Salerno and Marie of Hungary, king and queen of Naples, via their eldest child Charles Martel (1271–95), titular king of Hungary. Her older brother Károly Robert reigned as king of Hungary and Croatia from 1308 to 1342. Clemence's unusual given name – she was named after her German mother Klementia von Habsburg – caused some confusion in England: on 17 May 1316 (*Foedera 1307–27*, 290), Louis X's brother-in-law Edward II addressed a letter to Clemence as 'the most excellent lady, Lady Elizabeth, by the grace of God queen of France and Navarre'. Probably, the royal clerk who made this error had Edward's sister Elizabeth, countess of Hereford, in mind; she had passed away a few days earlier.
7. Brown, 'Philip the Fair of France and His Family's Disgrace', 75–6.
8. Elizabeth A.R. Brown, 'The Ceremonial of Royal Succession in Capetian France: The Double Funeral of Louis X', *Traditio*, 34 (1978), 228–29, 232.
9. Proctor-Tiffany, *Medieval Art in Motion*, 18. Clemence was raised in Naples by her long-lived paternal grandmother Marie of Hungary (d. 1323), queen consort of Naples, after her parents Charles Martel of Hungary and Klementia von Habsburg, daughter of the German king Rudolf I, both died in 1295 when she was a toddler: see Proctor-Tiffany, *Medieval Art in Motion*, 14–16. Charles Martel was an older brother of Robert 'the Wise', king of Naples, Philip of Taranto, and Charles de Valois's first wife Marguerite of Anjou-Naples. He died many years before his parents.
10. Brown, 'Double Funeral of Louis X', 264; Proctor-Tiffany, *Medieval Art in Motion*, 18.
11. Jeanne of France (1308–47) thus became, confusingly, both countess and duchess of Burgundy.
12. Brown, 'The King's Conundrum: Endowing Queens and Loyal Servants', 126.

Chapter 30: The Last Capetian King

1. Elizabeth A.R. Brown, 'The Funeral of Philip V', 269–71.
2. Brown, 'Philip the Fair and His Family', 181; Elizabeth A.R. Brown, 'The Children of Charles of La Marche and Blanche of Artois and Burgundy', *Medieval Prosopography*, 34 (2019), 151–74; Brown, 'Philip the Fair of France and His Family's Disgrace', 84, 102.
3. *The War of Saint-Sardos (1323–1325): Gascon Correspondence and Diplomatic Documents*, ed. Pierre Chaplais (1954), 189–90, which cites a letter sent to Edward II of England by some of his envoys to France on 10 July 1324, stating: '…*lui* [Charles IV] *trovasmes a Annet' le joedy prochain devant la feste de la Translacion de Seint Thomas, ou il avoit espouses mesmes le jour le* [sic] *soer le conte de Drews* [sic] *qore est*'.

4. *The War of Saint-Sardos*, ed. Chaplais, 199–200.
5. Brown, 'Philip the Fair of France and his Family's Disgrace', 78; Elizabeth A.R. Brown, 'Diplomacy, Adultery, and Domestic Politics at the Court of Philip the Fair: Queen Isabelle's Mission to the Court of France in 1314', *Essays in Medieval History Presented to George Peddy Cuttino*, ed. J.S. Hamilton and Patricia J. Bradley, 69–72.
6. Jean Lebeuf, Adrien Augier and Fernand Bournon, *Histoire de la Ville et de Tout le Diocèse de Paris*, vol. 2 (1883), p. 121. The second abbess of Maubuisson, from 1276 to her death in 1309, was the Brienne/Beaumonts' cousin Blanche de Brienne, daughter of Alphonse, count of Eu (d. 1270). Another Brienne/Beaumont sister, Marie, lady of Avaugour, also died in 1328, as did Clemence of Hungary, dowager queen of France, the widow of Louis X.

Part VI: Scotland

Chapter 31: The Red Fox Cub

1. *Anglo-Scottish Relations 1174–1328: Some Selected Documents*, ed. and trans. E.L.G. Stones (reprinted 1970), 12–23; *Foedera 1066–1272*, 59.
2. In 1979, Edith Pargeter (aka Ellis Peters) wrote a novel about her, *The Marriage of Meggotta*.
3. *John of Fordun's Chronicle of the Scottish Nation*, ed. William F. Skene (1872), 284; *Calendar of Documents Relating to Scotland 1108–1272*, no. 508; *Anglo-Scottish Relations 1174–1328*, 24–27.
4. *CDS 1108–1272*, no. 518; *Oxford Dictionary of National Biography*. Joan of England was a much younger first cousin of Berenguela of Castile, queen of León and her sister Blanche, queen of France, and of Otto von Welf, Holy Roman Emperor. Her mother the dowager queen of England, Isabelle of Angoulême, and her stepfather Hugues X de Lusignan had nine children, some of whom moved to England and became close to their half-brother Henry III.
5. *CDs 1108–1272*, nos. 805–06.
6. John of *Fordun's Chronicle*, 287; *Calendar of Liberate Rolls 1226–40*, 316–17; *CDS 1108–1272*, nos. 1692–93, 1701, 1902, 1948, 2555.
7. *Calendar of Liberate Rolls 1240–45*, 306, and *1245–51*, 156; *CDS 1108–1272*, nos. 1626, 1670. Rather confusingly, Queen Joan had a much older half-sister also called Joan, an illegitimate daughter of King John, who married Llywelyn ap Iorwerth, prince of Wales.

Chapter 32: The Young King of Scotland

1. *John of Fordun's Chronicle*, 288–89.
2. *CDS 1108–1272*, nos. 1785, 1791, 1795, 1804, 1807; *John of Fordun's Chronicle*, 290–91; D.E.R. Watt, 'The Minority of Alexander III of Scotland', *Transactions of the Royal Historical Society*, 21 (1971), 8. Queen Margaret was also an ancestor of the English royal family via her daughter Edith/Matilda of Scotland, who married William the Conqueror's son Henry I and was the grandmother of Henry II.
3. *CDS 1108–1272*, nos. 1815, 1825, 1829, 1844, 1848; *Foedera 1066–1272*, 278–79; Marion Campbell, *Alexander III, King of Scots* (1999), 37–39; Peter Hammond, *Food and Feast in Medieval England* (1993), 125–26.
4. *CDS 1108–1272*, no. 1854; Campbell, *Alexander III*, 38.
5. *CDS 1108–1272*, nos. 1826–27, 1841.
6. *CDS 1108–1272*, nos. 1824, 1828, 1848; *John of Fordun's Chronicle*, 291.
7. Campbell, *Alexander III*, 41, 65.

8. *CDS 1108–1272*, no. 1935.
9. *CDS 1108–1272*, nos. 1986–90, 1995–96, 2001–02, 2004; *Foedera 1066–1272*, 327; Watt, 'Minority of Alexander III', 13. The earl of Gloucester was Richard de Clare, b. 1222, once briefly married to Alexander III's cousin Meggotta de Burgh.
10. *CDS 1108–1272*, no. 2012, dated 20 September 1255; Hilda Johnstone, *Edward of Carnarvon 1284–1307* (1946), 24.
11. *CDS 1108–1272*, nos. 2053, 2055.

Chapter 33: Queen Marie and John de Brienne the Younger

1. *Foedera 1066–1272*, 357–58; *CDS 1108–1272*, nos. 2064, 2083–84, 2139–40; Watt, 'Minority of Alexander III', 18–19; Perry, *The Briennes*, 81, 165.
2. *CDS 1108–1272*, nos. 2139–40; *Memorial Histórico Español: Colección de Documentos*, nos. 60, 63. On 13 September 1258 (no. 66), Alphonse and Louis de Brienne witnessed another document of Alfonso X, and rather confusingly Louis was called 'count of Montfort', John's title, rather than 'count of Beaumont'.
3. *Scotichronicon, Volume 5, Books IX-X: New Edition in Latin and English with Notes and Indexes*, ed. D.E.R. Watt (1990; reissued as an e-book 2022), 368 (*fugiens a viro suo, venit in Scocia de partibus transmarinis*).
4. *CDS 1108–1272*, nos. 2206, 2229; *Foedera 1066–1272*, 402.
5. *CDS 1272–1307*, nos. 185, 204, 253; TNA SC 1/20 nos. 143–68.
6. Campbell, *Alexander III*, 243.
7. *John of Fordun's Chronicle*, 299–300, narrates the story of Marjorie's marriage to Robert Bruce (b. 1243) but mistakenly assumes that it was Marjorie and Adam's daughter Martha who married him.
8. *The Chronicle of Lanercost 1272–1346*, ed. H. Maxwell (1913), 8–9.

Chapter 34: The Lord Had Shaken His Sword Against Him

1. *John of Fordun's Chronicle*, 300; G.W.S. Barrow, 'A Kingdom in Crisis: Scotland and the Maid of Norway', *The Scottish Historical Review*, 69, part 2, *Studies Commemorative of the Anniversary of the Death of the Maid of Norway* (1990), 124. Eleanor de Montfort was the only daughter of Henry III's youngest sister Eleanor (1215–75) and Simon de Montfort, earl of Leicester; she died in June 1282 after giving birth to her only child, Gwenllian (d. 1337).
2. G.W.S. Barrow, *Robert Bruce and the Community of the Realm of Scotland* (second edition, 1976), 17.
3. *The Chronicle of Lanercost 1272–1346*, ed. Maxwell, 9, 32, 39–41.
4. *CDS 1272–1307*, no. 197.
5. *Foedera 1272–1307*, 579–80; Campbell, *Alexander III*, 215.
6. *John of Fordun's Chronicle*, 302.
7. *CDS 1272–1307*, no. 250; *Anglo-Scottish Relations 1174–1328: Some Selected Documents*, 84–87; Campbell, *Alexander III*, 220–21.
8. Barrow, 'Kingdom in Crisis', 121.
9. *Lanercost*, 41. Yoleta's paternal grandfather John, count of Dreux, died in Cyprus in 1249 during Louis IX's first crusade.

Chapter 35: The Great Cause

1. *John of Fordun's Chronicle*, 304.
2. *Lanercost*, 41–2; Barrow, *Robert Bruce*, 21.
3. *CDS 1272–1307*, no. 248; Barrow, 'Kingdom in Crisis', 126.

4. Arthur II of Brittany, b. 1262, was the nephew of Alexander III's first wife Margaret of England, being the son of her sister Beatrice. Yoleta's grandson John (b. 1339) eventually succeeded as Duke John IV of Brittany.
5. Her father King Eirik took another Scottish woman as his second wife in 1293: Isabel Bruce, one of the sisters of Robert Bruce (b. 1274), later earl of Carrick and king of Scotland. Eirik was succeeded by his younger brother Haakon, as his second marriage also produced one daughter, Ingeborg, duchess of Finland, though no sons.
6. *Foedera 1272–1307*, 741.
7. William, Malcolm and David's father was Henry of Scotland, earl of Northumbria and Huntingdon, who died in 1152 the year before his father David I, king of Scotland.
8. Barrow, 'Maid of Norway', 120.
9. *Foedera 1272–1307*, 742.

Chapter 36: Toom Tabard

1. Marc Morris, *A Great and Terrible King: Edward I and the Forging of Britain* (2008), 264–65; Michael Prestwich, Edward I (1988), 380.
2. *Nouvelles Preuves de l'Histoire de Chypre sous le Règne des Princes de la Maison de Lusignan*, vol. 1, ed. M.L. de Mas Latrie (1873), 41. John's sister Empress Marie of Constantinople also spelt his name 'Jehan' or 'Jehans': Roger, *La Noblesse de France aux Croisades*, 121–22. Roger Mortimer, first earl of March, was the son of Marguerite de Fiennes, elder daughter of John's daughter Blanche de Brienne; Margaret Wake was the daughter of Blanche's younger daughter Jeanne de Fiennes.
3. Barrow, *Robert Bruce*, 104.
4. Margaret married Edward I's youngest son Edmund, earl of Kent, in late 1325, a few years after John was killed at the battle of Bannockburn in 1314, fighting for Edward II against Robert Bruce. Margaret and John's son Aymer Comyn died as a child in 1316.
5. *CCR 1307–13*, 203, and see also Chapter 38.
6. https://www.nrscotland.gov.uk/Declaration, accessed 19 April 2023,

Part VII: England

Chapter 37: The Brienne/Beaumonts Move to England

1. TNA E 101/393/10; *Issues of the Exchequer*, ed. Friedrich Devon, 172.
2. Friedrich Lewis Weis and Walter Lee Sheppard Jr., *Ancestral Roots of Certain American Colonists Who Came to America Before 1700*, eighth edition (2008), 114.
3. *Memorial Histórico Español: Colección de Documentos*, nos. 98, 100, 106, 109, 111, 124, 126–28, 130.
4. *The Complete Peerage of England, Scotland, Ireland, Great Britain and the United Kingdom*, vol. 12b (1959), 279.
5. *Calendar of Fine Rolls 1272–1307*, 528.
6. *Calendar of Entries in the Papal Registers Relating to Great Britain and Ireland: Papal Letters*, vol. 1, 1198–1304, 544; *Memorial Histórico Español*, no. 124.
7. *Oxford Dictionary of National Biography*.
8. *Chronicle of Lanercost*, ed. Maxwell, 217; *Adae Murimuth Continuatio Chronicarum*, ed. E.M. Thompson (1889), 25.
9. Jacob Larwood, *The Book of Clerical Anecdotes* (1871), 108. 'Saint Louis' means the Brienne/Beaumonts' kinsman King Louis IX of France, canonised in 1297.
10. See John Carmi Parsons' post 'De Beaumont information' in www.soc.genealogy.medieval, dated November 2004, citing The National Archives C 47/4/5, fos. 26r, 46r.

11. *Calendar of Documents Relating to Scotland 1272–1307*, no. 730; *Oxford Dictionary of National Biography*.

Chapter 38: In the New King's Favour

1. *Calendar of Charter Rolls 1300–26*, 107; *Calendar of Close Rolls 1307–13*, 2, 10, 163.
2. *Calendar of Patent Rolls 1307–13*, 457.
3. http://www.gatehouse-gazetteer.info/English%20sites/1812.html, accessed 5 March 2023.
4. *CPR 1307–13*, 26, 38.
5. *CPR 1307–13*, 20, 44; *The Household Book of Queen Isabella of England for the Fifth Regnal Year of Edward II, 8th July 1311 to 7th July 1312*, ed. F.D. Blackley and G. Hermansen, xiv, xxiv.
6. *Calendar of Documents Relating to Scotland 1307–57*, no. 47.
7. *CPR 1307–13*, 209, 214–15; *Calendar of Documents Relating to Scotland*, vol. 5 (Supplementary), no. 566.
8. *CCR 1307–13*, 203.
9. *CPR 1307–13*, 300.
10. *CCR 1307–13*, 258; *CChR 1300–26*, 153.
11. *Calendar of Inquisitions Miscellaneous 1308–48*, no. 111; *CCR 1307–13*, 376–77, 431, 462.
12. *CPR 1307–13*, 267; *CCR 1307–13*, 409.
13. *CPR 1307–13*, 267, 514; *CCR 1307–13*, 340–41; *Calendar of Chancery Warrants 1244–1326*, 349.
14. In April 1340, John was said to be either 'twenty-two years on Christmas Day last' or 'twenty-one years at the feast of St Andrew last', or simply 'twenty-two years and more'. *Calendar of Inquisitions Post Mortem* 1336–46, no. 271; *CPR 1317–21*, 71. *Calendar of Inquisitions Post Mortem* 1347–52, no. 415, gives Thomas's approximate date of birth.
15. *Calendar of Inquisitions Post Mortem* 1384–92, nos. 1062–76; *CCR 1389–92*, pp. 394–97; *Calendar of Inquisitions Post Mortem* 1399–1405, nos. 477–84; *Testamenta Vetusta: Being Illustrations from Wills*, vol. 1, ed. N.H. Nicholas (1826), 152.

Chapter 39: Not a Good Englishman

1. *CFR 1307–19*, 107.
2. *English Historical Documents*, vol. 3, 1189–1327, ed. Harry Rothwell (1995), 537–38.
3. *Annales Londonienses 1195–1330*, in ed. W. Stubbs, *Chronicles of the Reigns of Edward I and Edward II*, vol. 1 (1882), 201.
4. *CCR 1307–13*, 401–2; *CFR 1307–19*, 87, 121, 177–78.
5. *CCR 1307–13*, 414, 417, 423–24, 426, 461, 543, 547; *CChR 1300–26*, 192; TNA C 53/98, nos. 6, 7, 13; TNA C 53/99, nos. 52–3, 64, 67–8.
6. TNA SC 1/49/9; *CPR 1307–13*, 484; *CCR 1307–13*, 579.

Chapter 40: A Defence Like a Stone Wall

1. *CPR 1313–17*, 85–7.
2. *CPR 1313–17*, 169.
3. *CDS*, vol. 5 (Supplementary), nos. 610, 626; *CPR 1313–17*, 371, 451, 458, 545; TNA C 53/103, nos. 37–39, 43.
4. Lisa Benz St John, 'In the Best Interest of the Queen: Isabella of France, Edward II and the Image of a Functional Relationship', *Fourteenth Century England VIII*, ed. Jeffrey Hamilton, 35.
5. *CCR 1318–23*, 697.

6. *Chronicle of Lanercost*, ed. Maxwell, 217.
7. *Calendar of Entries in the Papal Registers Relating to Great Britain and Ireland: Papal Letters*, vol. 2, 1305–41, 136, 166, 168, 414, 440–41; Thomas Stapleton, 'A Brief Summary of the Wardrobe Accounts of the Tenth, Eleventh, and Fourteenth Years of King Edward the Second', *Archaeologia*, 26 (1836), 326–30.
8. *CCR 1318–23*, 717.
9. *CCR 1318–23*, 697.
10. *Le Livere de Reis de Britanie e le Livere de Reis de Engletere* (1865), ed. John Glover, 354–55; *Croniques de London* (1844), ed. J.G. Aungier, 49; G.A. Holmes, 'The Judgement on the Younger Despenser, 1326', *English Historical Review*, 70 (1955), 266; *CCR 1323–27*, 593; *CFR 1319–27*, 418.
11. *CCR 1327–30*, 98, 100.
12. *CFR 1327–37*, 13–14. Henry was with the king on 16 February: *CPR 1327–30*, 13.
13. *CCR 1327–30*, 120; *CPR 1327–30*, 95.

Chapter 41: The Catch of the Century

1. Wake was, like Roger Mortimer, a great-grandson of John de Brienne the younger (d. 1296), via his mother Jeanne de Fiennes and her mother Blanche de Brienne.
2. Sonja Cameron, and Alasdair Ross, 'The Treaty of Edinburgh and the Disinherited, 1328–1332', *History*, 84 (1999), 237–56.
3. *CCR 1327–30*, 425, 443–4, 471, 528–31.
4. *A Descriptive Catalogue of Ancient Deeds*, ed. H. C. Maxwell-Lyte, vol. 3, no. D.293; Adae Murimuth *Continuatio Chronicarum*, ed. Thompson, 256; *CCR 1327–30*, 425; TNA DL [Duchy of Lancaster] 25/3468; *Documents Parisiens du Règne de Philippe de Valois, 1328–1350*, ed. Jules Viard (1900), vol. 1, 84–5.
5. Adae Murimuth, 255–57.
6. *Adae Murimuth*, 256. The archbishop of York's letter is now held in Warwickshire County Record Office.
7. *Adae Murimuth*, 256; *CPR 1327–30*, 544, 563, 570–72; *CCR 1330–33*, 147, 151.
8. *CPR 1327–30*, 549–54.
9. Kenneth Fowler, *The King's Lieutenant: Henry of Grosmont, First Duke of Lancaster 1310–1361* (1969), 256 notes 14, 16.
10. *CCR 1327–30*, 90.
11. *CPR 1330–34*, 20; CCR 1330–33, 74–7.

Chapter 42: Cohabiting Continually

1. *Wills and Inventories Illustrative of the History, Manners, Language, Statistics etc of the Northern Counties of England, from the Eleventh Century Downwards*, part 1, ed. James Raine (1835), 23.
2. *Abstracts of the Charters and Other Documents Contained in the Chartulary of the Priory of Bridlington in the East Riding of the County of York*, ed. W.T. Lancaster (1912), pp. 422–23.
3. *Calendar of Inquisitions Post Mortem* 1327–36, no. 622; *CPR 1334–38*, 457; *CFR 1327–37*, 419, 427, 435.
4. *CPR 1340–43*, 72–3, 175. Henry was 'of full age' by 14 January 1361: *CCR 1360–64*, 91.
5. *CPR 1340–43*, 72–3; *CPR 1350–54*, 63; *Calendar of Inquisitions Post Mortem* 1347–52, no. 415.
6. TNA DL 25/1869/1539.
7. *Chronicle of Lanercost*, 320; *The Anonimalle Chronicle 1333 to 1381*, ed. V.H. Galbraith (1927), 15; *Early Lincoln Wills: An Abstract of All the Wills and Administrations Recorded*

in the Episcopal Registers of the Old Diocese of Lincoln, 1280–1547, ed. Alfred Gibbons (1888), 14; *Calendar of Inquisitions Post Mortem* 1336–46, no. 271; *CCR 1339–41*, 413.

8. *Calendar of Inquisitions Post Mortem* 1361–65, no. 118.
9. *Adae Murimuth*, ed. Thompson, 142.
10. *CPR 1340–43*, 428.
11. *Calendar of Inquisitions Post Mortem* 1336–46, no. 381; *CFR 1337–47*, 288, 386; *CCR 1341–43*, 441, 578; *CPR 1340–43*, 506.
12. *Calendar of Inquisitions Post Mortem* 1336–46, no. 381.
13. *CPR 1343–45*, 557.
14. *Calendar of Inquisitions Post Mortem* 1327–36, no. 379; *Calendar of Inquisitions Post Mortem* 1352–60, no. 638.
15. *Calendar of Inquisitions Post Mortem* 1365–69, no. 321; *Calendar of Inquisitions Post Mortem 1377–84*, no. 889.
16. *Early Lincoln Wills*, 30–31, 111; *Calendar of Inquisitions Post Mortem 1399–1405*, no. 998.

Bibliography

Primary Sources

Abstracts of the Charters and Other Documents Contained in the Chartulary of the Priory of Bridlington in the East Riding of the County of York, ed. W.T. Lancaster (1912)

Adae Murimuth Continuatio Chronicarum, ed. E. M.Thompson (1889)

Anglo-Scottish Relations 1174–1328: Some Selected Documents, ed. and trans. E.L.G. Stones (reprinted 1970)

Annales Londonienses 1195–1330, in ed. W. Stubbs, *Chronicles of the Reigns of Edward I and Edward II*, vol. 1 (1882)

The Anonimalle Chronicle 1333 to 1381, ed. V.H. Galbraith (1927)

The Art of Falconry, Being the De Arte Venandi cum Avibus of Friedrich II of Hohenstaufen, trans. Casey A. Wood and F. Marjorie Fyfe, two vols. (1943; reissued 2010)

A Descriptive Catalogue of Ancient Deeds, six vols., ed. H. C. Maxwell-Lyte (1890–1915)

Calendar of Chancery Warrants Preserved in the Public Record Office, 1244–1326 (1927)

Calendar of the Charter Rolls, 6 vols., 1226–1516 (1903–27)

Calendar of the Close Rolls, ten vols., 1279–1337 (1898–1902)

Calendar of Documents Relating to Scotland, three vols., 1108–1357, ed. Joseph Bain (1881–87)

Calendar of the Fine Rolls, six vols., 1272–1356 (1911–21)

Calendar of Inquisitions Miscellaneous, vol. 2, 1308–48 (1916)

Calendar of Inquisitions Post Mortem, eight vols., 1272–1352 (1906–16)

Calendar of the Liberate Rolls, six vols., 1226–1272 (1916–64)

Calendar of Entries in the Papal Registers Relating to Great Britain and Ireland: Papal Letters, four vols., 1198 to 1404, ed. W.H. Bliss, C. Johnson and J.A. Twemlow (1893–1902)

Calendar of the Patent Rolls, twelve vols., 1272–1343 (1891–1905)

Chronicles of the Crusades: Contemporary Narratives of the Crusade of Richard Coeur de Lion by Richard of Devizes and Geoffrey de Vinsauf, and of the Crusade of Saint Louis by Lord John de Joinville, ed. Margaret R.B. Shaw (1903)

The Chronicle of Lanercost 1272–1346, ed. H. Maxwell (1913)

Chronique de Ramon Muntaner, Traduite pour la Première Fois du Catalan, vols. 1 and 2, ed. J.A. Buchon (1827)

The Conquest of Constantinople: Robert of Clari, trans. Edgar Holmes McNeal (1936)

La Conquête de Constantinople par Geoffroi de Villehardouin, ed. M. Natalis de Wailly (1872)

Constitutiones et Acta Publica Imperatorum et Regum, vol. 2, 1198–1272, ed. Ludwig von Weiland (1896)

Crónica del Señor Rey Don Juan, Segundo de Este Nombre, en Castilla y en León, compiled by Fernán Pérez de Guzmán, amended by Lorenzo Galíndez de Carvajal (1779)

Crónicas de los Reyes de Castilla desde Don Alfonso el Sabio hasta los Católicos Don Fernando y Doña Isabel, ed. Cayetano Rosell, vol. 2 (1877)

Crónicas de los Reyes de Castilla Don Pedro, Don Enrique II, Don Juan I, Don Enrique III por D. Pedro López de Ayala, ed. Don Eugenio de Llaguno Amirola, vol. 1 (1779)

Croniques de London (1844), ed. J.G. Aungier

The Crusade of Friedrich Barbarossa: The History of the Expedition of the Emperor Friedrich and Related Texts, ed. G.A. Loud (2010)

Documents Illustrative of the History of Scotland from the Death of Alexander the Third to the Accession of Robert Bruce, two vols., ed. Joseph Stevenson (1870)

Documents Parisiens du Règne de Philippe de Valois, 1328–1350, ed. Jules Viard, vol. 1 (1900)

Early Lincoln Wills: An Abstract of All the Wills and Administrations Recorded in the Episcopal Registers of the Old Diocese of Lincoln, 1280–1547, ed. Alfred Gibbons (1888)

English Historical Documents, vol. 3, 1189–1327, ed. Harry Rothwell (1995)

Estoire d'Eracles: the Old French Continuation of William of Tyre, extracts translated by G.A. Loud, available online at https://ims.leeds.ac.uk/wp-content/uploads/sites/29/2019/10/Estoire-dEracles.pdf

Foedera, Conventiones, Litterae, et Cujuscunque Acta Publica, six vols., 1066–1377, ed. Thomas Rymer (1816–30)

A History of Deeds Done Beyond the Sea, by William, Archbishop of Tyre, vols. 1 and 2, translated and annotated by Emily Atwater Babcock and A.C. Krey (1943)

The Household Book of Queen Isabella of England for the Fifth Regnal Year of Edward II, 8th July 1311 to 7th July 1312, ed. F.D. Blackley and G. Hermansen (1971)

Issues of the Exchequer, ed. Friedrich Devon (1837)

John of Fordun's Chronicle of the Scottish Nation, ed. William F. Skene (1872)

Joinville and Villehardouin: Chronicles of the Crusades, trans. M.R.B. Shaw (1963)

Le Livere de Reis de Britanie e le Livere de Reis de Engletere (1865), ed. John Glover

Memorial Histórico Español: Colección de Documentos, Opúsculos y Antigüedades que Publica la Real Academia de la Historia, vol. 1 (1851)

Nouvelles Preuves de l'Histoire de Chypre sous le Règne des Princes de la Maison de Lusignan, ed. M.L. de Mas Latrie, vol. 1 (1873)

O City of Byzantium: Annals of Niketas Choniatēs, ed. Harry J. Magoulias (1984)

Pruebas de la Historia de la Casa de Lara, ed. Luis Salazar y Castro (1694)

Ryccardi de Sancti Germano Notarii Chronica, ed. Georgius Heinricus Pertz (1864)

Scalacronica: The Reigns of Edward I, Edward II and Edward III as Recorded by Sir Thomas Gray, ed. Herbert Maxwell (1907)

Scotichronicon, Volume 5, Books IX–X: New Edition in Latin and English with Notes and Indexes, ed. D.E.R. Watt (1990; reissued as an e-book 2022)

Testamenta Vetusta: Being Illustrations from Wills, vol. 1, ed. N.H. Nicholas (1826)

The National Archives records

Vita Edwardi Secundi Monachi Cuiusdam Malmesberiensis, ed. N. Denholm-Young (1957)

The War of Saint-Sardos (1323–1325): Gascon Correspondence and Diplomatic Documents, ed. Pierre Chaplais (1954)

Wills and Inventories Illustrative of the History, Manners, Language, Statistics etc of the Northern Counties of England, from the Eleventh Century Downwards, part 1, ed. James Raine (1835)

Selected Secondary Sources

Abulafia, David, *Friedrich II: A Medieval Emperor* (1992)

Agrait, Nicholás, 'The Reconquest During the Reign of Alfonso XI (1312–1350)', *Essays in Honour of Joseph F. O'Callaghan*, ed. Donald J. Kagay and Theresa M. Vann (1998), 149–65

Angold, Michael, 'The Latin Empire of Constantinople, 1204–1261: Marriage Strategies', Identities and Allegiances in the Eastern Mediterranean after 1204, ed. Judith Herrin and Guillaume Saint-Guillain (2011), 47–68

Armenia, John, *Armenian Cilicia XII-XIV Century: Dawn, Splendor and Twilight of a Christian Kingdom in the Near East During the Crusades* (2010)
Asbridge, Thomas, *The First Crusade: A New History* (2004)
Aurell, Jaume, 'The Self-Coronations of Iberian Kings: A Crooked Line', *Imago Temporis: Medium Aevum*, 8 (2014), 151–75
Barber, Richard, *Magnificence and Princely Splendour in the Middle Ages* (2020)
Barrow, G.W.S., 'A Kingdom in Crisis: Scotland and the Maid of Norway', *The Scottish Historical Review*, 69, part 2, *Studies Commemorative of the Anniversary of the Death of the Maid of Norway* (1990), 120–41
Barrow, G.W.S., *Robert Bruce and the Community of the Realm of Scotland* (second edition, 1976)
Benz St John, Lisa, 'In the Best Interest of the Queen: Isabella of France, Edward II and the Image of a Functional Relationship', *Fourteenth Century England VIII*, ed. Jeffrey Hamilton, 21–41
Bianchini, Janna, *The Queen's Hand: Power and Authority in the Reign of Berenguela of Castile* (2012)
Boase, T.S.R., 'The History of the Kingdom', in ed. T.S.R. Boase, *The Cilician Kingdom of Armenia* (1978), 1–33
Bradbury, Jim, *The Capetians: Kings of France 987–1328* (2007)
Brown, Elizabeth A.R., 'The Ceremonial of Royal Succession in Capetian France: The Double Funeral of Louis X', *Traditio*, 34 (1978), 227–71
Brown, Elizabeth A.R., 'The Ceremonial of Royal Succession in Capetian France: The Funeral of Philip V', *Speculum*, 55 (1980), 266–93
Brown, Elizabeth A.R., 'The Children of Charles of La Marche and Blanche of Artois and Burgundy', *Medieval Prosopography*, 34 (2019), 151–74
Brown, Elizabeth A.R., 'Diplomacy, Adultery, and Domestic Politics at the Court of Philip the Fair: Queen Isabelle's Mission to the Court of France in 1314', *Essays in Medieval History Presented to George Peddy Cuttino*, ed. J.S. Hamilton and Patricia J. Bradley (1989), 53–83
Brown, Elizabeth A.R., 'Moral Imperatives and Conundrums of Conscience: Reflections on Philip the Fair of France', *Speculum*, 87 (2012), 1–36
Brown, Elizabeth A.R., 'The Political Repercussions of Marriage Ties in the Early Fourteenth Century: The Marriage of Edward II of England and Isabelle of France', *Speculum*, 63 (1988), 573–95
Brown, Elizabeth A.R., 'The King's Conundrum: Endowing Queens and Loyal Servants, Ensuring Salvation, and Protecting the Patrimony in Fourteenth-Century France', *Medieval Futures: Attitudes to the Future in the Middle Ages*, ed. Ian P. Wei and John Anthony Burrow (2000), 115–66
Brown, Elizabeth A.R., 'Philip the Fair and His Family: His Sons, Their Marriages, and Their Wives', *Medieval Prosopography*, 32 (2017), 125–185
Brown, Elizabeth A.R., 'Philip the Fair of France and His Family's Disgrace: The Adultery Scandal Revealed, Recounted, Reimagined, and Redated', *Mediaevistik*, 32 (2019), 71–103
Brown, Elizabeth A.R., 'Philip the Fair's Sons, Their Statuses, and Their Landed Endowments', *Medieval Prosopography*, 32 (2017), 186–227
Buckley, James Michael, 'The Problematic Octogenarianism of John of Brienne', *Speculum*, 32 (1957), 315–22
Burgtorf, Jochen, 'The Antiochene War of Succession', *The Crusader World*, ed. Adrian J. Boas (2015), 196–211
Cameron, Sonja and Alasdair Ross, 'The Treaty of Edinburgh and the Disinherited, 1328–1332', *History*, 84 (1999), 237–56

Campbell, Marion, *Alexander III, King of Scots* (1999)

Carpenter, David, *Henry III: The Rise to Power and Personal Rule, 1207–1258* (2020)

Childs, W.R., 'England in Europe in the Reign of Edward II', *The Reign of Edward II: New Perspectives*, ed. Gwilym Dodd and Anthony Musson (2006), 97–118

Chrissis, Nikoloas G., 'A Diversion that Never Was: Thibaut IV of Champagne, Richard of Cornwall and Pope Gregory IX's Crusading Plans for Constantinople, 1235–1239', *Crusades*, 9 (2010), 123–45

Cockerill, Sara, *Eleanor of Castile: The Shadow Queen* (2014)

Crowley, Roger, *Accursed Tower: The Crusaders' Last Battle for the Holy Land* (2019)

Cuttler, S.H., *The Law of Treason and Treason Trials in Later Medieval France* (1981)

Daumet, Georges, *Mémoire sur les Relations de la France et de la Castille de 1255 à 1320* (1913)

Davis, John Paul, *The Gothic King: A Biography of Henry III* (2013)

Davis, John Paul, *King John, Henry III, and England's Lost Civil War* (2021)

Deneckere, Gita, and Jeroen Deploige, *Mystifying the Monarch: Studies on Discourse, Power, and History* (2006)

Denholm-Young, N., *Richard of Cornwall* (1947)

Doubleday, Simon, *The Wise King: A Christian Prince, Muslim Spain, and the Birth of the Renaissance* (2015)

Dunbabin, Jean, *Charles I of Anjou. Power, Kingship and State-Making in Thirteenth-Century Europe* (1998)

Edbury, Peter W., *The Kingdom of Cyprus and the Crusades, 1191–1374* (1993)

Edbury, Peter W., and John Gordon Rowe, *William of Tyre: Historian of the Latin East* (1991)

Estepa, Carlos, 'The Strengthening of Royal Power in Castile Under Alfonso XI', *Building Legitimacy: Political Discourses and Forms of Legitimacy in Medieval Societies*, ed. Isabel Alfonso Antón, Hugh Kennedy and Julio Escalona Monge (2004), 179–222

Estow, Clara, *Pedro the Cruel of Castile 1350–1369* (1996)

Fine, John V.A., *The Late Medieval Balkans: A Critical Survey from the Late Twelfth Century to the Ottoman Conquest* (1994)

Folda, Jaroslav, *Crusader Art in the Holy Land, From the Third Crusade to the Fall of Acre* (2005)

Fowler, Kenneth, 'Henry of Grosmont, First Duke of Lancaster 1310–1361', Univ. of Leeds PhD thesis, 1961

Fowler, Kenneth, *The King's Lieutenant: Henry of Grosmont, First Duke of Lancaster 1310–1361* (1969)

Frankopan, Peter, *The Silk Roads: A New History of the World* (2015)

Fröhlich, Walter, 'The Marriage of Henry VI and Constance of Sicily: Prelude and Consequences', *Anglo-Norman Studies*, 15 (1992), 99–115

García Fernández, Manuel, 'Alfonso XI y Andalucía. Un Rey en Tierra de Frontera (1312–1350)', *Andalucía en la Historia*, 38 (2012), 42–47

Garland, Lynda, *Byzantine Empresses: Women and Power in Byzantium, AD 527–1204* (1999)

Gaulle, Julien Philippe de, and Charles Nodier, *Nouvelle Histoire de Paris et de Ses Environs*, vol. 1 (1839)

Ghazarian, Jacob G., *The Armenian Kingdom in Cilicia During the Crusades: The Integration of Cilician Armenians with the Latins (1080–1393)* (2000)

Gibbs, V., and H.A. Doubleday, *The Complete Peerage of England, Scotland, Ireland, Great Britain and the United Kingdom*, 14 vols. (1910–59)

Gilchrist, M.M., 'Conrad de Monferrat in English-Language Fiction and Popular Histories', *Bollettino del Marchesato*, 6 (2005), 5–13

Goldstone, Nancy, *Four Queens: The Provençal Sisters Who Ruled Europe* (2007)

González Mínguez, César, 'La Minoría de Fernando IV de Castilla (1295–1301)', *História: Revista Da Faculdade De Letras Da Universidade Do Porto*, 15 (2019), 1071–84

Hamilton, Bernard, *The Leper King and his Heirs: Baldwin IV and the Crusader Kingdom of Jerusalem* (2005)

Hamilton, Bernard, 'Queen Alice of Cyprus', *The Crusader World*, ed. Adrian J. Boas (2016), 225–40

Hamilton, Bernard, 'Women in the Crusader States: The Queens of Jerusalem (1100–1190)', *Studies in Church History Subsidia*, 1 (1978), 143–74

Hanley, Catherine, *Louis: The French Prince who Invaded England* (2016)

Harris, Jonathan, *Byzantium and the Crusades* (2003)

Harvey, L.P., *Islamic Spain, 1250 to 1500* (1990)

Hinojosa Montalvo, José, *Jaime II y el Esplendor de la Corona de Aragón* (2005)

Hodgson, Natasha R., *Women, Crusading and the Holy Land in Historical Narrative* (2007)

Holmes, G.A., 'The Judgement on the Younger Despenser, 1326', *English Historical Review*, 70 (1955), 263–67

Howell, Margaret, *Eleanor of Provence: Queenship in Thirteenth-Century England* (1998)

Ismail, Dana Celest Asmoui, 'A History of the Counts of Brienne (950–1210)', PhD thesis, Royal Holloway, Univ. of London (2013)

Jeffreys, Michael, 'The Vernacular Εἰσιτήριοι for Agnes of France', *Proceedings of the First Australian Byzantine Studies Conference, Canberra, 17–19 May 1978* (1981), 101–15

Johnstone, Hilda, *Edward of Carnarvon 1284–1307* (1946)

Jones, Dan, *Crusaders: An Epic History of the Wars for the Holy Lands* (2019)

Kennedy, Kirstin, *Alfonso X of Castile-León: Royal Patronage, Self-Promotion and Manuscripts in Thirteenth-Century Spain* (2019)

Kinkade, Richard P., 'Violante of Aragón (1236?-1300?): An Historical Overview', *Exemplaria Hispanica*, 2 (1992–93), 1–37

Kurkjian, Vahan M., *The Armenian Kingdom of Cilicia* (1919)

Lambert, Malcolm, *Crusade and Jihad: Origins, History and Aftermath* (2016)

Lambert, Sarah, 'Queen or Consort: Rulership and Politics in the Latin East, 1118–1228', *Queens and Queenship in Medieval Europe*, ed. Anne J. Duggan (1995), 153–69

Larwood, Jacob, *The Book of Clerical Anecdotes* (1871)

La Zouche, Lucy, *Beaumont Crusaders and Campaigners* (2019)

Lebeuf, Jean, Adrien Augier and Fernand Bournon, *Histoire de la Ville et de Tout le Diocèse de Paris,* vol. 2 (1883)

Le Fèvre, Antoine-Martial, *Calendrier Historique et Chronologique de l'Église de Paris, Contenant l'Origine des Paroisses, Abbayes, Monastères, Prieurés, Collégiales &c. de Paris* (1847)

Lincoln, Kyle, '*Una Cum Uxore Mea*: Alfonso VIII, Leonor Plantagenet, and Marriage Alliances at the Court of Castile', *Revista Chilena de Estudios Medievales*, 4 (2013), 11–32

Linehan, Peter, 'The English Mission of Cardinal Petrus Hispanus, the Chronicle of Walter of Guisborough, and News from Castile at Carlisle (1307)', *English Historical Review*, 117 (2002), 605–21

Lock, Peter, *The Franks in the Aegean, 1204–1500* (1995)

Madden, Thomas F., 'The Latin Empire of Constantinople's Fractured Foundation: The Rift between Boniface of Montferrat and Baldwin of Flanders', *The Fourth Crusade: Event, Aftermath, and Perceptions*, ed. Thomas F. Madden (2017), 45–52

Magdalino, Paul, *The Empire of Manuel I Komnenos, 1143*–1180 (1993)

Martínez, Salvador H., *Berenguela the Great and Her Times (1180–1246)* (2021)

Martínez, Salvador H., *Alfonso X, the Learned: A Biography* (2010)

Meri, Josef W., ed., *Medieval Islamic Civilization: An Encyclopedia, volume 2, L-Z, index* (2006)

Mitchell, Linda E., 'Isabella de Vescy and the Lords Ordainer: Marital Politics and the Crown, 1272–1327', in her *Portraits of Medieval Women: Family, Marriage, and Politics in England, 1225–1350* (2003), 93–104

Morris, Marc, *A Great and Terrible King: Edward I and the Forging of Britain* (2008)

Mortimer, Ian, *The Fears of Henry IV: The Life of England's Self-Made King* (2007)

Murray, Alan V., 'Women in the Royal Succession of the Latin Kingdom of Jerusalem (1099–1291)', *Mächtige Frauen? Königinnen und Fürstinnen im europäischen Mittelalter*, ed. Claudia Zey (2015), 131–62

Neagu, David-Linus-Emanuel, 'The War of the Antiochene Succession: Lewon I's Game of Diplomacy', *Revue des Études Sud-Est Européenes*, 57 (2019), 221–50

Newman, Sharan, *Defending the City of God: A Medieval Queen, The First Crusades, and the Quest for Peace in Jerusalem* (2014)

Pangonis, Katherine, *Queens of Jerusalem: The Women Who Dared to Rule* (2021)

Pepin, Paulette, 'A Case Study: Contract and its Consequences for the Kingdom of Castile-León', *The Historian*, 75 (2013), 806–19

Pepin, Paulette Lynn, *María de Molina, Queen and Regent: Life and Rule in Castile-León, 1259–1321* (2016)

Perry, Guy, 'A King of Jerusalem in England: The Visit of John of Brienne in 1223', *History*, 100 (2015), 627–39

Perry, Guy, 'Isabella II or Yolanda? The Name of the Queen of Jerusalem and the Spouse of the Emperor Friedrich II', *Medieval Prosopography*, 30 (2015), 73–86

Perry, Guy, *John of Brienne: King of Jerusalem, Emperor of Constantinople, c. 1175–1237* (2013)

Perry, Guy, *The Briennes: The Rise and Fall of a Champenois Dynasty in the Age of the Crusades, c. 950–1356* (2018)

Phillips, Jonathan, *The Fourth Crusade and the Sack of Constantinople* (2004)

Phillips, Jonathan, *Holy Warriors: A Modern History of the Crusades* (2009)

Phillips, Jonathan, *The Life and Legend of the Sultan Saladin* (2019)

Pollock, M.A., *Scotland, England and France after the Loss of Normandy, 1204–1296: 'Auld Amitie'* (2015)

Powicke, F.M., *King Henry III and the Lord Edward: The Community of the Realm in the Thirteenth Century* (1947)

Prestwich, Michael, *Edward I* (1988)

Prestwich, Michael, 'Edward I and the Maid of Norway', *The Scottish Historical Review*, 69, part 2, *Studies Commemorative of the Anniversary of the Death of the Maid of Norway* (1990), 157–74

Proctor-Tiffany, Mariah, *Medieval Art in Motion: The Inventory and Gift Giving of Queen Clémence de Hongrie* (2019)

Rhodes, Walter, 'Edmund, Earl of Lancaster', *English Historical Review*, 10 (1895), 19–40

Rhodes, Walter, 'Edmund, Earl of Lancaster (Continued)', *English Historical Review*, 10 (1895), 209–37

Roche, T.W.E., *The King of Almayne: A Thirteenth-Century Englishman in Europe* (1966)

Roger, Paul André, *La Noblesse de France aux Croisades* (1845)

Rosser, John Hutchins, *Historical Dictionary of Byzantium* (2012)

Ruiz, Teofilo F., *Spain's Centuries of Crisis 1300–1474* (2007)

Runciman, Steven, *A History of the Crusades*, vols. 2 and 3 (1987)

Runciman, Steven, *The Sicilian Vespers: A History of the Mediterranean World in the Later Thirteenth Century* (1958)

Rudt de Collenberg, W.H., 'L'Empereur Isaac de Chypre et Sa Fille (1155–1207)', *Byzantion*, 38 (1968), 123–79
Schrader, Helena P., *The Holy Land in the Era of the Crusades: Kingdoms at the Crossroads of Civilizations, 1100–1300* (2022)
Simpson, Alicia, *Niketas Choniates: A Historiographical Study* (2013)
Stapleton, Thomas, 'A Brief Summary of the Wardrobe Accounts of the Tenth, Eleventh, and Fourteenth Years of King Edward the Second', *Archaeologia*, 26 (1836), 318–45
Stephenson, Paul, *Byzantium's Balkan Frontier: A Political Study of the Northern Balkans* (2000)
Strayer, Joseph R., *The Reign of Philip the Fair* (1980)
Sturcken, H.T., 'The Unconsummated Marriage of Jaime of Aragón and Leonor of Castile (October 1319)', *Journal of Medieval History*, 5 (1979), 185–201
Tricht, Filip Van, trans. Peter Longbottom, *The Latin Renovatio of Byzantium* (2011)
Tyerman, Christopher, *God's War: A New History of the Crusades* (2007)
Vasiliev, Alexander A., 'The Foundation of the Empire of Trebizond (1204–1222), *Speculum*, 11 (1936), 3–37
Verity, Brad, 'The First English Duchess: Isabel de Beaumont, Duchess of Lancaster (*c.*1318-*c.*1359)', *Foundations*, 1 (2004), 307–23
Watt, D.E.R., 'The Minority of Alexander III of Scotland', *Transactions of the Royal Historical Society*, 21 (1971), 1–23
Weiler, Björn K.U., *Henry III of England and the Staufen Empire, 1216–1272* (2006)
Weiler, Björn, 'The Negotium Terrae Sanctae in the Political Discourse of Latin Christendom, 1215–1311', *The International History Review*, 25 (2003), 1–36
Weis, Friedrich Lewis, and Walter Lee Sheppard Jr., *Ancestral Roots of Certain American Colonists Who Came to America Before 1700*, eighth edition (2008)
Williams, Kelsey Jackson, 'A Genealogy of the Grand Komnenoi of Trebizond', *Foundations*, 2 (2006), 171–89
Wilson, Peter H., *The Holy Roman Empire: A Thousand Years of Europe's History* (2016)
Wilson, Samuel James, 'The Latin Principality of Antioch and Its Relationship with the Armenian Kingdom of Cilicia, 1188–1268', Nottingham Trent University PhD thesis (2016)
Wolff, Robert Lee, 'Baldwin of Flanders and Hainaut, First Latin Emperor of Constantinople: His Life, Death, and Resurrection, 1172–1225', *Speculum*, 27 (1952), 281–322
Wolff, Robert Lee, Harry M. Hazard and Kenneth M. Setton, *A History of the Crusades, Volume Two: The Later Crusades, 1189–1311* (1969)
Wolff, Robert Lee, 'Mortgage and Redemption of an Emperor's Son: Castile and the Latin Empire of Constantinople', *Speculum*, 29 (1954), 45–84
Woodacre, Elena, *The Queens Regnant of Navarre: Succession, Politics, and Partnership, 1274–1512* (2013)

Index